I0117158

HARNESSING THE **POWER** OF

COLLECTIVE
TEACHER EFFICACY

A **5**-STEP PROCESS
for Developing
Strong Teams in a
PLC AT WORK®

JAMIE VIRGA

Solution Tree | Press

a division of
Solution Tree

Copyright © 2025 by Solution Tree Press

Materials appearing here are copyrighted. With one exception, all rights are reserved. Readers may reproduce only those pages marked "Reproducible." Otherwise, no part of this book may be reproduced or transmitted in any form or by any means (electronic, photocopying, recording, or otherwise) without prior written permission of the publisher.

555 North Morton Street
Bloomington, IN 47404
800.733.6786 (toll free) / 812.336.7700
FAX: 812.336.7790

email: info@SolutionTree.com
SolutionTree.com
Visit **go.SolutionTree.com/PLCbooks** to download the free reproducibles in this book.

Printed in the United States of America

FSC
www.fsc.org
MIX
Paper | Supporting
responsible forestry
FSC® C008955

Library of Congress Cataloging-in-Publication Data

Names: Virga, Jamie, author.
Title: Harnessing the power of collective teacher efficacy : a five-step
  process for developing strong teams in a PLC at Work / Jamie Virga.
Other titles: 5-step process for developing strong teams in a PLC at Work
Description: Bloomington, IN : Solution Tree Press, [2025] | Includes
  bibliographical references and index.
Identifiers: LCCN 2024022380 (print) | LCCN 2024022381 (ebook) | ISBN
  9781960574268 (paperback) | ISBN 9781960574275 (ebook)
Subjects: LCSH: Professional learning communities. | Educational
  leadership. | Group work in education. | Team learning approach in
  education. | School improvement programs. | Educational change.
Classification: LCC LB1731 .V487 2025 (print) | LCC LB1731 (ebook) | DDC
  371.14/8—dc23/eng/20240618
LC record available at https://lccn.loc.gov/2024022380
LC ebook record available at https://lccn.loc.gov/2024022381

Solution Tree
Jeffrey C. Jones, CEO
Edmund M. Ackerman, President

Solution Tree Press
President and Publisher: Douglas M. Rife
Associate Publishers: Todd Brakke and Kendra Slayton
Editorial Director: Laurel Hecker
Art Director: Rian Anderson
Copy Chief: Jessi Finn
Production Editor: Kate St. Ives
Text and Cover Designer: Kelsey Hoover
Acquisitions Editors: Carol Collins and Hilary Goff
Content Development Specialist: Amy Rubenstein
Associate Editors: Sarah Ludwig and Elijah Oates
Editorial Assistant: Madison Chartier

ACKNOWLEDGMENTS

THE JOURNEY OF writing this, my first book, was possible because of so many individuals whose kindness, generosity, wisdom, and support inspired me to get started, convinced me that I was capable, and provided feedback to help me complete the task.

First and foremost, my wonderful family. Andrea, the love of my life, who passed away ten years ago, and our three children, Michael, Lizzie, and Jack. You believed in me and supported me through so much. You are my world, and I love you to the moon and back.

Next, I need to acknowledge Rick DuFour, whose vision for making schools work for students transformed how I approached educational leadership and working with teacher teams. My knowledge and understanding grew through hearing Rick, Becky DuFour, and Bob Eaker deliver a consistent message about how to make schools work for all learners.

I am very grateful to Jeff Jones, Ed Ackerman, Shannon Ritz, and the whole family at Solution Tree who gave me the opportunity to work as a Solution Tree associate. I would not have been able to write this book without the rich learning experiences I have had working throughout the United States as a Solution Tree associate for the past fifteen years.

I am so thankful for the encouragement from wonderful individuals like Claudia Wheatley, Douglas Rife, Mike Mattos, Kim Bailey, and so many more, who increased my self-efficacy for writing a book by repeatedly expressing their belief in me. This book would not have happened without the patient support of editor Kate St. Ives and the wonderful team at Solution Tree Press.

Finally, I would like to acknowledge the many frontline educators—classroom teachers, teacher leaders, school administrators, district coaches, and superintendents—who let me be a part of their story during the last fifteen years in my work as a consultant. In schools from Vermont to California and Washington to Florida, I have had the honor of working with hundreds of caring educators who are giving their all every day for students and their learning. I have learned so much from you about working through difficulty, keeping the focus on students, and organizing teacher teams to make great things happen for students. It is through that work that I was able to formulate what has become the CLEAR process to build the collective efficacy of teacher teams. I am awed by the amazing work that you do every day.

It is my deepest hope that this book helps educational leaders and coaches of all types to build the collective efficacy of their teacher teams and thereby ensure high levels of learning for all students.

Solution Tree Press would like to thank the following reviewers:

Doug Crowley
Assistant Principal
DeForest Area High School
DeForest, Wisconsin

Shanna Martin
Middle School Teacher
 & Instructional Coach
School District of Lomira
Lomira, Wisconsin

Lindsey Matkin
Principal
Kinard Middle School
Fort Collins, Colorado

Jennifer Renegar
Data & Assessment Specialist
Republic School District
Republic, Missouri

Steven Weber
Assistant Principal
Rogers Heritage High School
Rogers, Arkansas

Visit **go.SolutionTree.com/PLCbooks** to download the free reproducibles in this book.

TABLE OF CONTENTS

Reproducible pages are in italics.

CHAPTER THREE

Step 1 of the CLEAR Process: Clarify the Why, the What, and the How   57

CHAPTER FOUR

Step 2 of the CLEAR Process: Listen to Teachers' Fears, Anxieties, Questions, and Concerns   89

CHAPTER FIVE

Step 3 of the CLEAR Process: Explore Examples, Models, Best Practices, and Proven Processes   117

CHAPTER SIX

Step 4 of the CLEAR Process: Activate New Learning Through Coaching, Practice, and Implementation 141

CHAPTER SEVEN

Step 5 of the CLEAR Process: Review Results, Celebrate Growth, and Set New Targets 171

ABOUT THE AUTHOR

Jamie Virga, EdD, has over forty years of experience as a teacher, principal, professional developer, principal coach, and associate school superintendent. He has worked as a Solution Tree associate for fifteen years and has provided professional development and coaching to a wide variety of schools and districts in over thirty states.

As a Solution Tree associate, Jamie works to support schools and districts with implementing Professional Learning Communities at Work® and RTI at Work™ processes. As principal of Viers Mill Elementary in Montgomery County, Maryland, a Title I school with students from forty-two countries who spoke thirty-two different languages, Jamie led staff efforts to create a professional learning community (PLC) culture. Due to outstanding student achievement growth and results, Viers Mill was named a National Blue Ribbon School of Excellence in 2005.

Jamie holds master's degrees in education from Towson University and Johns Hopkins University. He earned a doctorate in educational policy and leadership at the University of Maryland.

To book Jamie Virga for professional development, contact pd@SolutionTree.com.

INTRODUCTION

*T*HE HEADLINES ARE scary.

"The Pandemic Has Had Devastating Impacts on Learning"
>—Brookings Institution, March 2022
(Kuhfeld, Soland, Lewis, & Morton, 2022)

"Teacher Job Satisfaction Hits an All-Time Low"
>—*Education Week*, April 2022 (Will, 2022b)

"Teacher Turnover Hits New Highs Across the U.S."
>—*USA Today*, March 2023 (Barnum, 2023)

"Fewer People Are Getting Teacher Degrees. Prep Programs Sound the Alarm."
>—*Education Week*, March 2022 (Will, 2022a)

"Teachers Are Calling It Quits Amid Rising School Violence, Burnout, and Stagnating Salaries"
>—*CNN*, May 2023 (Choi, 2023)

"No More Teachers: The Epic Crisis Facing Education in 2024"
>—*Forbes*, January 2024 (Perna, 2024)

As K–12 educators approach the second quarter of the 21st century, they are encountering some of the greatest challenges ever to face the teaching profession. These include concerns about student achievement levels after the pandemic interrupted instruction, worries about student behavior and violence in schools, historically low levels of teacher morale, high teacher turnover rates in many districts, and a national shortage of qualified teachers (Barnum, 2023; Broom, 2022; Choi, 2023; Kuhfeld et al., 2022; Perna, 2024).

Despite this challenging environment in K–12 education, particularly in public schools, teachers and administrators are expected to meet the needs of all students and prepare them to be successful in a complex and demanding world.

To make matters even more difficult, the world is still working its way out of the effects of the most devastating worldwide pandemic in a century. The age of COVID-19 brought school closures, a whiplash shift to virtual instruction and unprecedented interruptions to classroom learning that had a powerfully negative impact on student learning. Even after schools were reopened and returned to normal functioning, data reflect that student achievement after the pandemic is lower than pre-COVID-19 levels (Broom, 2022; Di Pietro, 2023). This is especially true of students in high-poverty schools. A Brown University study found that achievement gaps between students in low-poverty and high-poverty elementary schools grew substantially from 2020 to 2022; furthermore, they determined that these declines related to COVID-19 were greater than during other school disruptions, including Hurricane Katrina in 2005 (Kuhfeld et al., 2022).

Teachers also face historically low levels of morale due to the impact of the pandemic and other factors. In the beginning stages of the pandemic, teachers were hailed as heroes who demonstrated commitment to their students by making adjustments and finding ways to meet the needs of students. Over time, frustration about school closures and other restrictions led many people to find fault with the teachers whose efforts they had praised just months before (Grosse, 2023).

This combination of stressors has an impact on teacher recruitment and retention. Teachers in record numbers report that they are considering leaving the profession. Educators who are leaving teaching cite a variety of factors, including student behavior, growing workloads, insufficient pay, lack of support from school leadership, and overall stress (Diliberti, Schwartz, & Grant, 2021; Farmer, 2020; Smith, 2022). Indeed, a significant percentage of teachers have retired or resigned from their teaching positions (Chambers Mack, Johnson, Jones-Rincon, Tsatenawa, & Howard, 2019; Perna, 2024; Santoro, 2021). Simultaneously, colleges and universities report that there has been a significant decrease in the number of college students choosing to major in education (Choate, Goldhaber, & Theobald, 2021). Interviews with teachers leaving the profession around the country reflect some common themes: teaching has become harder than ever, teachers are not being compensated fairly for their hard work, and now they are dealing with new levels of distrust and disrespect from different groups, including some parents, policy makers, politicians, and pundits (Amitai & Van Houtte, 2022; Santoro, 2021; Smith, 2022).

Educational leaders find themselves facing daunting scenarios. Leaders in districts and schools must ask themselves, "How do we respond to the challenges educators are facing—interrupted student learning, reduced student achievement, low morale among teachers, teacher exhaustion and burnout, teacher turnover, high numbers of teachers leaving the profession and fewer entering it—and, at the same time, support educators and ensure high levels of learning for students?"

In this book, I make the argument that there is a powerful answer to this question: collective teacher efficacy. In a nutshell, *collective teacher efficacy* is what happens when a group of educators believes that when they work together, they can positively influence students and their learning—and then they see concrete evidence that they have. When collective efficacy flourishes in a teaching community, the teachers embrace a mindset that, when they truly collaborate, they have a more powerful effect on student learning than any other factor. But in practice, collective teacher efficacy is even more: it's a commitment, a group of collective actions, a guiding value system—a research-based culture that principals, professional developers, teacher coaches, department chairs, and other education leaders can develop in their schools. And when collective teacher efficacy grows strong in a school building, it can help leaders and coaches to address all the issues facing educators, including concerns about student learning, teacher morale, teacher retention, and school culture.

Collective teacher efficacy is consistently linked to higher levels of teacher morale, increases in teacher commitment, and growth in student achievement (Buonomo, Fiorilli, & Benevene, 2020; Donohoo, 2018; Goddard, Bailes, & Kim, 2021; Tschannen-Moran & Barr, 2004; Zee & Koomen, 2016). When collective teacher efficacy flourishes in a school environment, students learn more, teachers and teams feel more purposeful and powerful, and the overall school culture improves. The challenge with regard to collective teacher efficacy is *how* to make it happen. In this book, I present the CLEAR process, a research-based five-step process to build collective efficacy. Each of the letters in the CLEAR acronym stands for a critical action that leaders and coaches can take to intentionally and strategically build the collective efficacy of their teacher teams.

1. **C**larify the *why*, the *what*, and the *how*
2. **L**isten to teachers' fears, anxieties, questions, and concerns
3. **E**xplore examples, models, best practices, and proven processes
4. **A**ctivate new learning through coaching, practice, and implementation
5. **R**eview results, celebrate growth, and set new targets

Each of these steps is based on research about how we, as people, develop our self-efficacy and collective efficacy beliefs. When leaders and coaches implement the steps of the CLEAR process with their teacher teams and use methods and tools that are aligned with the efficacy research, they increase their chances of developing high levels of collective teacher efficacy in their schools and districts.

My goal is to provide school leaders and coaches who work with teacher teams of all types with the plan, strategies, and tools they need to build collective efficacy in their teacher teams and thereby increase student learning, retain and empower teachers, and transform their school cultures.

My Story

My personal journey with collective teacher efficacy started before I even knew the term. Let me explain: In 1998, I was a first-year principal in Montgomery County, Maryland. After years as a general music teacher, assistant principal, and principal intern, I was thrilled to have my first principalship at Viers Mill Elementary School in Silver Spring, Maryland, just twenty minutes north of Washington, D.C.

At Viers Mill, approximately 70 percent of our students were economically disadvantaged, and 65 percent were English language learners. A good number of our students were immigrants who had experienced interrupted schooling and trauma as a result of unrest and warfare in their home countries.

We had a great community and terrific staff at Viers Mill, but our students were struggling to become proficient readers. When I arrived at Viers Mill, less than 50 percent of our students were meeting the proficiency target on the Maryland School Assessment (MSA). The results were even more concerning for our students who qualified for additional supports. For example, only 10 percent of our students who qualified for English for speakers of other languages (ESOL) support were meeting the proficiency standard for reading. The percentage of our students who were proficient and receiving special education supports was even lower, at 9 percent. We were faced with many student learning challenges.

In addition, we were struggling with teacher recruitment and retention. As a Title I school in the southeastern portion of the county, it was difficult to attract teachers to our diverse school. Getting to our location usually involved a longer commute, and traffic in Washington D.C. and Maryland was not very cooperative. To be frank, most prospective applicants also understood that working with the students at Viers Mill would be a challenge and require a high level of effort.

In my first two years as principal, I worked hard, along with my teachers and community members, to address our challenges. Despite our best efforts, we did not see much evidence of growth. Then, in the summer of 2000, something important happened that set us on a course for positive change. Our district held a summer training institute for all school principals. The featured speaker was a school superintendent from the Chicago area who had written a book about how schools can work as "professional learning communities" (PLCs) His name, of course, was Rick DuFour. He presented a simple but compelling message. The way people had "done school" for the past 150 years was not working for current students— or for teachers, for that matter. He shared practical, common-sense ideas that were also inspirational and motivating. Teaching was not educators' fundamental purpose, he said. Ensuring high levels of learning for all students was our true purpose, and we should organize our schools to make that happen every day. The long-standing, deeply entrenched tradition of having teachers work in isolation was an archaic model that was not meeting the challenges of the day. We needed to work collaboratively and organize teachers into high-performing teams that would focus on student learning and allow teachers to learn from each other in the process. And we needed to focus on results, actual evidence of student learning, to drive our work. We needed to have a plan for how we would monitor student learning on a daily basis, not just to put a grade in a book, but to ensure that our students were learning and growing. He encouraged us to build our schools in alignment with what he called the three big ideas of PLCs (DuFour et al., 2024).

- Big idea #1: Our fundamental purpose is not teaching—it is ensuring high levels of learning for all students.

- Big idea #2: We cannot work in isolation anymore. We must work collaboratively to meet the needs of our students.

- Big idea #3: We have to focus on results and work strategically to increase student achievement every day. (p. 18)

He also challenged us to steer the work of our teacher teams with four commonsense questions (DuFour et al., 2024).

- What do our students need to know and be able to do?
- How will we know when they've learned it?
- How will we respond when they don't learn?
- How will we respond when they already know it? (p. 67)

By lunchtime of the first day of the institute, I was calling some of my teacher leaders and asking them to join me at the sessions. They were not technically invited to attend, so we snuck them in. Rick continued to share practical wisdom and authoritative research, wrapped in Midwestern humor and captivating stories. By the end of the two days, we had a new vision for how we needed to work at Viers Mill. It was not about working harder; it was about working differently.

After that experience, we built shared knowledge by reading and attending other institutes. We collaborated on plans to live by the three big ideas and organize around high-performing teacher teams. We learned to use the four critical questions to focus our instruction, refine our assessment strategies, and provide interventions for students who needed them. We started to see results. Beginning with glimmers in the classrooms, we began to see evidence of higher levels of student learning. Gradually, these increases in student achievement were evident in district and state assessments. Five years later, in 2005, Viers Mill Elementary School was named a National Blue Ribbon School of Excellence in recognition of outstanding increases in student achievement. The percentage of students meeting the standard on the state test in reading had risen to over 80 percent, and it would surpass 90 percent in the ensuing years.

When people ask me how we were able to accomplish this success, I tell them that there are many factors, including the support of the community and the students themselves. But I believe the greatest factor was our high-performing teacher teams who embraced the process and worked hard every day to ensure high levels of learning for all students. They were committed to true collaboration and focused on results. Over those five years, our student demographics did not change. We still served a community with a high percentage of students who were economically disadvantaged, affected by interrupted schooling, and learning to speak English as a second language. What changed was the way we worked, how we collaborated, how we focused our work, and, most of all, what we believed was possible.

As I noted, I did not know the term *collective efficacy* when I was principal at Viers Mill during our period of transformation. It wasn't until years later, when I was working on my doctorate at the University of Maryland, that I learned about Albert Bandura, the research on self-efficacy beliefs, and the beginning research on the collective efficacy of groups. In my dissertation, I studied the sources and perceptions of the self-efficacy beliefs of principals of high-performing schools. I learned about how individuals form their self-efficacy beliefs through mastery experiences, vicarious experiences, social persuasion, and affective states from Bandura's works, especially *Self-Efficacy in Changing Societies* (1995) and *Self-Efficacy:*

The Exercise of Control (1997). I also came across the research into collective teacher efficacy and the impact it could have in schools. For example, I read the influential 2004 study by Roger D. Goddard, Wayne K. Hoy, and Anita Woolfolk Hoy, researchers at Ohio State University, that helped to define what collective teacher efficacy was and how it could influence student learning and teacher commitment. I also read the study by Megan Tschannen-Moran and Marilyn Barr that documented connections between higher levels of collective teacher efficacy and student performance in writing (Tschannen-Moran & Barr, 2004).

Once I understood what collective efficacy was and what it could do, it was easy for me to connect it back to what I had experienced at Viers Mill. As our teacher teams embraced the PLC process, they developed a high level of collective efficacy. They believed collectively that they could make a profound difference in students' learning, and they had confidence that they could overcome any barrier. They collaborated at a deep level and had a common vision for student learning. They worked with intentionality every day to achieve that vision. They reached goals and lived up to their vision by focusing on student learning, using common formative assessments (CFAs) at a high level, and by being hungry for evidence of student learning every day. When they saw that their efforts were resulting in higher levels of learning, that made them even more motivated to stay on track and strive for higher results. The culture of collective efficacy also made a difference in other areas. As teams became stronger and more invested in our students' growth, teachers were less likely to leave, and average tenure at the school increased every year. In addition, word got around that teaching at Viers Mill was exciting and rewarding because you got to work as part of an amazing teacher team that was accomplishing great things for students. This helped tremendously with recruiting, and more candidates applied for open positions than ever before. Successes in teacher retention and recruiting were also reflective of a high level of teacher morale. Teachers at Viers Mill worked very hard, and some days were very challenging, but they had a high level of enthusiasm for the work because they were doing it with trusted colleagues, and they saw that it was working. And when you work at an elementary school and you have evidence that all your students are learning at high levels, you know you are changing lives. The collective efficacy of teacher teams at Viers Mill is an essential part of the school's story.

I share the story of Viers Mill's transformation because it demonstrates the power of collective efficacy to improve a learning and work environment, and because we are now at an inflection point in education. We are coming out of a very difficult and disruptive time and face many challenges. The greatest problems involve student learning and teacher capacity. In terms of student learning, we must rally as educators to respond to the interrupted schooling that so many students experienced and use the best research-based strategies to ensure high levels of learning for all students. We also must respond to the data and reports that show that teacher morale is historically low and that more teachers are leaving the profession and fewer are choosing education as a career. How do we address these areas of need? We work strategically and deliberately to build the collective efficacy of our teacher teams.

Collective teacher efficacy is associated with high levels of student learning (Donohoo, 2018; Eells, 2011; Goddard, Skrla, & Salloum, 2017; Tschannen-Moran & Barr, 2004). Collective teacher efficacy is also linked to higher levels of teacher morale, higher teacher retention, and increased teacher commitment (Buonomo et al., 2020; Donohoo, 2018; Qadach, Schechter, & Da'as, 2020). Thus, collective teacher efficacy has the potential to address two main challenges for educators. Collective teacher efficacy is the win-win that educators need as we enter the second quarter of the 21st century.

About This Book

Every time leaders and coaches work with a teacher team to improve practice, try a new technique, implement a new approach, or refine a current strategy, they have an opportunity to deliberately and strategically build the collective efficacy of that team. Within the work of continuous improvement and the dogged pursuit of higher levels of student learning, there are endless opportunities to build collective teacher efficacy if we know the steps to take. However, recognizing those opportunities, and knowing when and how to take them, can be difficult. This is because much of the collective efficacy research focuses on its relationship to other factors, including student learning, student behavior, teacher morale, and teacher retention (Bandura, 1993; Donohoo, 2018; Goddard, Hoy, & Woolfolk Hoy, 2000; Stroud, 2022). There has been less research done on the practical task of how to generate and sustain collective teacher efficacy in the schools of today.

There is a need for some "how-to" guidance on building collective teacher efficacy. I am a practitioner at heart, and as I work with superintendents, principals, teacher leaders, and teacher teams across the country, I find that busy and committed educators want and need practical advice and tools to do their jobs and meet the challenges they face every day at work.

This is a guidebook of practical research-supported advice and tools for those frontline leaders, including principals, department chairs, instructional coaches, teacher leaders, and any other person acting as a coach or leader in a school or district setting. The CLEAR process provides insights, strategies, and tools that educational leaders of all kinds can infuse and apply in their work with teachers; working intentionally and strategically to build the collective efficacy of their teacher teams.

As I explain the research and offer practical steps for implementing the CLEAR process in each chapter, my aim is to provide information that is valuable for any school leader in any type of school that seeks to build the collective efficacy of teacher teams. However, because of my commitment to the PLC process and schools that are working to implement PLC practices, I will also be making frequent reference to how the CLEAR process can be implemented in schools that are in different places on the PLC journey.

I have implemented the PLC process as a principal, district administrator, and professional developer, and I have supported PLC growth as a Solution Tree associate in dozens of schools and districts in thirty states since 2010. I have reviewed the research regarding the PLC process, culture, and strategies, and I firmly believe functioning as a PLC gives educators the best opportunity to provide students the education they need and deserve. I have also seen in my practice that adopting PLC principles helps to create the conditions for collective teacher efficacy to flourish in your school or district. Engaging teacher teams in high-level collaboration that is focused on student learning places them in an ideal environment for them to build their collective efficacy. Likewise, increasing the collective efficacy of teacher teams makes them better equipped to implement the strategies necessary to function as a high-performing team in a PLC. This book shows readers how to build that collective efficacy with teachers in a practical, iterative, step-by-step way, whether they are just starting their PLC journey or are in high-performing PLCs and looking to deepen practice. To this end, I provide examples and scenarios inspired by real-life work with schools and educators that allow all leaders and coaches to see themselves in the role of building collective efficacy with their teams and I describe schools at different points of the PLC journey, from the very beginning steps ("What does PLC stand for again?") to the highest level of implementation.

This book contains eight chapters and an epilogue. Chapter 1 provides the foundation for the CLEAR process: an overview of the research on self-efficacy beliefs, collective efficacy, and implications for both in today's schools.

Chapter 2 presents the CLEAR process, the practical five-step plan for intentionally building the collective efficacy of teacher teams in a PLC. The chapter also explains the research base for each step of the CLEAR process and provides an overview of how the entire process is implemented.

In chapters 3–7, I devote one chapter to each step of the CLEAR process, providing an in-depth look at the research behind each step and practical tools for implementing each part of the process. Each of these chapters follows the same structure and contains the following sections.

- **Meet the Team:** A real-world-inspired scenario describing a team that is struggling with a real-life task or challenge related to the CLEAR process step addressed in the chapter.

- **What the Research Says:** An exploration into the pertinent research that supports this step in the CLEAR process.

- **Making It CLEAR:** Practical guidance for implementing this step of the CLEAR process with today's teams. This section breaks down implementation into three substeps—(1) *preparation*, (2) *engagement*, and (3) *follow-through*—and includes tools, resources, and strategies for practitioners to use in their work.

- **Team Update:** An updated version of the real-world-inspired scenario from earlier in the chapter reflecting how the team benefited from leaders and coaches implementing the CLEAR process. These team updates will help to illustrate how each step of the CLEAR process helps teams to move toward collective efficacy and how the full five-step process is designed to hard-wire collective teacher efficacy into collaborative teams.

- **CLEAR Thoughts and Next Steps:** A user-friendly summary of the key points of the chapter along with opportunities to reflect on the content and plan action steps.

In chapter 8, I provide scenarios that describe how the full five-step CLEAR process could be implemented by individuals in different roles (principal, teacher coach, team leader), at various grade levels (K–12) and at different spots on the PLC journey (beginning, intermediate, advanced), and to support collective efficacy with the critical tasks for teams. These scenarios are provided to help all practitioners see themselves in the book, and to enable them to envision and plan how they would implement the CLEAR process in their own unique situation.

In addition to the contents of the chapters, this book contains numerous reproducible tools to help make implementing the CLEAR process easy, efficient, and customizable. There is also an appendix with planning tools that leaders and coaches can use to implement the process.

As we enter the second quarter of the 21st century and face unprecedented challenges in education, we need hope. Specifically, we need hope anchored in practical change methods. Winston Churchill is credited with saying, "The pessimist sees the difficulty in every opportunity. The optimist sees the opportunity in every difficulty" (BrainyQuote, n.d.). One of the great opportunities that we have in K–12 education today centers on building the collective efficacy of teacher teams and maximizing its positive effects. The CLEAR process provides practical guidance and tools to do that work. Let's get started.

CHAPTER ONE

The Power and Promise of Collective Teacher Efficacy

*F*OLLOWING IS A tale of two teams.

The sixth-grade literacy team at Low Valley Middle School was struggling. In what had become an annual rite of stress and disappointment, their principal, Ms. Adams, had just shared the scores of the state test their students had taken last spring. She tried to be encouraging and positive, but the results were frankly heart-breaking. The teachers on the team had worked so hard, but the scores had actually gone down compared to the year before! How was that possible? The teachers felt defeated and dejected. A sense of hopelessness was starting to grip them. They knew the tests were important, and they worked hard to increase performance, but their efforts had failed. It was always difficult to predict how students would do on the state test, but they had really hoped they would get a bump in the scores this year. Feeling a little embarrassed, each teacher privately looked more closely at the scores to see if maybe their individual students had done better than the group as a whole. A few of the teachers had tried some special lessons that they kept to themselves in hopes that their scores would improve. Each found, however, that students scored poorly across all classrooms. They felt sad for their students. They also felt increasing stress as professionals. These scores were part of their annual evaluation. Each teacher privately started to think about finding another school or leaving teaching altogether.

The sixth-grade literacy team at Rising Crest Middle School was soaring. The school principal, Ms. Brooks, had just shared results from the state test, and the sixth graders crushed it! They not only had the highest percentage to ever hit the proficiency target on the test, but the gaps between different student groups had narrowed. This was not a surprise to the team, because they had been carefully monitoring student progress throughout the school year with their own CFAs. They had reviewed student work together and shared instructional strategies. They had also maximized the school's system for interventions and extensions to make sure their students were receiving all the supports they needed. It had not always been easy. There were rough spots when they felt overwhelmed and were tempted to give up, but they persisted because they knew that they had to come through for their students. They also got wonderful support from their coaches and administrators who provided feedback, guidance, and encouragement. They worked through difficulties together and kept their eyes, minds, and hearts focused on the students and their learning. Gradually, the evidence that they reviewed every day—student work, CFAs, unit tests, and so on, started to show that their efforts were paying off. Students were learning more, and the teachers were excited about their progress. As the team began to see the evidence that students were, indeed, learning more and performing at a higher level than ever before, their confidence grew. They started to believe that they, as a team, could do what was necessary to help all their students learn at high levels. This encouraged them to look for additional ways to support students and their learning. Their team meetings became powerful professional learning experiences, as they looked at student work together and shared instructional strategies and techniques. Egos were left at the door as they worked interdependently to ensure success for all their students. They set clear goals for student learning that were specific, measurable, attainable, results-oriented, and timebound (SMART), and they monitored progress toward those goals. They were beyond thrilled when they met their end-of-year goals by February! They enthusiastically set new goals and blasted through those targets as well. They felt reconnected to why they had become teachers in the first place and were so happy to be part of a supportive collaborative team. They were already looking forward to the next school year and the possibilities ahead.

These two scenarios capture the differences between a team that has developed collective teacher efficacy and a team that is still working in stressful isolation with little hope for better student results.

The team at Rising Crest embodies a collective belief that their actions will positively affect their students' learning. Their collective efficacy is fed by compelling evidence that their students are making academic gains, not just on the state test but in regular classroom assessments and daily checks for understanding. When a student or class is having difficulty mastering a new skill, they bring it back to their team, confident that the group, as a whole, will come up with an effective strategy. When an individual student or a group of students is performing below grade level, they redouble their efforts, determined to find an approach that will make a difference. Through hard work, persistent effort, and mutual trust, they have developed collective teacher efficacy, a deeply held belief that, as a group, they can perform the actions necessary to positively influence student learning.

Like the teachers at Rising Crest, those at Low Valley also care about their students and want them to do well. They also put in many hours and work very hard, trying to get better student results, but they are repeatedly frustrated by their students' lack of progress. In their team meetings, they talk about how they wish their students had more support at home and commiserate about how so many of their students don't care about schoolwork. When a student or class struggles with a concept or skill, they wonder why the teachers in the previous grade level didn't adequately prepare the students for their grade-level curriculum. They desperately want their students to do well, but they are at a loss to understand what they can do about it. They lack a sense of teacher self-efficacy—their own personal ability to positively affect student learning—and, as a group, they question their collective ability to make a difference. They lack collective teacher efficacy. In truth, their collaborative meetings have become negative venting sessions that reinforce their shared belief that they can do nothing to ensure that all their students meet grade-level targets.

These two scenarios, as noted, illustrate the differences between a teacher team that has a high degree of collective efficacy and a team that does not. So, what is collective teacher efficacy and why is it so important?

Collective efficacy is "a group's shared belief in its conjoint capabilities to organize and execute the courses of action required to produce given levels of attainment" (Bandura, 1997, p. 477). Researchers have found collective efficacy is associated with positive workflow and improved productivity across a variety of fields and disciplines (Butel & Braun, 2019; Higgins & Hunt, 2016; Jugert, Greenaway, Barth, Büchner, Eisentraut, & Fritsche, 2016; Salanova, Llorens, & Schaufeli, 2011). In a school setting, Megan Tschannen-Moran and Marilyn Barr (2004) describe collective teacher efficacy as "the collective self-perception that teachers in a given school make an educational difference to their students over and above the educational impact of their homes and communities" (p. 189). When a team of teachers believes in their ability to positively impact student learning and then sees evidence that they are, it produces many positive effects in schools.

Research has shown that collective teacher efficacy is a powerful influence on teacher morale, teacher retention, positive teaching behaviors, and student achievement (Donohoo, 2018). Studies show that when collective efficacy is nurtured and supported in a school, it has a measurable impact on school culture and student learning (Donohoo, Hattie, & Eells, 2018; Hoogsteen, 2020; Stroud, 2022). To understand the power of collective teacher efficacy, it is helpful to review some of the history and research that led to our current understanding.

In this chapter, I trace the development of the collective teacher efficacy research from the early studies of individual self-efficacy beliefs and how they are formed. We explore the impact of self-efficacy beliefs, particularly in terms of how they affect individual teachers and their teaching. Then, we examine how the research on self-efficacy for individuals applies to groups of people as well, including teams of teachers. We review the compelling research on collective teacher efficacy and its impact on schools and discuss the challenge of developing collective teacher efficacy in schools today, which is, of course, the central theme of this book. This chapter concludes with the CLEAR Thoughts and Next Steps section, which offers leaders and coaches an opportunity to reflect on the key points of the chapter and plan an action step.

What Self-Efficacy Beliefs Are

Why do people do what they do? Researchers have long been intrigued by influences on human behavior and performance. Behaviorism, as a branch of psychology, arose in the early 1900s, largely as a reaction to and rejection of the psychoanalytic psychology promoted by Sigmund Freud (Tarzian, Ndrio, & Fakoya, 2023). In 1913, John Watson, often called the father of behaviorism, argued that psychologists should focus on observable behavior, rather than unobservable events that take place in a person's mind (Watson, 1913). Behaviorism, therefore, focuses on observing behavior as a means to study how the human mind works. In 1938, B. F. Skinner wrote *The Behavior of Organisms*, and presented his theory of operant conditioning, arguing that behavior is learned responses to the environment, based on rewards and punishments that occur (Skinner, 1938, 2019). Much of this research focused on a stimulus-response view of human behavior—the idea that people do what they do as a reaction to stimuli.

Stanford psychologist Albert Bandura (1925–2021) was influenced by earlier thinkers' research, but he wanted to combine elements of cognitive psychology, social psychology, and behaviorism into one coherent theory that explained human behavior and learning. He developed his social learning theory as a framework to understand motivation, thought, and action (Bandura, 1977).

A central idea in Bandura's theory is that individuals have the ability to self-regulate thoughts and behaviors, rather than simply react to the environment around them. In other words, people have more control than we guessed over their thoughts, feelings, motivations, and actions. Bandura also believed that individuals could influence their environments through their thoughts and behaviors. Bandura (1997) saw human agency as a dynamic interaction of behavior, interpersonal factors (cognitive, affective, and biological), and the external environment, with each component affecting the other two. It follows, then, that an individual's interpersonal beliefs play a critical role in his or her motivation and behavior. Bandura (1997) called these "self-efficacy beliefs," defining them as "a person's beliefs that they have the necessary skills and attributes to achieve an expected outcome" (p. 3). So how do our self-efficacy beliefs affect our daily attitudes, choices, and actions?

As humans, we are constantly presented with tasks to complete. During the course of every day, life confronts us with a myriad of duties and responsibilities. Bandura (1986) first explained that self-efficacy beliefs are task specific. Other researchers have confirmed that we have varying degrees of self-efficacy for different tasks we encounter in our lives, based on functional area, domains, and context of the task (Bong & Skaalvik, 2003; C. Wang, Kim, Bai, & Hu, 2014). In this way, self-efficacy beliefs are different than broader concepts like self-esteem, which is more about how we value ourselves in general, rather than how we perceive our competence for a particular task. When people are presented with a task, they conduct a personal assessment of how confident they feel about performing that task successfully. Our level of self-efficacy has a significant influence on our willingness to tackle the task, whether or not we will persevere if the task is difficult, and, indeed, our ability to complete the task successfully. In other words, "by enabling us to master our thoughts, motivations, emotions, and decisions, self-efficacy is key to recognizing our ability to shape the world around us" (Moore, 2016).

The Sources of Self-Efficacy Beliefs

Where do self-efficacy beliefs come from? Bandura (1997) explains that our self-efficacy beliefs are formed through the intersection of four main influences.

1. **Mastery experiences:** Having success with a task

2. **Vicarious experiences:** Seeing others having success with a task

3. **Social persuasion:** Having trusted coaches tell you that you can be successful

4. **Affective states:** Emotional and physiological responses to tasks

As we engage with our environment and encounter tasks to complete, we make judgments about our own self-efficacy, based on how successful we have been with the task in the past (mastery experiences), observations of others who are successful with the task (vicarious experiences), encouragement from trusted individuals that we will be successful with the task (social persuasion), and our own physiological reactions to the task (affective states). Understanding how each of these sources works will help us to understand how to build self-efficacy and collective efficacy in others—important skills for an educational leader to have. Let's take a deeper look at each of the four sources of efficacy beliefs and how they affect teachers and teaching.

Mastery Experiences

The most powerful influences on self-efficacy beliefs are *mastery experiences*. Bandura (1997) states, "Mastery experiences are the most influential source of efficacy information because they provide the most authentic evidence of whether one can muster whatever it takes to succeed. Successes build a robust belief in one's personal efficacy" (p. 80).

This makes sense, right? When we are presented with a task, if it is something we have done successfully in the past, we are more likely to have a strong belief that we can do it again. This increases with the number of successful experiences we have had. If it is something that we have done dozens, hundreds, even thousands of times with success, memories of those successes flood in and we think "I got this!" This is especially true if we have received positive feedback, appreciation, or rewards of some type for these successes. On the other hand, if we are presented with a task that we associate with failure because of past experiences, we will have a diminished confidence in our ability to complete the task effectively (Bandura, 1997). Researchers have found that mastery experiences increase the self-efficacy beliefs of individuals in many contexts, including those involving medical students, athletes, musicians, and patients working to adopt healthier habits (Buckworth, 2017; O'Neil, 2023; Wilson, Marks Woolfson, & Durkin, 2020; Wu, Li, Zheng, & Guo, 2020; Zelenak, 2015).

Let's look at how mastery experiences, or the lack of them, influence the self-efficacy beliefs of two elementary teachers preparing to teach fractions to their students.

Mrs. Johnson is a veteran teacher who has been teaching third grade for ten years. Over that time, she has had success teaching her students about fractions. Because of this, she approaches the upcoming fractions unit with a sense of confidence. She recalls the lessons and activities that worked and remembers how "the light bulb went on" for students as they grasped the tricky concepts. She can visualize herself teaching the content effectively and this makes her feel confident as she prepares to teach. Mrs. Johnson is approaching the upcoming unit with excitement and energy as a result of her mastery experiences; she has high self-efficacy for teaching fractions. Though she knows the fractions unit is always a challenge, she is enthusiastic about presenting the content again.

Ms. Bailey is a novice teacher in her second year of teaching third grade. She struggled to get the concepts across to students in her first delivery of the fractions unit last year. She is anxious about the upcoming unit as it approaches on the pacing guide. She remembers how her lessons failed and how students became more and more confused. This reduces her confidence as she prepares to teach. She is feeling stressed and is dreading the start of the unit. Ms. Bailey feels anxious and unprepared as a result of her struggles in the past. She does not have mastery experiences to draw on, so she has a low sense of self-efficacy for teaching fractions.

When we experience mastery with a task, it gives a turbo boost to our self-efficacy. We associate that task with success and that affects our approach to it. If, on the other hand, we have experienced failure with a task, our self-efficacy is diminished. Leaders and coaches who work with teachers must be aware of, and sensitive to, their teachers' self-efficacy beliefs about critical teaching tasks. Leaders can help to build teacher self-efficacy by providing targeted supports and genuine opportunities for teachers to demonstrate mastery.

Vicarious Experiences

The second most powerful influence on self-efficacy beliefs, according to Bandura, is what he calls *vicarious experiences*. Bandura (1997) explains, "Seeing people similar to oneself succeed by sustained effort raises observers' beliefs that they too possess the capabilities to master comparable activities to succeed" (p. 87). In other words, even if you have not personally experienced mastery with a task, if you see someone else complete it, that can positively influence your self-efficacy. Think of this as, "If they can do it, so can I!" Vicarious experiences are most powerful when we can identify with the person completing the task and see them as having similar skills and attributes. Researchers have shown that vicarious experiences play an important role in developing self-efficacy beliefs of people in a variety of roles, including science students, student-athletes, new mothers, female entrepreneurs, and university professors (Bartle & Harvey, 2017; Capa-Aydin, Uzuntiryaki-Kondakci, & Ceylandag, 2018; Dempsey & Jennings, 2014; Haddad & Taleb, 2016; Rintaugu, Mwangi, & Toriola, 2018).

Let's see how vicarious experiences, or the lack of them, can have an impact on teachers who are trying to demystify fractions for their third graders.

Mrs. Johnson did not always have a high sense of self-efficacy for teaching fractions. In her first few years of teaching, she felt much more comfortable teaching reading. Mathematics instruction was harder for her, and the fractions unit was particularly challenging. Then, the principal arranged for her to observe a more experienced teacher delivering fractions lessons. Seeing someone else teach the content to students helped Mrs. Johnson to build her own self-efficacy. In addition, she had the opportunity to attend some targeted professional development on teaching grade three mathematics. As she implemented her new learning, she saw that students were grasping the concepts. Mrs. Johnson's self-efficacy for teaching fractions grew as a result of her vicarious experiences.

Ms. Bailey, on the other hand, has not had opportunities to observe other teachers successfully teaching fractions. She has really been on her own to find resources and activities for teaching the fractions content. As a result, her self-efficacy remains low.

When we see another person perform a task successfully, and we see that person as similar to ourselves, we interpret that information as an increase in our own self-efficacy. The vicarious experience of simply observing someone completing a task can increase our own self-efficacy. Principals and teacher leaders can maximize this source of self-efficacy by providing teachers and teams with multiple opportunities to observe successful teachers and teams, consult with them, or even just review their work products.

Social Persuasion

The next most powerful influence on self-efficacy beliefs is *social persuasion* or *verbal persuasion*. Our confidence about completing a task can be positively influenced by a trusted mentor or colleague who tells us they believe we can do it. Bandura (1997) explains, "It is easier to sustain a sense of self-efficacy, especially when struggling with difficulties, if significant others express faith in one's capabilities than if they convey doubts" (p. 101). When a person we respect and admire, someone whose opinion and judgment we value, expresses confidence in our ability to do something, we will feel better about our chances to be successful. We are also more likely to exert a higher level of effort when we receive this type of social persuasion (Bandura, 1997). This is not as powerful as the mastery experience itself, but it can help in the development of self-efficacy. Researchers have found that social persuasion plays an important role in the development of self-efficacy beliefs for people in a variety of contexts, including engineering students, cancer patients, and doctoral students (Chin, Tseng, Chao, Wang, Wu, & Liang, 2021; Dortch, 2016; Lazarides & Warner, 2020; Loo & Choy, 2013).

Social persuasion can be a powerful source of self-efficacy in the teaching world. Let's see how different experiences of coaching and encouragement affected the self-efficacy beliefs of our third-grade teachers.

Mrs. Johnson's self-efficacy for teaching fractions was enhanced by supportive coaching that she received from the principal at her school as well as from the district mathematics trainer. As she worked to implement new strategies, her coaches observed and provided feedback, pointing out the effective strategies she was using and making targeted suggestions about what to adapt. They encouraged Mrs. Johnson as she took risks and tried out new instructional strategies. Her self-efficacy for teaching the fractions content grew as a result of the social persuasion she received from her coaches.

Unfortunately, Ms. Bailey has not been provided with supportive coaching or targeted professional development. She has not received encouragement and feedback from trusted coaches. In fact, one time the principal visited her class while she was teaching fractions and did not appear to like the lesson. He didn't say anything negative, but Ms. Bailey got the impression that he wasn't pleased with what he saw. As a result, her self-efficacy for teaching fractions is limited.

When we receive specific and meaningful encouragement from a trusted mentor, it can help us to approach a task with a greater sense of self-efficacy. We believe in this person's judgment enough to count their opinion as evidence that we have what it takes to be successful. Principals and coaches who work with teachers or teacher teams should note how powerful social persuasion can be, while also remembering how damaging it can be to withhold encouragement and coaching, or worse, demoralize a teacher or team with harsh negative feedback.

Affective States

In his explanation of how self-efficacy beliefs affect human performance, Bandura (1997) also delves into what he calls "physiological and affective states" (p. 106). He explains that when people are making judgments about their self-efficacy for a task, emotions and physiology come into play: "In judging their capabilities, people rely partly on somatic information conveyed by physiological and emotional states" (Bandura, 1997, p. 106). If we are presented with a task that reminds us of struggle or failure, we might feel stress, anxiety, nervousness, even fear. The same way that memories of a mastery experience help to build our self-efficacy, remembering failures can immediately cause a pit in our stomach and feelings of dread. Our brain and physiology tell us, "I do not like this task, and I want to avoid it if I can." If we are required to perform the task, those feelings of stress and anxiety are likely to affect our performance in a negative way. This additional failure will further cement our low self-efficacy for the task, because this validates our lack of confidence: "I was right to think I couldn't do it!"

On the other hand, if we have had success with the task before, our physiological response may register as excitement and eagerness to show what we can do. We *love* the task because we associate it with success, praise, and satisfaction. We can't wait to get started—we are ready to go! Individuals with high levels of self-efficacy see problems as challenges that they can overcome, rather than immovable obstacles (Schwarzer & Warner, 2013).

Stress and anxiety can have a negative effect on self-efficacy beliefs. This is especially true in demanding jobs like teaching in K–12 schools. Let's see how physiological and emotional factors affect the self-efficacy beliefs of our two third-grade teachers.

Mrs. Johnson always feels a little nervous before the fractions unit. She knows the unit includes important skills that students need to master, not only to perform well on the state test but also to be prepared for grade 4 and beyond. As she thinks of previous classes and how well they have done, her nervousness becomes eagerness to tackle the challenge again. The self-efficacy that she has gained through the guidance of coaches (social persuasion), targeted modeling, observations, and professional development (vicarious experiences), and mastery experiences (previous success and evidence of student learning) helps her to meet the challenge with confidence. Even if this year's class struggles a little, Mrs. Johnson has enough self-efficacy to persevere and help the students learn.

Ms. Bailey has not had the coaching, modeling, or success that Mrs. Johnson has, so the arrival of the fractions unit only fills her with fear. This stress and anxiety are likely to negatively affect her planning and delivery of instruction. The prospect for high levels of student learning is low.

When we are presented with a task, we will have a physiological reaction based on our prior experiences. It may be subtle or pronounced, but there will be a reaction. If we have had some positive experiences, or if we get the right kinds of support (coaching and encouragement), we can learn to see these tasks as exciting challenges to take on. If we have had negative experiences and are not provided with helpful supports, we are prone to see the task as an overwhelming obstacle that we cannot conquer. Leaders and coaches working with teachers and teams must be aware of this aspect of self-efficacy and collective efficacy beliefs. If we understand and anticipate how individuals react to new challenges, we can plan the right types of supports so that they will be successful. Supervisors and coaches for Ms. Bailey could help her build her self-efficacy for teaching fractions if they provided her with effective models, strategic coaching, targeted professional learning, and ongoing support, for example.

It is important for educational leaders and coaches to understand the sources of self-efficacy, how they affect persons in a teaching environment, and how they can be used to support teacher growth and wellness. When those who work with teachers and teams have an understanding of where efficacy beliefs come from, they can infuse that knowledge into their support for individuals and teams. This will change how they interact with teams and lead to better results. Of course, many leaders and coaches exhibit some of these approaches at times in their work with teams based on their own experiences. We all know principals who try to help teachers and teams be successful (mastery experiences). We have seen administrators work to provide examples for teams to clarify expectations (vicarious experiences). We are aware of instructional facilitators who endeavor to support teams with responsive coaching and support (social persuasion). And we have hopefully seen principals who notice when teams are stressed and try to do something about it (affective states). Often, however, these efforts are reactions to situations and not intentional or strategic: A team has a need, and a good coach or leader works to respond.

SELF-EFFICACY AND LEARNING TO RIDE A BIKE

A helpful analogy to understand and remember the interaction of the four influences on self-efficacy beliefs is to consider the factors involved in teaching a child to ride a bicycle without training wheels for the first time.

When I work with teachers and teams, I share the story of teaching my son Jack to ride a bike.

Jack is the youngest of my three children and, when it came time to take off the training wheels, he was a little nervous. He worried about falling and hurting himself. He was afraid that other people might laugh if they saw him struggle. These feelings reflect Bandura's physiological and affective states. Jack's anxiety about failure threatened to negatively affect his performance. He questioned his ability to ride without training wheel support, and this made him hesitant to try. But there were other factors in play. Jack had some older friends who had learned to ride with no training wheels. His older brother and sister had learned to ride freely. This was a powerful influence. *If they can do it, I can do it!* This belief is an example of Bandura's vicarious experiences. And then Jack had my wife Andrea and me. We took turns performing that most awkward of parental duties, the combination of jog and crab walk, trotting beside your child pedaling the bike without training wheels for the first time—a completely unnatural physical task that I am sure results in multiple adult muscle strains, if not emergency room visits, for parents around the globe every day. But there you are, voicing calm encouragement for your five-year-old (while gasping for air), assuring them that they've got it and are doing great. Bandura would call this social persuasion. Finally, that amazing moment arrives when your child is balancing the bike and pedaling independently. For parents, it is a wonderful combination of pride and relief. For children, it is one of the most powerful mastery experiences in their young lives. It is an experience of freedom, and it resonates deep within. You know how people say you never forget how to ride a bicycle? That's because it is one of the first experiences of independence and personal power that we have. Understanding self-efficacy beliefs and how they are formed can help us to support quality coaching, teaching, and performance.

Self-Efficacy and Teachers

We can see how self-efficacy beliefs can play a significant role in a person's performance on any task. An individual's self-efficacy beliefs also have a big impact on their stress level and wellness in their work. Recent studies focused on workplaces in manufacturing, nursing, and education have found a link between high work stress and low self-efficacy (Dos Santos, 2020; Kumar Pradhan, Prasad Panigrahy, & Kesari Jena, 2021; Nixon, Ebert, Boß, Angerer, Dragano, & Lehr, 2022). In any job, people are responsible for completing different tasks of various difficulty levels. If the person has a high degree of self-efficacy for those tasks, they are likely to feel successful, capable, motivated, and rewarded in their work. If, on the other, they find themselves in a job where they have to perform tasks for which they have a low level of self-efficacy, they are more likely to feel stressed, overwhelmed, exhausted, and unhappy. Persons with low self-efficacy for critical tasks "tend to experience self-doubt . . . perceive demanding tasks to be threatening . . . and are more vulnerable to stress and depression" (Schwarzer & Warner, 2013, p. 139). This can, of course, lead to poor performance in the workplace (Carter, Nesbit, Badham, Parker, & Sung, 2018).

We've already looked at the examples of how self-efficacy beliefs affect Mrs. Johnson and Ms. Bailey as they plan for the fractions unit; now let's take a deeper look into how self-efficacy beliefs might play out in the daily life of a classroom teacher who is juggling a multitude of roles and responsibilities. For our purposes, let's just concentrate on the following three common responsibilities for most teachers.

1. Managing classroom behavior and atmosphere

2. Planning instruction

3. Assessing student learning

For a teacher to be successful and happy in the profession, it is critical for them to have a high degree of self-efficacy for these critical tasks. Let's use the following example to consider a teacher with high self-efficacy beliefs in each of these areas.

Mr. Williams, a high school history teacher, looks forward to coming to school every day. Even when he is tired from his hard work as an educator, he looks forward to seeing his students and starting their day together. He has established clear expectations for behavior and has built positive relationships with his students. He welcomes students by name into an organized classroom where all students know the routines and what is expected of them. Mr. Williams has developed a repertoire of strategies to get and hold student attention and he knows how to get students back on task when they start to stray. When the occasional behavior flare-up occurs, Mr. Williams remains calm because he knows he has the skills to respond. He has planned engaging lessons to teach students the most important history content. Over time he has filled his toolbox with teaching strategies that work in a variety of situations and with students with different learning needs. Once in a while, a lesson doesn't go as planned. Mr. Williams doesn't get discouraged. He tries another approach or does some research to find a new strategy. He is always eager to learn more and add to his repertoire. Mr. Williams uses a variety of informal and formal strategies to check student understanding and monitor their learning. He has learned to use assessment as a tool to engage students, to provide them with feedback about their work, and to coach them to improve. Sometimes students don't do as well on an assessment as Mr. Williams hoped they would. He shakes off the disappointment and uses the results as an opportunity to learn more about his students and their learning so he can respond effectively. Over time, Mr. Williams is pleased to see abundant evidence that his students are learning and making progress. He is excited for every little breakthrough and cherishes those moments when students grasp a tricky history concept for the first time.

When Mr. Williams is confronted with a critical task related to teaching, he can draw on numerous mastery experiences, positive models he has seen, and encouraging coaching he has received. As a result, he approaches teaching with confidence and motivation.

Now imagine a teacher who has low self-efficacy beliefs for classroom management, instructional planning, and assessment.

Mr. Jackson, another high school history teacher, dreads going to school most days. He feels a pit in his stomach and often has a headache. He wants the best for his students, but he has not found a way to manage his classroom effectively. He thought he had a good plan going into the school year, but student behavior has been a problem since day one. He's tried a few ideas, but nothing has stuck. He knows that the principal has been getting complaints from parents and that just adds to the stress. The principal tells Mr. Jackson that he needs to do something about his classroom management, but she doesn't really offer guidance or support. Mr. Jackson is stressed about his lesson plans too. He tries to plan lessons that will motivate his students, but the lessons all seem to fall flat. He feels like he is failing at the key point of his job. When it comes to assessing students, he worries that he is not being accurate and fears that his grades will be questioned by the principal or by parents. The day-to-day stress is overwhelming, and it is wearing him down.

When Mr. Jackson is presented with a critical task related to teaching, he is immediately filled with anxiety as he remembers how much he has struggled with these tasks and how much he fears failing again. Mr. Jackson is overwhelmed, and it is negatively affecting his performance.

These illustrations of high and low self-efficacy in the lives of two teachers bring us face-to-face with a critical responsibility that all school leaders must address: How do we, as leaders, create the conditions for our teachers to approach their daily responsibilities with a high sense of self-efficacy? Anyone who has the opportunity to influence a teacher or teacher team can and should incorporate the research on efficacy beliefs into their work with staff. All educational leaders want their teachers to have the high self-efficacy Mr. Williams experiences. We want teachers to feel successful, capable, and confident in the profession. We want them to see evidence that their efforts are helping all students to learn. This is better for students and better for the teachers. However, there are many teachers like Mr. Jackson—hard-working teachers who are overwhelmed and struggling in the profession.

Leaders and coaches must provide teachers with vicarious experiences (modeling) and social persuasion (coaching) so that they can have mastery experiences. These mastery experiences will build their individual self-efficacy beliefs so that they are able to withstand self-doubts or stress (affective states) that they feel as they tackle their teaching responsibilities. Leaders must be strategic in planning how to assess, increase, and support the self-efficacy of their teachers. The research calls for principals and coaches to be intentional in providing effective modeling and responsive coaching so that teachers will experience mastery (Cansoy & Parlar, 2018; Francisco, 2019; Lazarides & Warner, 2020; Loughland & Ryan, 2022; Withy, 2019). The research also encourages leaders to be mindful of teacher wellness and to create working conditions and supports that result in teacher self-efficacy (Boogren, 2018; Meyer, Richter, & Hartung-Beck, 2022; Pierce, 2014). When principals and teacher leaders provide supports that are aligned with the research on efficacy beliefs, teacher self-efficacy increases.

The Impact of Teacher Self-Efficacy in Schools

Teacher self-efficacy beliefs not only offer positive benefits for individuals but are linked with positive effects in schools. Marjolein Zee and Helma M. Y. Koomen's (2016) comprehensive review of forty years of the research on teacher self-efficacy and its effects finds links between high levels of teacher self-efficacy and positive influences on students' academic achievement, student motivation, classroom quality, teacher well-being, job satisfaction, and teacher commitment. Their review also finds a correlation between low levels of teacher self-efficacy and teacher burnout. Gamze Kasalak and Miray Dagyar (2020) find that increased teacher self-efficacy is correlated with teacher commitment, job satisfaction, and resistance to burnout. Josef Künsting, Victoria Neuber, and Frank Lipowsky (2016) conclude that high teacher self-efficacy is predictive of instructional quality, supportive classroom climate, and effective classroom management. Numerous studies have shown that high levels of teacher self-efficacy are related to increases in student achievement (Althauser, 2015; Shahzad & Naureen, 2017; L. Wang, 2022). Clearly, high levels of teacher self-efficacy have a positive effect on teachers, schools, and students.

Now imagine taking individual teachers, who each deeply believe in their ability to positively impact student learning and combining them into a cohesive collaborative team that maximizes their collective knowledge, commitment, and skill. This is the amazing potential of collective teacher efficacy.

Collective Teacher Efficacy

In *Self-Efficacy: The Exercise of Control*, Bandura (1997) defined collective efficacy as "a group's shared belief in its conjoint capabilities to organize and execute the courses of action required to produce given levels of attainment" (p. 477). Just as a person can have individual self-efficacy beliefs, a group of people can develop a collective sense of their ability to take action and achieve goals. Researchers have found collective efficacy is associated with positive workflow and improved productivity across a variety of fields and disciplines (Butel & Braun, 2019; Jugert et al., 2016; Salanova, Rodríguez-Sánchez, Schaufeli, & Cifre, 2014). Studies have shown that collective efficacy can play a role in many scenarios, including the success of athletic teams, the productivity of workers, the social climate of neighborhoods, and how communities will react during a disaster (Chow & Feltz, 2014; Drury, 2018; Higgins & Hunt, 2016; Leo, Sánchez-Miguel, Sánchez-Oliva, Amado, & García-Calvo, 2013; Tasa, Sears, & Schat, 2011).

When a team of teachers has collective efficacy, it means that they believe they have the skills and attributes, as a group, to take the actions necessary for their students to learn and grow. Collective teacher efficacy grows out of repeated mastery experiences where a team implements effective strategies and then sees student learning increases as a result (Donohoo, 2018; Donohoo & Katz, 2017; Hoogsteen, 2020; Stroud, 2022). When collective efficacy is developed in a group of teachers, the impact on schools is profound. Bandura (1995) explains, "Schools in which staff members collectively judge themselves capable of promoting academic success imbue their schools with a positive atmosphere for development" (pp. 20–21). He points out that the opposite is true, as well. "Schools in which the staffs collectively judge themselves as powerless to get difficult students to achieve academic success convey a group sense of academic futility that can pervade the entire life of the school" (Bandura, 1995, p. 20). Bandura (1993) also finds that a high level of collective teacher efficacy in a school outweighs the potential negative effects of low socioeconomic status.

Bandura's research was carried forward by Goddard, Hoy, and Woolfolk Hoy (2000), who have studied the effects of collective teacher efficacy for several decades. In an oft-cited report published in 2000, they studied collective teacher efficacy levels and student achievement in forty-seven schools in a Midwest school district. They found that high levels of collective teacher efficacy were associated with higher levels of student performance in reading and mathematics. Furthermore, they found that the collective efficacy of teachers was a more significant predictor of student achievement than demographic features like socioeconomic status, race, or gender (Goddard et al., 2000).

John Hattie, researcher and author of *Visible Learning*, first published in 2009, regularly conducts meta-analyses of educational studies to determine the effect size of dozens of factors on student learning. Effect size refers to the impact a factor has on student learning. Researchers examine the data to pinpoint the level of student learning when the factor is implemented or present, compared to student learning in the absence of the factor. Researchers then assign an effect size score to each factor, based on its impact. A factor with an effect size of 0.1 to 0.4 is considered to have minimal impact. A factor with an effect size of 0.4 or greater is considered to have a significant influence on student learning. In 2015, Hattie and his researchers determined that collective teacher efficacy had an effect size of 1.57, which reflects a powerful influence on student achievement. In fact, collective teacher efficacy was found to have the highest effect score of over 200 factors that were studied (Hattie, 2017). See figure 1.1.

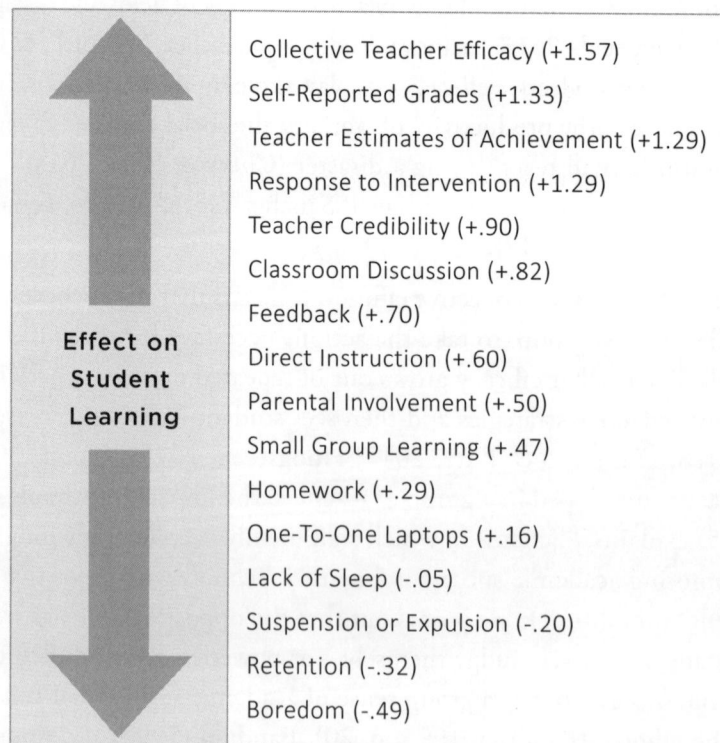

Effect on Student Learning

Collective Teacher Efficacy (+1.57)
Self-Reported Grades (+1.33)
Teacher Estimates of Achievement (+1.29)
Response to Intervention (+1.29)
Teacher Credibility (+.90)
Classroom Discussion (+.82)
Feedback (+.70)
Direct Instruction (+.60)
Parental Involvement (+.50)
Small Group Learning (+.47)
Homework (+.29)
One-To-One Laptops (+.16)
Lack of Sleep (-.05)
Suspension or Expulsion (-.20)
Retention (-.32)
Boredom (-.49)

Source: Hattie, 2017.

Figure 1.1: COLLECTIVE TEACHER EFFICACY AND EFFECT SIZE.

As Hattie and his researchers have continued their review of thousands of studies since 2015, they have consistently found collective teacher efficacy to have a significant impact on student learning. The 2023 publication of Hattie's list show collective teacher efficacy with an effect size of 1.36. This type of effect size translates into practical learning. Higher effect sizes increase the likelihood that students can make more than one year's growth in one year's time. Hattie (2023) is quick to point out that collective teacher efficacy is more than just having a common positive outlook.

In a video posted online in 2018, Hattie argues:

> The message I want to get across is . . . [collective teacher efficacy] isn't just growth mindset. It's not just "rah-rah" thinking. It's not just "Oh, we can make a difference!" But it *is* that combined belief that it is *us* that causes learning. It's not the students. It's not the students from particular social backgrounds. It's not all the barriers out there.
>
> Because when you fundamentally believe you can make the difference, and then you feed it with the evidence you *are*, then that is dramatically powerful. (The Learning Pit, 2018)

Hattie confirms that the collective teacher efficacy belief must be fueled by evidence that students are, indeed, learning at higher levels. Numerous studies have reinforced the connection between collective teacher efficacy and student achievement (Donohoo, 2018; Donohoo & Katz, 2017; Eells, 2011; Goddard et al., 2017; Hoogsteen, 2020; Stroud, 2022).

Jenni Donohoo (2016), author of *Collective Efficacy: How Educators' Beliefs Impact Student Learning*, highlights John Hattie's studies and asserts that, based on the effect sizes, collective teacher efficacy is more than three times more influential and predictive of student learning than socioeconomic status. She also points out that the data show collective teacher efficacy is significantly more impactful than student motivation and engagement (Donohoo, 2016). Based on these findings, Donohoo defines collective teacher efficacy as "a staff's shared belief that through their collective action, they can positively influence student outcomes, including those who are disengaged and/or disadvantaged" (Donohoo, 2016, p. 1). And further, she notes that "if a school staff shares a sense of collective efficacy, then they have a greater likelihood of positively impacting student learning, over and above any other influence" (Donohoo, 2016, p. 1).

Other studies show the link between high levels of collective teacher efficacy and positive effects on student engagement, teacher-student relationships, instructional practices, classroom management, and student behavior (Sørlie & Torsheim, 2011; Yin, Tam, & Lau, 2022). Collective teacher efficacy has also been linked to positive outcomes for teachers, including job satisfaction, teacher commitment, teacher retention, and reductions in burnout (Donohoo, 2018; Qadach et al., 2020; Ware & Kitsantas, 2007; Yurt, 2022). When teachers are working in a school environment characterized by collective teacher efficacy, it serves as a shield against low morale, crippling stress, and teacher burnout. When teachers are working as members of high-performing collaborative teams that labor together, trust each other, and are getting student learning results, they are excited about the work, fulfilled in their mission, and more committed to their team and school.

How to Build Collective Teacher Efficacy

The research conducted by Bandura, Goddard, Hattie, Donohoo, and others confirms that there is a strong positive relationship between high levels of collective teacher efficacy and many positive outcomes that benefit teachers and students, including increases in teacher morale, teacher retention, and student achievement. Accordingly, collective teacher efficacy has the potential to help educators at all levels to address some of the biggest challenges we are currently facing in K–12 schools. There is widespread agreement that a high level of collective teacher efficacy is a desired characteristic for schools today. So how do educational leaders, principals, and coaches make this happen in their buildings? What is the recipe to create this powerful force within our schools?

Previously we explored the four sources of efficacy beliefs (mastery experiences, vicarious experiences, social persuasion, and affective states) and how they contribute to an individual person's level of self-efficacy (page 15). These same four sources are the primary influence on the collective efficacy of a group or team. The research about these sources provides a roadmap for leaders and coaches to use in strategically building the collective efficacy of teacher teams. The CLEAR process clarifies that road map and provides a pragmatic guide for putting the research into practice. The recipe is this combination of research-supported actions and practicality. Table 1.1 shows how the four sources of efficacy beliefs align with the five steps of the CLEAR process.

Table 1.1: ALIGNMENT OF THE CLEAR PROCESS WITH THE FOUR SOURCES OF EFFICACY BELIEFS

The CLEAR Process	The Sources of Self- and Collective Efficacy
Step 1—Clarify the why, what, and how	We build our efficacy beliefs on a foundation of why we are performing a task, what the task involves, and how we will know if we have been successful with the task.
Step 2—Listen to teachers' fears, anxieties, questions, and concerns	Affective states—To help teachers build collective efficacy, we need to anticipate anxiety and have a strategy to hear and address concerns and questions.
Step 3—Explore examples, models, best practices, and proven processes	Vicarious experiences—To help teachers build collective efficacy, we have to provide them with powerful models and examples so that they can visualize what success looks like and believe they can achieve it.
Step 4—Activate new learning through coaching, practice, and implementation	Social persuasion—To help teachers build collective efficacy, we have to provide them with careful guidance, encouragement, and feedback as they apply what they have learned.
Step 5—Review results, celebrate growth, and set new targets	Mastery experiences—To help teachers build collective efficacy, we have to help them to see that their efforts are making a difference. We guide them to see the connection between their work and student results.

Let's look at how several prominent researchers have approached the challenge of creating collective teacher efficacy in schools and how the CLEAR process builds on or differs from those approaches. Donohoo (2016) establishes the following *six enabling conditions* for collective teacher efficacy:

1. Advanced teacher influence—teacher involvement in schoolwide decisions

2. Goal consensus—agreement on school goals

3. Teachers' knowledge about one another's work—teacher familiarity with other's practice

4. Cohesive staff—the degree to which teachers agree with each other on fundamental educational issues

5. Responsiveness of leadership—leaders who show concern and respect and protect teachers from issues that detract from their teaching time and focus

6. Effective systems of intervention—systems that ensure students are successful (p. 5)

Donohoo encourages all schools and school boards to undertake strategic efforts to create these conditions so that collective teacher efficacy will develop. However, she also acknowledges the limitations of this approach: "While enabling conditions do not cause things to happen, they increase the likelihood that things will turn out as expected" (Donohoo, 2016, p. 5). The emphasis is on creating positive conditions (teacher influence, cohesive staff, responsive leadership) that will indirectly foster the growth of collective teacher efficacy among staff. The CLEAR process presented in this book is an attempt to take direct action and use the research to deliberately construct collective efficacy within teacher teams.

Peter DeWitt, researcher and author of *School Climate: Leading With Collective Efficacy* (2018) and other books, wrote an article in 2019, "How Collective Teacher Efficacy Develops." In the article, DeWitt acknowledges the power of collective teacher efficacy and proposes several leadership strategies for engaging teachers and using their input. He argues that school administrators can help to develop collective efficacy by engaging teacher teams in action research—setting goals, implementing practices, and reviewing results. DeWitt (2019) also stresses the importance of providing feedback to leadership teams. DeWitt's approach to building collective teacher efficacy is focused on activities that leaders can use to engage teams and create the environment for teachers to grow. Several of his recommendations are aligned with the enabling conditions identified by Donohoo, but they have no direct connection to the four sources of efficacy beliefs.

T. J. Hoogsteen is a school administrator and researcher based in Saskatchewan, Canada. In "Collective Efficacy: Toward a New Narrative of Its Development and Role in Achievement" (Hoogsteen, 2020), he references the work of Donohoo and DeWitt and argues that collective efficacy should not be seen as "an end in itself"; further, he asserts that excitement about the effects of collective teacher efficacy has led to a "misguided attempt to treat [collective teacher efficacy] as the main catalyst for enacting school improvement" (p. 1). Hoogsteen proposes a new theory of action. He believes that rather than focusing on creating the conditions for collective efficacy to flourish in the hopes that this will result in increased student achievement, leaders should concentrate on proven school processes that are correlated with improvement in student performance, including effective leadership and goal setting. He argues that when these effective processes are in place, student learning will increase. The gains in student learning will then inspire collective teacher efficacy and growth in collective teacher efficacy will make it more possible to sustain the effective processes (Hoogsteen, 2020). Hoogsteen extends his critique of Goddard, Donohoo, DeWitt, and others, claiming that their models do not acknowledge how the sources of collective efficacy beliefs (mastery experiences, vicarious experiences, social persuasion, affective states) are employed in schools or how efficacy "is affected by and interacts with school processes" (Hoogsteen, 2020, p. 4). Hoogsteen (2020) concludes that this approach leads to a belief that "schools should focus on efficacy building to improve schools instead of creating the structures known to be a factor in successful schools" (p. 4). In some ways, this is a bit of a "chicken and the egg" situation. Which comes first? Student achievement or collective teacher efficacy?

Matt Navo and Jared J. Savage (2021), the authors of *Collective Efficacy in a PLC at Work*, add to the research by connecting leadership of collective teacher efficacy efforts more directly to the four sources of efficacy beliefs and the real-life world of teacher teams in a PLC. Navo and Savage tell the story of school district transformation in Sanger, California under the umbrella of collective efficacy. Like Donohoo, DeWitt, and Hoogsteen, Navo and Savage describe how building certain conditions (culture, vision, purpose, accountability, collaboration, autonomy) helped to create collective efficacy in Sanger schools and led to dramatic increases in student learning. Navo and Savage (2021) go a step further and offer a theory of action that provides leaders with tools to "identify the types of challenges teams have in relationship to collective teacher efficacy" and "identify the experiences they need to create for teams to overcome those barriers" (p. 143). They also specifically tie their recommendations to the four sources of efficacy beliefs, describing the "efficacy-shaping experiences" teachers might need in terms of mastery experiences, vicarious experiences, social persuasion, and affective states. Navo and Savage (2021) offer practitioners what they call *degree quadrant tools* that help leaders to assess where their teams are in terms of their collective efficacy and plan the types of professional development their teams need to build their efficacy beliefs. For the educational leader working to build the collective efficacy of their teacher teams, Navo and Savage's work provides some of the most practical strategies to date. Their work helps leaders to pinpoint why a teacher team is struggling (for example, difficulty with collaboration) and then plan a type of experience (mastery, vicarious, and so on) to address their needs and build their collective efficacy.

In the CLEAR process, I aim to build on this work and take another step to package the research and tools into a practical process that leaders of all types (principals, professional developers, instructional coaches, department chairs, and so on) could use to intentionally build the collective efficacy of the teams they lead or support.

In summary, education researchers agree on the power of collective teacher efficacy, but there are varying ideas about how to create collective efficacy in schools. Some say that the best strategy for building collective efficacy is to concentrate on creating the school and district conditions that allow it to flourish (Donohoo, 2017). Others say the emphasis on building collective efficacy is somewhat misguided and we should concentrate on implementing processes that are proven to increase learning, which will, in turn, bolster the collective efficacy of teachers (Hoogsteen, 2020). Still others say that leaders must be specific in analyzing team needs to provide targeted experiences that will help teacher teams to develop their collective belief in themselves (Navo & Savage, 2021).

In this book, I seek to take the best of these arguments and combine them into a practical tool for leaders and coaches. I believe that it is possible to have an approach in which educational leaders work intentionally to create the conditions for collective teacher efficacy to flourish and also strategically work through proven school processes, like goal setting, to make it happen. Furthermore, I believe that leaders and coaches must be purposeful in planning learning experiences—professional development, job-embedded collaborative teamwork, and coaching—that are aligned with the research about the sources of efficacy beliefs if we expect our teacher teams to increase their collective efficacy.

CLEAR Thoughts and Next Steps

Teacher teams today need a clear understanding of what they are being asked to do, what they are expected to achieve, and how they will get it done (step 1 of the CLEAR process). They need leaders who are aware of the stresses and anxieties that teachers and teams feel and who then respond by listening, responding to needs, and building trust (step 2). Today's teacher teams need vicarious experiences like observing effective colleagues, reviewing models and examples, and learning from each other (step 3). They need social persuasion experiences that come through effective coaching and support (step 4). Finally, teacher teams need genuine mastery experiences that grow out of examining data, identifying needs, implementing a strategy, and reviewing results (step 5). These are the experiences that the research shows lead to high levels of collective teacher efficacy and, in turn, improved teacher morale, increased teacher retention, and higher levels of student learning. How can today's leaders, with the enormous demands placed on them, organize and provide these types of supports for their teacher teams? The CLEAR process is designed to meet this need by providing educational leaders with a step-by-step guide for planning and implementing targeted supports for their teacher teams that will result in high levels of collective teacher efficacy. As we conclude chapter 1, we'll review critical takeaways, reflect on the implications for our work, and plan an action step.

Let's review critical takeaways.

- Self-efficacy is a person's belief in their ability to complete a given task. Self-efficacy beliefs have a significant influence on human attitude, behavior, and performance.

- An individual teacher's self-efficacy about critical tasks in teaching can have a significant influence on the teacher's emotions, stress level, confidence, persistence, and performance.

- Collective efficacy is the collective belief of a group that they can perform a given task.

- Collective teacher efficacy is the collective belief of a group of teachers that they believe they can positively influence student learning and that their collaborative efforts have more impact than other factors, including the students' socioeconomic status.

- Collective teacher efficacy has been linked to higher levels of teacher morale, increased teacher retention, and higher levels of student learning.

- The four main sources of self-efficacy and collective efficacy beliefs are mastery experiences, vicarious experiences, social persuasion, and affective states.

- Considerable research has been conducted about the effects of collective teacher efficacy, but less has been written about the practical aspects of creating collective teacher efficacy in a school.

- The CLEAR process is a five-step process that leaders and coaches can use to build the collective efficacy of their teacher teams.

Let's reflect on the content from this chapter.

1. Before picking up this book, how much had you heard about collective efficacy and collective teacher efficacy? What had you heard? What were your main takeaways? What was your base knowledge about collective teacher efficacy before starting to read about the CLEAR process?

2. Now that you have been presented with the research about self-efficacy, the sources of efficacy beliefs, collective efficacy, and the potential impact of collective teacher efficacy in schools, how does it affect your thinking and your planning?

3. How could you apply what you have learned already in your work with teachers, teams, and schools? Try to think of one to three concrete actions you could take this week to apply what you have learned about collective teacher efficacy.

4. As we head into chapter 2 and a more thorough description of the CLEAR process to build collective teacher efficacy, what are your main questions? What are you hoping to learn about? What kinds of challenges are you having with teams that you hope the CLEAR process might address?

Let's plan an action step.

Start by considering the four sources of efficacy beliefs: (1) mastery experiences, (2) vicarious experiences, (3) social persuasion, and (4) affective states. How have you used them before (or not used them) in building the capacity of your teachers and teams?

_____

_____

_____

_____

_____

_____

_____

_____

_____

_____

_____

Do a full review of staff meetings and professional development plans that you have implemented since the beginning of the year. Have those plans used the four sources of efficacy to help teachers? Why or why not?

_____

_____

_____

_____

_____

_____

_____

_____

_____

_____

_____

CHAPTER TWO

How to Build Collective Teacher Efficacy Through the CLEAR Process

*I*T'S A FRIDAY in November, and principal Arthur King is frustrated and confused. As he sits in his office after school, Mr. King reflects on the week. On Monday, he had a staff meeting and reminded his teacher teams, *again*, about what they were expected to do during classroom instruction for their middle school students. He reviewed district expectations about student engagement and rigorous instruction. He reiterated that these expectations were important and encouraged his teachers to implement them at a high level. On Tuesday, Wednesday, and Thursday, Mr. King visited classrooms during instructional blocks. He was disappointed with what he saw. In most classrooms, he saw no evidence of the recommended strategies. Teachers were teaching the same way they had before, which was not producing student learning results. When he followed up with teachers about what he had observed, he reminded them of the expectations and asked why the recommended strategies were not evident in their instruction. The teacher responses ranged from timid confusion ("I know I should be doing those strategies, but I'm really not clear about how to do them in my subject."), to candid inquiry ("Forgive me for being blunt, but if the district really wanted us to use these strategies, shouldn't they provide some kind of training? No one has taught us what to do.") to frustrated resistance ("I am doing what I thinks works for my students. Why does the district think these strategies will work for my students? Why should I change what I am doing?"). Mr. King calls one of his trusted colleagues and mentors, Mrs. Merlin, the principal at another middle school, to share his frustration and to ask for advice. She listens to Mr. King's retelling of the week. She empathizes with his frustration because she has been there too. Mrs. Merlin says, "I used to feel that way, and then I really reflected on what I needed to do differently. I asked myself some hard questions.

- "Have I really explained to my teachers why I am asking them to do what I'm asking them to do? Have I given them a compelling reason to change?"

- "Have I clearly explained what they need to do and provided training, guidance, and support to help them do it?"

- "Have I explained how we will measure whether or not these strategies work?"

- "Have I given teachers and teams the opportunity to ask questions and even share what is stressing them about the change in practice?"

- "Have I provided them with models and examples of how this can be done, and maybe even an opportunity to observe others doing it?"

- "Have I provided ongoing coaching, support, and encouragement to help them with implementation?"

- "Have I helped them acknowledge their growth and celebrated their successes, even the little wins?"

Mrs. Merlin explains that, when she took the time to ask herself these questions and then followed through with focused actions, she found that teachers and teams were more willing to try new strategies. They persevered as they were implementing new techniques, they were more successful at integrating new practices in their classrooms, they helped each other to be consistent, and they achieved better results. These positive results then inspired them to put even more effort into implementing the strategy. Mr. King reflects and thinks about the next steps he can take to help his teams.

In chapter 1 (page 11), I established that collective teacher efficacy is strongly linked to increases in teacher morale, teacher commitment, and student achievement (Bandura, 1997; Donohoo, 2018; Eells, 2011; Goddard et al., 2017; Stroud, 2022). This is why collective teacher efficacy can help leaders address their greatest concerns about retaining high-quality teachers in the profession and providing students with the engaging and rigorous instruction they need to be successful in the world today. Collective teacher efficacy is the win-win needed in education as educators strive to meet the unique challenges of the 21st century.

So how do K–12 leaders in schools and districts make collective efficacy happen?

What are the steps? What is the plan?

How can leaders and coaches take the work they are already doing and infuse it with proven research on efficacy beliefs so that they strategically build the collective efficacy of their teacher teams?

In this chapter, I outline the CLEAR process, a practical, five-step plan for intentionally and strategically building the collective efficacy of teacher teams in schools, in detail. I explain each of the steps of the process, examine how each step is rooted in the research on efficacy beliefs, and preview what leaders do to implement each step with teams. This chapter provides an overview of the full process. The chapter concludes with the CLEAR Thoughts and Next Steps section, which offers a review of the key takeaways of the chapter, reflection questions for leaders and coaches, and guidance for planning an action step.

As educators, we must be committed to continuous improvement. We must be continually looking for ways to help our students learn more and to make sure that all students are learning at high levels. This work involves examining current methods, trying new strategies, refining practices, and experimenting with new ideas. By its nature, the continuous improvement work in schools involves trying new things and taking on new tasks. Each time that leaders ask teachers and teams to do something new or to refine a current practice, they have a golden opportunity to build the collective efficacy of teachers and teams. The CLEAR process is designed to help school leaders, coaches, and teacher leaders of all kinds maximize the opportunities for building the collective efficacy of teacher teams by providing a practical research-based approach. Whatever work you are doing with your teams and whatever role you play, you can infuse your work with research-based strategies that will nurture and develop the collective efficacy beliefs of your teachers as you work with them.

The CLEAR Process

To build the collective efficacy of teacher teams, coaches, district leaders, and school leaders must take the following five steps.

1. **Clarify the why, what, and how**—The step reflects the research that shows that teams build collective efficacy when they have a clear understanding of why they are implementing a change (the why), what the change involves (the what), and how the change will be measured (the how). Without this foundation, teams will struggle to implement practices at a high level and, consequently, will not develop a high level of collective efficacy.

2. **Listen to teachers' fears, anxieties, questions, and concerns**—This step is rooted in the research about how affective states and physiological reactions have a powerful impact on individual and collective efficacy beliefs. Leaders must anticipate these reactions and have a plan to address them if they hope to have their teams develop a high sense of collective efficacy. When leaders skip this step, they risk the very real possibility that teacher stress and anxiety will undermine their efforts to help teams to be successful.

3. **Explore examples, models, best practices, and proven processes**—The step reflects that vicarious experiences, observing others, is a significant source of efficacy beliefs. When leaders provide their teams with evidence that a task is "doable" and has been completed by similar teams, it boosts the collective efficacy of their own teams. When leaders give teams an opportunity to observe another team completing a task at a high level, it helps them to believe that they can be successful as well. Consulting with a successful team or reviewing their work can also increase a team's belief in itself. Without these models and examples, teams may doubt their ability and their collective efficacy will not grow.

4. **Activate new learning through coaching, practice, and implementation**—This step shows that social persuasion can have a significant impact on the efficacy beliefs of a person or group. When leaders and coaches provide skilled coaching, then encouragement and targeted support to their teams, they build

trust and collective efficacy. In the absence of trusted guidance and social persuasion, many teams will flounder in their efforts to build collective efficacy.

5. **Review results, celebrate growth, and set new targets**—This step is rooted in the research that confirms that mastery experiences are the most powerful source of efficacy beliefs. When leaders and coaches engage their teams in reviewing data and evidence of growth, it reinforces their collective belief in themselves. This increase in collective efficacy inspires teams to take on even more challenging goals. If, however, teams are not led to establish clear goals and monitor progress, they miss an excellent opportunity to build their collective efficacy.

See figure 2.1 for a sense of the sequence and interrelationship of the five steps of the CLEAR process (page 35; also available as reproducible in the appendix, page 216, and online at **go.solutiontree.com/PLCbooks**).

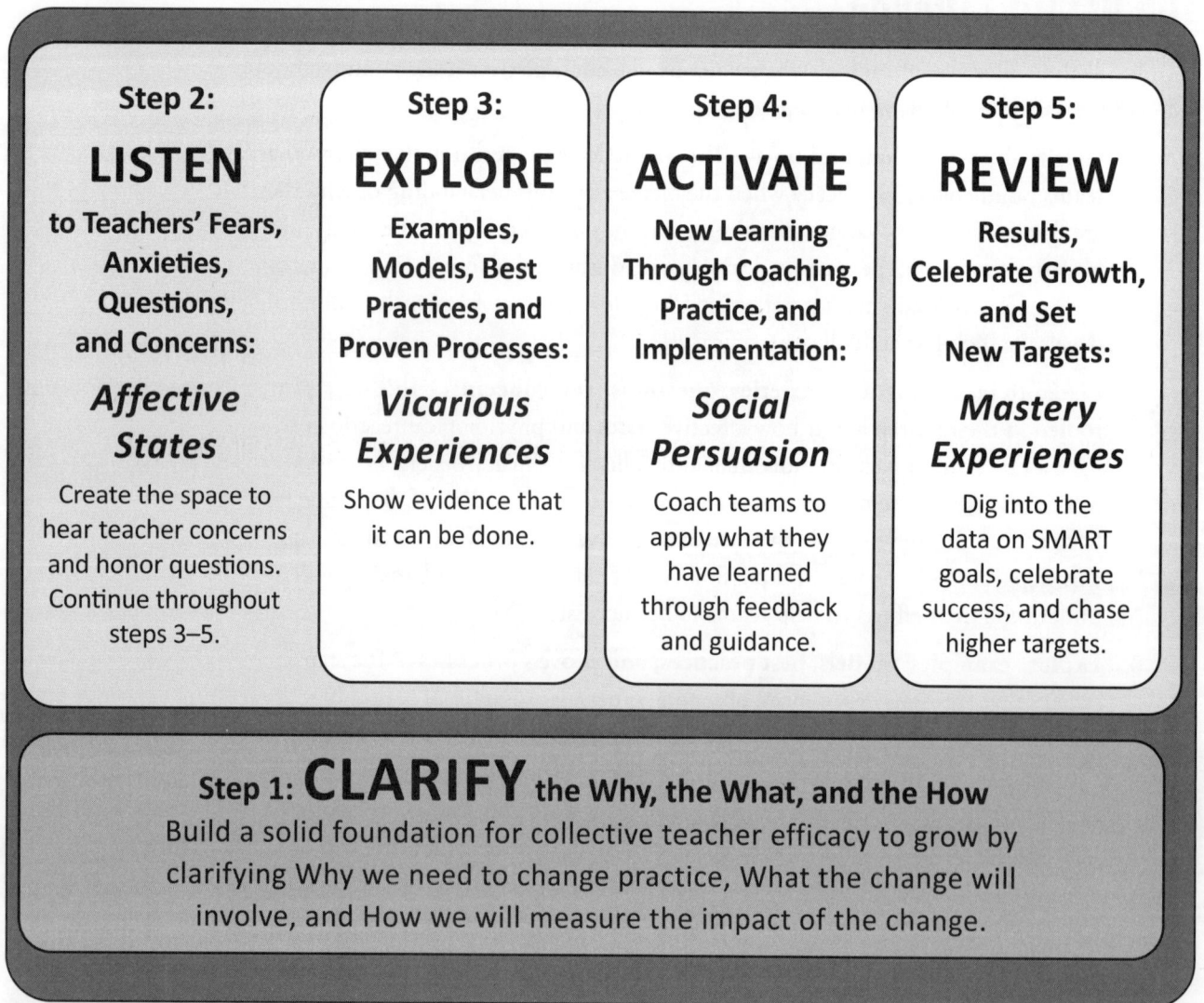

Step 2: LISTEN	Step 3: EXPLORE	Step 4: ACTIVATE	Step 5: REVIEW
to Teachers' Fears, Anxieties, Questions, and Concerns: *Affective States* — Create the space to hear teacher concerns and honor questions. Continue throughout steps 3–5.	Examples, Models, Best Practices, and Proven Processes: *Vicarious Experiences* — Show evidence that it can be done.	New Learning Through Coaching, Practice, and Implementation: *Social Persuasion* — Coach teams to apply what they have learned through feedback and guidance.	Results, Celebrate Growth, and Set New Targets: *Mastery Experiences* — Dig into the data on SMART goals, celebrate success, and chase higher targets.

Step 1: CLARIFY the Why, the What, and the How
Build a solid foundation for collective teacher efficacy to grow by clarifying Why we need to change practice, What the change will involve, and How we will measure the impact of the change.

Figure 2.1: CLEAR PROCESS GRAPHIC.

Visit **go.SolutionTree.com/PLCbooks** *for a free reproducible version of this figure.*

Each of the five steps is based on extensive research and provides critical support to teams as they develop collective efficacy (Bandura, 1997; Capa-Aydin et al., 2018; Chin et al., 2021; Lazarides & Warner, 2020; Wilson et al., 2020). In the preceding figure, step 1 is shown as the foundation of the rest of the process. This is because clarifying why we are making a change, what the change involves, and how we will measure success provides the basis for the other steps to happen. Step 1 is the underpinning of the whole process, thus, it is pictured as the base for the other steps. Steps 2–5 are shown as supported by step 1. The sequence of the steps is deliberate as well, since teams must have a clear understanding of what, what, and how *before* they can identify their questions and concerns; they must have their fears and stress addressed (affective states) *before* they can benefit from examples; they must have time exploring examples (vicarious experiences) *before* they will benefit from the coaching that will help them to integrate new learning into their own practice; and they must receive differentiated coaching (social persuasion) and implement at a high level *before* they can review results and celebrate growth (mastery experiences). Step 2, please note, is depicted as a wider, inclusive step that stretches through steps 3, 4, and 5. This is because coaches and leaders who are working to build the collective efficacy of their teams must monitor the emotional health and well-being of their teacher teams throughout the full process.

Equipped with this five-step process, educational leaders of all types can develop and execute a plan to build the collective efficacy of their teacher teams. Let's take an in-depth look at each step to gain a greater understanding of the CLEAR Process.

Step 1: Clarify the Why, the What, and the How

Leaders and coaches who are trying to build the collective efficacy of their teacher teams must begin by clarifying *why* there needs to be a change (the compelling student learning needs that must be addressed), *what* the change will involve (the strategies that will be implemented to address the student learning need), and *how* they will measure the impact of the change (the goals for implementation and achievement).

Together the why, the what, and the how give teacher teams the foundation they need to undertake a new challenge. Leaders and coaches must be diligent in providing teams with this foundation if they hope to build the collective efficacy of their teams. A firm understanding of why they are being asked to do something, what is involved in the change, and how they will measure it, serves as a launch pad for all the other work they will do. If leaders do not provide this clear foundation for their teacher teams, they are building on an unstable platform that is unlikely to produce high levels of collective efficacy.

If, as Bandura (1997) says, collective efficacy is "a group's shared belief in its conjoint capabilities to organize and execute the courses of action required to produce given levels of attainment" (p. 477), then it is logical that the group needs to understand why they are taking on a task (the reason for "organizing" and "executing"), what the task will involve ("the courses of action required" by the task), and how success with the task will be measured (by reaching "given levels of attainment").

Step 1:

CLARIFY

the Why, the What, and the How

Build a solid foundation for collective teacher efficacy to grow by clarifying Why we need to change practice, What the change will involve, and How we will measure the impact of the change.

Clarifying the why, what, and how for employees is key to overall performance, as well as recruitment, development, and retention of staff (Dhingra, Samo, Schaninger, & Schrimper, 2021). The McKinsey group surveyed over 1000 employees and found that it was essential for managers to help workers to connect to personal purpose in their work for the company. They found that employees who get the purpose they want from work reported better outcomes at work and in life than their less-satisfied peers. The implications for leaders are stark. As the article's authors warned: "Help your employees find purpose—or watch them leave" (Dhingra et al., 2021, p. 1).

In a school setting, teacher teams must have a clear understanding of why they are being asked to change an instructional or collaborative practice, what the change in practice involves, and how they will measure whether or not the change is working. Let's look at each of these components of step 1 in greater depth.

Clarify the Why—Rationale

Leaders and coaches who are working to build the collective efficacy of their teacher teams start by clarifying why there needs to be a change. Leaders and coaches should not recommend or demand change unless there is a compelling reason. Clarifying the why is the first stone in the foundation for building collective efficacy. Collective efficacy in a school setting starts with evidence that there is a compelling student learning need—that students aren't achieving at the levels we want and expect. This is where the leader's work begins. Leaders and coaches should share compelling data and anticipate the questions that teachers will have. These questions may include the following.

- Why do we need to change?
- Why should we change what we are currently doing?
- Why are you asking us to do something new?

Leaders working to build the collective efficacy of their teams must have a plan to explain why a change is necessary. This plan will include strategies for presenting the why to staff and also responding to pushback from teachers or teams. I cover this more deeply in chapter 3 (page 57).

In a PLC, the need for change will always be driven by information about students and their learning. School leaders and teams must review information like performance data from state tests and district-level assessments, school-level data like CFA data, unit test performance, student proficiency levels in reading and mathematics, observation data, surveys completed by staff, students, and parents, and other sources that the school uses to evaluate their work on behalf of students.

For example, when I was principal at Viers Mill, the compelling information was data that showed that our students were not reading at proficient levels. This fact was our why as we worked to modify our practices to get better results. In my time as principal at Seven Locks Elementary, a more affluent school, the vast majority of our students were performing at high levels, but there were specific groups of students who were not achieving at the level of their peers. Our why was data that showed that our instructional program was not working for all our students. Our why lets us know that we need to change our practice.

In schools that are actively working to grow as PLCs, clarifying the why ties directly to Big Idea #1—our fundamental purpose is to ensure high levels of learning for all students.

Making a clear difference in their students' learning is a powerful source of collective efficacy for teachers (Donohoo, 2017; Hattie et al., 2015). That's why the first step to building the collective efficacy of teacher teams requires us to take a long hard look at the data about how our students are learning (the why). When the data show that there are areas of need, the school and staff have a commitment to address those needs and make any necessary changes to ensure those students will be successful. Leaders work to create urgency about the student learning needs so that teachers will understand why a change is necessary.

Clarify the What—Strategies

Once teachers have a clear idea of why they need to change, then the next question becomes what the change will involve. Again, leaders should anticipate the likely questions that teachers will have about the new strategy.

- What will we have to do differently?
- What are the specific tasks that are involved?
- What strategies have been proven to work?

Leaders must be prepared to provide clear answers to these questions. Research confirms that leaders are more successful in implementing change when they provide clear details about what the new strategies are and, subsequently, ensure ongoing training to support implementation (Kotter, 2012; Muhammad & Cruz, 2019). In practical terms, school leaders must do the homework of engaging staff in the study of research-based instructional strategies to address their students' needs and then follow that up with high-quality, job-embedded professional development to support implementation. Whether they are introducing a new reading strategy, new lessons for social-emotional learning, a revised school approach to managing student behavior, or a mathematics curriculum, leaders and coaches need to clarify the *what*.

In schools that are actively working to grow as PLCs, clarifying the what ties directly to Big Idea #2—we must work collaboratively to meet the needs of our students. We must work in collaborative teacher teams and implement strategies that will ensure student learning.

Leaders and coaches in a PLC help teacher teams to implement the specific strategies that research has shown to increase student achievement. As we learned in chapter 1 (page 11), efficacy beliefs are task-specific, so it is crucial for leaders and coaches to be clear about the specific tasks that teams need to master to thrive as high-performing teams in a PLC. Clarity about the tasks to be mastered will help leaders and coaches to focus their work and build the collective efficacy of their teacher teams.

So, what are the critical tasks that teams in a true PLC must accomplish? Many PLC authors, experts, and practitioners have addressed this question about the critical tasks of collaborative teams in a PLC in a variety of ways. The aim of each of these explanations is to help teams understand, remember, and implement the most critical actions.

Rick DuFour (2016), one of the primary architects of the PLC at Work Process, addresses this question by identifying five aspects that must be "tight" or nonnegotiable for a school to call itself a PLC:

1. Educators work in collaborative teams and take collective responsibility for student learning rather than working in isolation. As members of a team, they work interdependently to achieve common SMART goals for which members are mutually accountable.

2. Collaborative teams implement a guaranteed and viable curriculum, unit by unit.

3. Collaborative teams monitor student learning through an ongoing assessment process that includes frequent, team-developed CFAs.

4. Educators use the results of common assessments to:

   a. Improve individual practice

   b. Build the team's capacity to achieve its goals

   c. Intervene or extend on behalf of individual students

5. The school provides a systematic process for intervention and enrichment. Intervention is timely, directive (not invitational), and diagnostic (focusing on specific skills), and it does not remove a student from new direct instruction. (p. 33)

These five elements capture the essence of a PLC. A PLC is built on collaborative teams of teachers dedicated to students learning who set clear goals and monitor progress. When teacher teams are clear about what students need to know and be able to do, they reflect that in the guaranteed, viable curriculum they deliver. Teams monitor student progress on the essential learning through frequent CFAs that they use to inform their own teaching, to learn from each other, and to identify students who need intervention or extension. And finally, the school as a whole has a system for meeting the needs of students who struggle to learn the essential outcomes as well as students who have already mastered standards and skills. If the teams in a school consistently execute these tight practices, they are functioning as a PLC.

While it is important to remember these tight elements of a PLC, they do not capture all the specific tasks that collaborative teams in a PLC must complete to ensure high levels of learning for all students. For example, the tight element of "ensure a guaranteed and viable curriculum" involves multiple tasks, including studying curriculum, unpacking standards and learning targets, and clarifying expectations for proficiency. Likewise, "assess and monitor regularly with CFAs" involves agreeing on proficiency targets, developing the actual assessment, administering the assessment, and critically reviewing results. To strategically build the collective efficacy of teacher teams, particularly in a PLC, leaders and coaches must be specific about the tasks they expect teams to complete. Any effort to build the collective efficacy of teacher teams will be based on helping teams to master specific collaborative team tasks.

Numerous authors and experts have worked to clarify and define the critical tasks that teacher teams must complete to be successful. These include the critical issues for team consideration in *Learning By Doing* (DuFour et al., 2024) and the pathways tools in *Amplify Your Impact* (Many, Maffoni, Sparks, & Thomas, 2018). Consider these works as well to capture the essential work of teams in a PLC. They are research-based, helpful, and applicable in different coaching settings and circumstances. All of this work helps us to better understand the critical work of teams in a PLC.

When we understand the critical tasks that we are asking teams to complete, we are in a better position to provide the targeted support that teams need to build collective efficacy, because efficacy beliefs are task-specific. When we can organize our work to build the collective efficacy of our team around critical tasks, we are more likely to have a focused and successful plan. The CLEAR process is designed to strategically build the collective efficacy of teacher teams in a PLC as they learn and implement the critical collaborative tasks that support student learning.

For the leaders and coaches implementing the CLEAR process, I want a targeted and manageable list of defined tasks that captures that essential work of collaborative teams in a PLC and apply that specifically to the arena of building collective teacher efficacy. I have taken the wisdom from the earlier works and boiled it down to what I call the *top ten tasks* of teams in a PLC. The emphasis on the task is deliberate, as we want to keep our focus on building efficacy beliefs around specific tasks that teams must complete.

1. **Establishing and using team norms:** Collaborative teams in a PLC clearly establish and commit to a limited number of norms they will use to guide their work together.

2. **Establishing and using clear team SMART goals:** Collaborative teams in a PLC establish strategic, measurable, attainable, results-oriented, and timebound (SMART; Conzemius & O'Neill, 2013) goals, both short-term and long-term, to assess how they are impacting students and their learning. Teams use these goals to monitor their progress.

3. **Identifying and focusing on a limited number of essential standards, a guaranteed and viable curriculum:** Teams review curricula and determine a limited number of essential standards that students must learn in their subject, grade level, or course. Teams commit to ensuring that all students learn these essential standards and skills.

4. **Determining proficiency expectations for students on essential standards:** Teams agree and document their expectations for student proficiency for the essential standards. They work to build consistency in how they evaluate student work.

5. **Planning units of instruction to ensure learning of essential standards:** Collaborative teams in a PLC plan units of instruction to ensure that they are teaching, and students are learning, the essential standards. They plan pacing and the timing of assessments, so that they stay in sync while teaching students the critical content.

6. **Developing common assessments (both formative and summative):** Collaborative teams in a PLC give the same formative and summative

assessments to their students to ensure a common expectation of proficiency on the essential standards. Teams strive to give the common assessments within the same timeframe so that they can compare like results.

7. **Reviewing common assessment data to inform instruction and teaching practice:** Soon after giving the common assessment, collaborative teams in a PLC gather to review student work together. They use the data from the common assessment to inform their teaching. Did one teacher have exceptional results? What strategies did that teacher use to get those results?

8. **Reviewing common assessment data to identify students for support and extension:** Soon after giving a common assessment, collaborative teams in a PLC review student work together. They use the data to identify students who are struggling to demonstrate proficiency and assign them to an appropriate intervention. They identify students who are demonstrating proficiency and advanced work and provide them extension and enrichment supports.

9. **Planning and delivering interventions and extensions:** A school that is functioning as a PLC establishes systematic interventions and extensions to meet the needs of all students. This is not left to individual teachers or teams. There is a schoolwide system.

10. **Measuring, evaluating, and modifying interventions and extensions:** A school that is functioning as a PLC monitors the effectiveness of interventions and extensions and makes adjustments as needed.

I selected these ten tasks because they reflect a synthesis of the best thinking and research about what teams must do to be successful in a PLC. The tasks include foundational teamwork like setting and using team norms as well as in-depth instructional tasks like planning units of instruction to ensure students learn essential standards. These are also observable tasks that provide opportunities for leaders and coaches to provide feedback and guidance. As a result, these ten specific tasks provide the ideal framework for building the collective efficacy of teacher teams. Focusing on these top ten tasks will help coaches and leaders to clarify the what. While it is beyond the scope of this book to provide detailed instruction for each of these ten tasks, I will point readers to additional resources when appropriate.

As teachers and teams gain an understanding about what they are expected to do, it is natural for them to wonder how this new work they will be doing will be measured—How will we know this is working?

Clarify the How—Goals

Once teachers have a clear idea of why they must collectively make a change and what that change involves, they will likely want to understand what the goals are for implementing the new strategy. Leaders should anticipate questions such as the following.

- How will we know if this is working?
- How will we measure success?
- How will we monitor progress along the way?

Setting goals for change work is essential. If educators do not set aspirational goals and monitor progress toward them, the work of identifying why they must change and what they must do to bring about those changes will lack focus and direction. Clear aspirational goals are motivating and unifying. Leaders and coaches must be prepared to help teams aspire to better results and guide them to set effective goals.

In a PLC, teacher teams implement Big Idea #3—focus on results, by setting student achievement goals based on baseline data. Then they carefully monitor student progress as they review student work and assessment data together.

Researchers find that shared goals are a vital component in working to build the collective efficacy of teacher teams. Clear goals, and progress toward them, help individuals to boost their self-efficacy (Bandura, 1997). Clear targets are critical as well in the work of building collective efficacy in groups. Donohoo (2016) lists "goal consensus" as one of the six enabling conditions for collective teacher efficacy to flourish in a school, arguing that when teachers are clear about the shared goals of their school and their team, it helps them to believe in their collective efforts. Hoogsteen (2020) asserts that when school leaders work to set goals with teachers, followed by careful monitoring and celebrations of growth, collective teacher efficacy is enhanced.

In a practical sense, the work of school leaders to clarify and set goals involves engaging teacher teams in deep examination of the current state of the learning environment and setting goals that are specific, measurable, attainable, results-oriented, and timebound (SMART) and establishing processes for monitoring progress (Conzemius & O'Neill, 2013).

At its heart, collective teacher efficacy occurs when a group of teachers see evidence that their work together has had an undeniable positive impact on student learning. Seeing this evidence helps the team to see that their collective efforts are powerful. For teacher teams to see this evidence, they must set clear goals and monitor progress. Without a process to monitor growth and celebrate success, teacher teams cannot develop collective efficacy. Thus, clarifying how we will measure the impact of the change is an essential stone in the foundation for collective teacher efficacy.

To complete the foundation of step 1 of the CLEAR process, leaders and coaches guide teams to set SMART goals that will serve as their motivation and beacon as they work collaboratively to ensure student learning. Teacher teams will set specific team goals that they will review at every team meeting. As they see they are making progress on these goals, it will help to build their collective efficacy.

In step 1 of the CLEAR process, leaders and coaches clarify why a change is necessary, what the change entails, and how the change will be measured. These elements provide the foundation for collective teacher efficacy to grow. The clarity of this foundation is more important than ever.

Teachers today are dealing with more demands and pressures than ever before, and there isn't enough time for them to successfully complete the multitude of tasks they are being asked to accomplish. In a recent study, 92 percent of teachers reported that they "always" or "frequently" do not have enough time to prepare effective instruction (Earp, 2022). As a result, teachers are very protective of their time and have little patience for new requirements, especially if it is not clear why there needs to be a change, what the change will involve, and how the change will be measured. If, however, the leaders and coaches who are steering the CLEAR process are diligent in their explanation of the why, what, and how, most teachers and teams will give the initiative a solid effort.

Let's imagine a first-grade team of three teachers. Their principal and literacy coach are presenting new research-based instructional strategies for primary reading. They expect teams to begin implementing these strategies in the coming school year. If the teachers think this change is a pet project or random ask from the administration, they will resist changing their practice. The principal makes sure the change is not perceived as part of an arbitrary or personal agenda by sharing compelling data that show that reading fluency is a significant need for the first-grade students in their school. The principal then presents evidence that there are research-based instructional strategies that have generated significant learning gains for primary students in other similar schools. She provides details about the reading strategies and commits to providing ongoing training. Lastly, she establishes clear goals for their efforts, especially as they relate to first-grade students and their learning, As a result of the principal's actions, the teachers will have a better understanding of the reasons for the change (concerns about student reading levels), what they will do to make the change effective (learn and implement research-based strategies), and how the change will be evaluated (clear goals for student learning and processes for monitoring). Because of this facilitated understanding, they are more likely to give the new strategy a full effort.

The establishment of the why (our data show that we need to make a change to fulfill our fundamental purpose), the what (we have identified selected research-based strategies that will help us to operate as high-performing teams in a PLC to address our students' learning need), and the how (we have clear school goals, clear team goals that are aligned with our school goals, and a plan for monitoring progress) confirms for every teacher and every team where the school's energy and focus are. Teachers and teams must be clear that everyone is expected, within their own individual and team practice, to address the why, the what, and the how. Teams will be expected to ask themselves the following questions.

- What can we do for our team to address our why (compelling student data) and make a difference in student learning?

- What will we do to learn, implement, and master the practices and strategies that will be implemented to improve student learning?

- How will we measure our own team's progress in improving student learning results and mastering research-based practices?

This clear understanding of purpose, strategy, and goals puts teams in a perfect position to take on challenging tasks and build their collective teacher efficacy. It is important to remember, however, that when schools establish the why, what, and how, it involves confronting difficult data, taking on new tasks, and setting ambitious goals. Each of these elements of step 1 can cause some anxiety in teachers and teams. In step 2, coaches take the time to listen to their teachers' fears, questions, and concerns because teacher anxiety is one of the greatest obstacles to building collective teacher efficacy.

Step 2: Listen to Teachers' Fears, Anxieties, Questions, and Concerns

When teachers and teams are presented with the need to modify practice, it is natural for them to feel some stress and anxiety about the change. Even if their coach or leader has clarified why the change is needed, what they will be doing differently, and how they will measure success, they are likely to have some concerns. Teachers may worry that the new practice will be too difficult or complicated. They may stress about the time it will take to learn the new techniques. They might even have a deep-seated fear that they will fail in implementing the new strategy. They are afraid they may be embarrassed in front of their colleagues. They may even fear that they will lose their jobs. Like a child learning to ride a bike for the first time, their fears and anxieties have a negative effect on their efficacy beliefs.

We can choose to ignore teacher anxiety and just move ahead with implementation, believing that teachers and teams will find ways to deal with their stress. But ignoring teacher anxiety doesn't make it go away. It will still percolate in teachers' minds and hearts, negatively affecting wellness and performance. Teachers whose stress is not addressed will conjure up negative outcomes (Bandura, 1977) because they have not been trained to transform their anxiety into enthusiasm for a positive change. If a coach takes time to let teachers share their worries and then explains a plan for addressing those feelings, teachers are much more likely to manage their stress effectively and perform at a higher level.

In step 2 of the CLEAR process for building the collective efficacy of teachers, coaches and leaders *listen* to teachers' fears, anxieties, questions, and concerns. The research on collective efficacy beliefs tells us that it is critically important for leaders to create the space for teachers to be able to be candid about their fears and anxieties. A team that has named its stressors and knows that they are working through them with the support of coaches and leaders will encourage and assist each other as they hit the rough spots. In doing so, they begin to develop a collective sense of power and effectiveness. Creating the space will involve providing a variety of settings and methods for teachers to express their stress. Leaders will need to facilitate open discussions in meetings with the full staff, at the team level, and even with individual teachers. In these sessions, leaders will have to truly listen to their teachers and be open to their questions and concerns. By doing this, the leader or coach works proactively to address how affective states, stress, and emotions, could negatively affect the collective efficacy of their teacher teams.

The purpose of taking the time to listen to teachers' fears, anxieties, questions, and concerns is to identify and address emotions and stress that might negatively affect the development of collective efficacy as teams act on the why, the what, and the how that have been established at the school. To be clear: step 2 is not about revisiting the why, what, and how or making changes in what the school and teams have committed to. Step 2 of the CLEAR process is about hearing teams' questions, concerns, fears, and anxieties, and responding to those concerns in a way that establishes a supportive environment for teams to develop collective efficacy. The most critical component of step 2 is effective listening.

Step 2:

LISTEN

to Teachers' Fears, Anxieties, Questions, and Concerns:

Affective States

Create the space to hear teacher concerns and honor questions. Continue throughout steps 3–5.

Effective leaders listen for content (what is actually being said), listen for meaning and intent (deep listening to discern the underlying meaning), and listen for feelings and values (the affective level of communication (Baker, Dunne-Moses, Calarco, & Gilkey, 2019). Principals, coaches, and team leaders must listen at all these levels to truly understand the state of their teams. Doing so will have a positive impact on their relationship with their teams and their overall school culture. In an examination of the role of active listening in the roles of international school leaders, Matthew R. Merritt (2021) asserts that "effective listening . . . lends itself to a humanistic approach to leadership and associates a leader with a professional culture based on trust, respect, and understanding" (p. 115).

When listening to teachers' fears, anxieties, questions, and concerns, coaches and leaders must be prepared to ask questions of teachers and teams to gauge their comfort level and to ensure that they understand what team members are trying to communicate. This reflects several characteristics of active listening, especially reflecting and clarifying. When meeting with both individuals and teams coaches and leaders should use questions like the following.

- How are you feeling about this change?
- What possibilities do you see in this change?
- What worries you about this change?
- What stresses you most about this change in practice?
- What questions do you have about implementing the new practice?
- How can I support you and your team with learning and implementing this new practice?

When coaches and leaders ask these questions, it creates the space for teachers and teams to be candid about their worries. Capturing and describing these anxieties will make it easier to address and overcome them. Coaches and leaders should also be prepared for the possibility that a team, or an individual teacher, may have an emotional or angry reaction to the new practice or the discussion about implementing it. I have been in the room with coaches when a discussion like this results in a teacher breaking into tears or angrily complaining about what they are being asked to do. In these cases, coaches and leaders can use techniques to try to diffuse the situation. They can ask the teacher why they are upset, give them time to explain their feelings, listen without interrupting, empathize with the teacher's feelings, and offer support. They can also then follow up individually with teachers at another time to hear their concerns.

Coaches and leaders can also gather information about teachers' fears, anxieties, questions, and concerns through anonymous surveys, comment walls, suggestion boxes, and other techniques that do not involve meeting face-to-face with teachers. This provides an avenue for teachers who are not comfortable sharing their questions and concerns in front of others with an avenue to share their concerns anonymously.

The bottom line is this: if we, as leaders and coaches, do not have specific leadership and communication strategies for listening to our teachers, especially in terms of their stresses and anxieties, we will not be able to achieve a high level of collective teacher efficacy in our schools.

Imagine a middle school mathematics team in a small rural school. Their principal is telling them that they must start working collaboratively to develop CFAs. The principal emphasizes that common assessment has been proven as an effective strategy to increase student achievement and build teacher-team effectiveness. But CFAs are something the teachers have never done before. They understand that they must do something to improve their students' performance in mathematics, but this idea about creating and using the same assessments in their courses is kind of scary. They wonder, doesn't the principal understand that they teach the content in their own way? Doesn't he trust each teacher to create a good and accurate assessment? If the teachers do not have an opportunity to share their questions and concerns, their fears will simmer and undermine their adoption of collaborative practices. But if they are given a chance to voice their stress, and their concerns are heard and addressed, there is a better chance that they will be open to trying the new practice.

An important note: although this is step 2 of the process, the work of monitoring teacher emotions and stress does not stop here. Coaches will need to be sensitive to teacher and team worries and anxiety through the entire five steps of the CLEAR process. When a coach sees that teachers or teams are stressed or feeling overwhelmed, he needs to respond by initiating conversations and addressing anxieties.

The first two steps of the CLEAR process provide (1) the foundation for collaborative teamwork (clarify the why, what, and how) and (2) address the stress that teacher teams are feeling (listen to teachers' fears, anxieties, questions, and concerns). This sets the table for the hands-on work to implement new tasks and strategies, which begins in step 3 with exploring examples, models, best practices, and proven processes.

Step 3: Explore Examples, Models, Best Practices, and Proven Processes

Once coaches have clarified why the change is needed, what the teams will be doing, and how success will be measured, and listened to teachers' fears and anxieties, it is critical to get down to the practical collaborative teamwork of unpacking and learning the new practices.

In step 3, coaches and leaders help teams to explore examples, models, best practices, and proven processes. Teachers who have embraced the idea that they are making a change that will help students and have had a chance to voice their questions and concerns will then have practical questions about implementing the new strategy. Coaches must anticipate and be ready to respond to teacher questions like the following.

> **Step 3:**
>
> **EXPLORE**
>
> **Examples, Models, Best Practices, and Proven Processes:**
>
> *Vicarious Experiences*
>
> Show evidence that it can be done!

- How do we know this is doable?

- What does this look like when it's done?

- Can we see an example of how another team has done it?

- Is there another school or another team similar to ours that has been successful with this? What did they do? What can we learn from them?

In step 3 of the CLEAR process, the coach's response to these questions is to facilitate team learning as they explore multiple examples, models, best practices, and proven processes. When coaches lead teams in studying exemplary models of excellent team process, they are providing their teams with what Bandura (1997) calls vicarious experiences or powerful models of success. Providing teams with samples of how other schools and teams have tackled this change helps them to visualize it for themselves. Giving teams an opportunity to consult with another team can provide a vicarious experience that boosts their collective confidence. Facilitating an opportunity for teams to observe other teachers implementing the practice is an even more powerful boost to collective efficacy. Coaches who are working strategically to build the collective efficacy of their teacher teams should have a plan for providing vicarious experiences to their teachers.

Models or examples are most powerful when a learner sees the models as comparable to themselves. A person working out in a gym who sees a much younger person performing an exercise or lifting a heavy weight will experience a limited influence on their self-efficacy beliefs about their own ability. They might say to themselves "I could never do that!" But if they see someone who is a similar age performing at a high level, they are more likely to think "If they can do it, I can do it!" This has important applications in work with teacher teams. When a team of teachers observes a successful team, consults with them, or reviews their work products, this inspires them to do their work at a high level. This is true even if they are already a proficient team. Bandura (1997) explains it this way: "Even those who are highly self-assured will raise their efficacy beliefs if models teach them even better ways of doing things" (p. 87).

Table 2.1 captures some of the different ways that an effective coach can build the collective efficacy of teacher teams through providing vicarious experiences.

Table 2.1: VICARIOUS EXPERIENCES TO BUILD COLLECTIVE TEACHER EFFICACY

Direct Observation	A teacher team is provided the opportunity to observe, in-person or virtually, a model team performing a critical collaborative team task, like reviewing the results of a CFA.
Consultation with Successful Teams	A teacher team is provided the opportunity to consult with a model team. They do not observe the team completing the task, but the team describes their process and answers questions. For example, the model team explains how they use a protocol to review CFA data.
Review of Successful Teams' Products	A teacher team is provided the opportunity to review the work products of a successful team. They do not observe the team performing the task or consult directly with the model team, but they have examples of the team's work to review. For example, they study the successful team's completed data protocol and action steps.

Imagine that the principal of a small rural high school has an English department with five teachers who all teach different grade levels and courses. Due to the small size of their school, many teachers are the only person on the staff that teaches their particular classes. For example, there is only one teacher who teaches ninth-grade English, so she does not have any ninth-grade English teaching colleagues at her school to collaborate with. In PLC language, she is referred to as a *singleton*. All of the teachers at this rural high school have been operating as singletons for as long as anyone can remember. When the principal approaches the team with research that shows that students do better when their teachers work collaboratively across courses and grade levels, rather than isolated from each other as singletons, the teachers on the team are likely to have questions like these.

- Has any other high school done this?
- Do they have the same circumstances and challenges as our school?
- How does it work?
- How did they figure out how to work across different courses and content?
- Can we see what they did?

If coaches respond to these questions by citing work done by teachers at an elementary school, for example, the high school English team is likely to dismiss the model as irrelevant. If, however, the principal and coaches can offer information about a similar high school that implemented cross-course collaboration, teachers are more likely to be open to the change. This is especially true if the model high school is similar in key characteristics like size and demographics. The coach could find stories from schools similar to theirs on All Things PLC (www.allthingsplc.info), where model PLCs share stories of their PLC journeys.

Implementing step 3 of the CLEAR process helps increase the team's belief in themselves by exploring models and best practices that provide evidence that other teams have been successful with the work. Step 3 sets the table for step 4, when coaches lead teams to a deeper implementation of practice and a higher level of collective efficacy.

Step 4: Activate New Learning Through Coaching, Practice, and Implementation

In step 4 of the CLEAR process, coaches activate new learning through coaching, practice, and implementation. Bandura (1997) cites social persuasion as a powerful influence on self-efficacy and collective efficacy. As individuals and groups consider their own ability to successfully complete a task, encouragement from a mentor or coach can be a big boost to their efficacy beliefs. This is especially true if the mentor is seen as knowledgeable and trustworthy (Bandura, 1997).

Athletic coaches at every level learn to get the best out of their teams by encouraging them and expressing their confidence in the team's ability to be successful. Coaches and mentors working with teachers can employ many of the same techniques to build the collective efficacy of teacher teams. Encouragement and support are essential as teams begin to adopt new practices and put them into action.

As coaches lead teams into this higher level of collaborative work, they must anticipate and be prepared to answer questions like these.

- What team processes did other schools use to implement this strategy at a high level?
- How did teams organize and use their time to accomplish implementation?

Step 4:

ACTIVATE

New Learning Through Coaching, Practice, and Implementation:

Social Persuasion

Coach teams to apply what they have learned through feedback and guidance.

- What is the most efficient and effective way to implement this practice?
- How can we best implement this practice here with our staff and our students?

At this step of the process, the teams will be working to take the examples and models they have seen and apply these new ideas to their unique situations. Every school is different. No "one size" that "fits all" exists. A school's size, organization, staff, students, demographics, and history must be considered when planning new initiatives. An effective coach will help their teacher teams to review models and examples and then customize them to meet the needs of their particular school.

For example, when schools and teams read and review stories of model PLC schools on the All Things PLC website, their response isn't usually "That's a great practice! We can do that exactly the way they do it." It is more likely that schools will find processes and strategies that intrigue them. Then they work through figuring out how the practice may be useful to them, asking themselves questions such as, "How can we apply this strategy with our school, with our teams, and with our students?" This is when the guidance of a trusted coach is so important. Coaches acting as guides and mentors help to provide teams with the social persuasion and encouragement that can increase their collective teacher efficacy. To accomplish this, coaches must establish their credibility and expertise, establish positive relationships with their teams, and provide effective, responsive coaching over time.

For a collaborative team of teachers, effective coaching involves careful diagnosis of a team's strengths and needs, development of clear short-term and long-term goals, a strategic coaching plan, encouragement, prompt and specific feedback, and support through the rough spots. Targeted coaching helps teams to build capacity and proficiency with key collaborative team tasks. Differentiated professional development guides teachers and teams to build their own strategies and processes for implementing change. When teachers see that their unified efforts are producing results, it builds the collective efficacy of the team.

Imagine a team of grade 2 teachers being asked to identify essential standards for the first time. They have reviewed examples and seen great models for how teams have organized their learning targets. However, the examples are from other states and different curricula. They are feeling a little overwhelmed by the complexity of the task. They ask about the process that teams used to get from the overwhelming curriculum documents to the clear and efficient team plans they reviewed. To implement this step of the CLEAR process, the coach would provide targeted coaching and help the second-grade team to apply proven protocols to identify, unpack, and clarify learning targets.

By providing social persuasion, the coach would help the teachers on the team to work through the challenges, take greater ownership, and boost their collective efficacy.

Effective coaching continues into step 5 of the CLEAR process, when coaches help teams to analyze their results and recognize their growth.

Step 5: Review Results, Celebrate Growth, and Set New Targets

In step 5 of the CLEAR process—review results, celebrate growth, and set new targets—coaches teach teams to review their goals, analyze data, reflect on challenges, acknowledge wins, and aim for new heights. By coaching teams on how to complete these critical steps, leaders and coaches help them to recognize and celebrate the impact that their collective work is having. This provides the teams with mastery experiences, the most powerful source of self-efficacy and collective efficacy beliefs. When a teacher team sees clear evidence that what they are doing is making a difference in student learning, and therefore in their lives, it is a mastery experience like when a child rides a bike independently for the first time.

In his research, Bandura explains why mastery experiences have such a great influence on efficacy beliefs. Once a person develops self-efficacy through mastery experiences, it changes the way that the person approaches tasks, "People who perceive themselves as highly efficacious act, think, and feel differently from those who perceive themselves as inefficacious. They produce their own future, rather than simply foretell it" (Bandura, 1986, p. 395). When people experience mastery of a task, it greatly increases their confidence that they will be successful with the task in the future. This is particularly true if the person knows that the task is difficult. Bandura (1997) explains, "If people experience only easy successes, they come to expect quick results and are easily discouraged by failure. A resilient sense of efficacy requires experience in overcoming obstacles through perseverant effort" (p. 80).

At this point in the CLEAR process, coaches should anticipate and be prepared to answer questions like these.

- How will we know if this is really working?
- How do we know we are doing the right thing?
- How will we know if we need to make an adjustment?
- What do we do if we don't reach our goal?
- What do we do if we do reach our goal?

As I discussed in step 1, coaches help teams develop collective efficacy by clarifying why they are implementing a task (to respond to student learning needs), what the task involves (the PLC practice or instructional strategy that we are implementing), and how they will measure the impact of what they do (clear long-term and short-term goals that we monitor carefully). The establishment of clear goals is critically important. Without a clear target, it will be difficult for teams to recognize and quantify their growth. Clear goals and regular progress monitoring help teams to have a mastery experience as they see clear evidence that their efforts are having a positive impact. Coaches help teams to develop collective efficacy by providing guidance in gathering baseline data, setting goals that are SMART (specific, measurable, attainable, results-oriented, and timebound), and then monitoring progress regularly (Conzemius & O'Neill, 2014).

> **Step 5:**
>
> ## REVIEW
>
> **Results, Celebrate Growth, and Set New Targets:**
>
> *Mastery Experiences*
>
> Dig into the data on SMART goals, celebrate success, and chase higher targets.

In step 5 of the CLEAR process, coaches lead teams through the process of collecting and analyzing data to determine how much progress they have made toward their goals. Reviewing progress ties back to the essential purpose—to ensure high levels of learning for all students. Coaches must help teams establish habits of honestly reviewing data, so that they can celebrate progress toward their goals and address areas where growth is not happening. Then, as teams achieve their goals, coaches make sure that teams keep momentum by setting new goals to achieve.

Let's look at reviewing results, celebrating growth, and resetting targets at the school level. Imagine a team of kindergarten teachers who are implementing new strategies for helping students master letter names, letter sounds, and reading beginning kindergarten sight words. The team assesses students at the beginning of the school year and finds that only 20 percent of students meet the grade-level targets. If they do not have a process for carefully monitoring and reviewing individual student progress and sharing that with each other, they will not have a clear picture of whether their efforts are having an impact. If, on the other hand, a coach helps them to review data and monitor progress on their SMART goals routinely, the team can celebrate the small wins as students begin to grow in skill. As the percentage of students meeting the target increases, the team sees the impact of their work and has a mastery experience that increases their collective efficacy.

CLEAR Thoughts and Next Steps

In this chapter, I have provided an overview of the CLEAR process for building the collective efficacy of teacher teams. As figure 2.1 (page 36) shows, the CLEAR process is a sequential process. Each step is carefully designed to build on the previous one. So, before we go deeper into each step of the process in chapters 3–7, here are a few suggestions.

The research we have reviewed supports step-by-step progression from clarifying why to make a change (compelling student data), explaining what the change involves (research-based strategies), and how to measure the change (setting and monitoring goals), to listening to fears and anxieties, to exploring models and processes, to activating new learning through coaching, to reviewing progress and setting new goals. The power of the CLEAR process is that it aligns with decades of research about how individuals and teams develop efficacy beliefs.

I strongly encourage coaches using this resource to follow all five of the steps and suggest that leaders and coaches use the process as described, completing the steps in the order they are presented while keeping in mind that step 2 (see figure 2.1, page 36) may stretch through the entire process and be needed at any point in which teachers reach a stressful moment in the process and need their fears, anxieties, questions, and concerns listened to. Similarly, effective leaders will use the foundation established in step 1 to support and drive the process throughout all five steps. As leaders and coaches work to build the collective efficacy of their teams, they will look for opportunities to reinforce the why (our students and their learning), the what (the actions we are taking together for our students), and the how (the aspirational goals we have set for our students and their success). When leading change and building the collective efficacy of their teacher teams, leaders must frequently remind staff why they are doing what they are doing. The most effective leaders will find ways to remind staff that all their hard work is about their students' learning and futures.

Life as an educational leader can be very stressful and there are often pressures to expedite processes or skip steps to save time. While I understand these pressures, I highly recommend following the process as written, and avoiding what Rick DuFour and colleagues would call "seductive shortcuts" (DuFour et al., 2024, p. 8).

- **Seductive Shortcut 1: Skipping over the WHY**—When implementing step 1, please be sure to spend time clarifying the why, as well as the what, and the how. Effective coaches will be sure to give clarifying the why (the reason for the change) the attention and time it deserves. Some leaders will feel the urgency to act and immediately rush to clarifying the strategy for making the change (the what) without adequately explaining why the teachers should make the change in the first place. This leaves staff without a compelling reason for implementing the strategies and goals for change, and it undercuts teacher understanding and commitment. When clarifying the why is solid and then followed by a clear explanation of the what and the how, teacher teams have the strong foundation they need to build their collective efficacy.

- **Seductive Shortcut 2: Skipping over step 2**—Some leaders and coaches will be tempted to skip from step 1 right to step 3, avoiding the work of listening to teachers' fears and anxieties. But skipping this step ignores a key piece of the research on how teams form collective efficacy beliefs. I understand that inviting teachers to share their fears and anxieties is a little scary for some leaders and coaches. Ironic, yes? But if we do not give teachers the space to share their thoughts, stresses, and questions, they will simmer under the surface and then blow up at some point in the process. Skipping step 2 also represents a missed opportunity to build trust with teachers and teams. When a leader or coach takes the time to listen to concerns, the teachers feel heard, and they are more likely to give a new initiative a solid effort.

- **Seductive Shortcut 3: Starting the process at step 4**—The most common scenario, unfortunately, is that the process that many leaders and coaches involves jumping directly to step 4. They tell the teachers that there needs to be a change (without a full explanation or building shared knowledge) and then start holding professional development sessions to drive home the requirements. Unfortunately, this approach appears to be rather common with directives that come from the state or the district level. This top-down approach is time-efficient and may generate some compliance, but it is unlikely to build commitment, competence, or collective efficacy. As we have discussed, step 1 lays the foundation and step 2 addresses affective states and clears the way for deep learning. Steps 3 and 4 are both critical because they provide powerful sources of collective efficacy (vicarious experiences and social persuasion) in the process of building toward mastery experiences for the team (step 5). Teams that have a foundation of effective models and differentiated coaching are more likely to achieve mountaintop breakthroughs that we all want for teachers and students.

Leaders and coaches who follow the CLEAR process as described will have the best chance of building the collective efficacy of their teacher teams and harnessing that power to benefit their students.

As we finish chapter 2 and a first exploration of the CLEAR process, we'll review critical takeaways, reflect on the implications for our work, and plan an action step.

Let's review the critical takeaways.

- To strategically build the collective efficacy of their teacher teams, leaders and coaches should plan their actions based on the research about how efficacy beliefs are formed and strengthened.

- The four sources of efficacy beliefs are mastery experiences, vicarious experiences, social persuasion, and affective states.

- The CLEAR process for building the collective efficacy of teacher teams in a PLC aligns with the research by clarifying the why, what, and how (step 1), listening to teachers' anxieties, fears, questions, and concerns (step 2), exploring examples, models, best practices, and proven processes (step 3), activating new learning through coaching, implementation, and practice (step 4), and reviewing progress, celebrating growth, and setting new targets (step 5).

- Leaders of all types and in varying school situations can use the CLEAR process to build the collective efficacy of their teacher teams.

- Leaders and coaches using the CLEAR process with their teams should be careful to implement all five steps in the sequence that is described. This will produce the best results.

Let's reflect on the content from this chapter.

1. Have you fully explained why you are asking your teacher teams to do what you are asking them to do?

2. Have you fully explained what they are expected to do and provided the necessary clarity, guidance, and training?

3. Have you fully explained how you will measure success?

4. Have you given teachers a chance to share their questions and concerns, as well as their fears and anxieties about what they are being asked to do?

5. Have you provided targeted coaching and ongoing support to help teachers implement what you are expecting?

6. Have you helped teacher teams to set clear goals, monitor growth, and celebrate success?

7. How could you enhance your work with teacher teams with strategies and tools that would deliberately build collective teacher efficacy?

8. What are the concrete steps you could take in your next sessions with your teacher teams?

Let's plan an action step.

When you reflect on the research about building collective efficacy, how could you be more intentional about clarifying the why, what, and how? How could you be more strategic about providing teams with vicarious experiences (models), targeted coaching (social persuasion), and celebration of growth (master experiences)? Are there ways that you could be more aware of how affective states (emotional arousal) might affect your teacher teams?

_____

_____

_____

_____

_____

_____

_____

_____

_____

Before heading into your next team meeting, consider reviewing the four sources of efficacy beliefs. Which is the most challenging for you to implement with your teams? Why?

_____

_____

_____

_____

_____

_____

_____

_____

_____

_____

CHAPTER THREE

Step 1 of the CLEAR Process:

Clarify the Why, the What, and the How

*F*OR LEADERS AND coaches working to build the collective teacher efficacy of collaborative teams, the first step is to establish a foundation for collective efficacy to grow. Teacher teams must understand why they are being asked to do something, what they are being asked to do, and how success will be measured. Thus, step 1 of the CLEAR process is to *clarify the why, the what, and the how*.

In this chapter, I provide an overview of the research on leading change at the school level, especially in terms of clarifying the rationale for change (why), communicating expectations about the change (what), and measuring the impact of the change (how). This is critical because clarifying the why, what, and how provides the foundation for building collective teacher efficacy and harnessing its power to transform schools. I describe strategies for implementing this work with today's teacher teams and provide tools that help leaders and coaches to plan and implement this step of the CLEAR process. A real-world-inspired scenario offers examples of a leader and team experiencing challenge and, ultimately, doing this work. At the end of the chapter, the CLEAR Thoughts and Next Steps section (page 86) provides reflection questions and action planning for leaders and coaches to move forward with the work.

Now, let's explore part 1 of our scenario, where a school principal is trying to implement a significant change with his teacher teams without providing them with the critical foundation of understanding the why, what, and how.

Meet the Team

At Einstein High School, it is a Tuesday in March, and the faculty lounge is buzzing. All the teachers are still reacting to yesterday's staff meeting. Dr. Brown, the principal, shared his plan to have all departments at Einstein meet regularly as collaborative teams next school year. This is a surprise and a real curve ball to everyone on the staff! For years, the teachers at Einstein have worked independently to plan instruction, deliver lessons, and grade students. This makes sense because most of the teachers at their small high school are the only teachers who teach their courses. Teachers enjoy the autonomy of planning their lessons to match their own interests and teaching styles. And the students are doing fine! Why would this new principal, still in his first year at Einstein, want to make a change like this? Some teachers are saying that he had attended a professional conference and "got all excited about teachers working in teams." But in the staff meeting, he hadn't really given a reason for why he thought the change was necessary. Does he think teachers at Einstein are not doing a good job? Doesn't he realize that everyone at Einstein is already overwhelmed with the many responsibilities that they have? Doesn't he know that teachers are feeling stressed out, and some are considering leaving teaching altogether? How can he think this is the right time to announce a new initiative? And why? We are doing fine! Most of the students are doing OK, we don't have a lot of behavior problems, and the majority of the parents are satisfied with what we are doing. Some teachers are already saying that they will resist the change and look to the teachers' union for support. Others are saying to wait and see if Dr. Brown shares more about his rationale for a change. Still others are saying, "This too shall pass," and they are ignoring what their young principal announced. The Einstein staff lounge is awash with confusion, frustration, anger, and apathy—not exactly the best building blocks for school improvement.

Dr. Brown means well, but he is making some critical leadership mistakes. He is trying to launch a significant change in practice without clearly explaining why the change is necessary. In addition, he is not providing details about what the change will involve. Finally, he has not been clear about how they will measure whether or not the change is working. To build the collective efficacy of teacher teams in a PLC, leaders must start by *clarifying the why, the what, and the how.*

What the Research Says

The research that supports step 1 of the CLEAR process—clarify the why, the what, and the how—is found throughout the literature on leading change in organizations, including schools and school systems (Bandura, 1997; Collins, 2001; Donohoo, 2017; Errida & Lotfi, 2021; Hoogsteen, 2020; Kotter, 2007). Leaders who are working to implement change in their organizations are more successful when they explain a purpose for the change, provide details about what the change involves, and explain how they plan to measure success (Collins, 2001; Errida & Lotfi, 2021; Kotter, 2007). In an educational setting, school leaders and coaches who are attempting to lead their schools through change are also more successful when they take the time to provide a powerful purpose, a clear strategy, and common goals (Donohoo, 2017; Eaker, Hagadone, Keating, & Rhoades, 2021; Muhammad & Cruz, 2019). When these educational leaders are working to build the collective efficacy of teacher teams, the same principles apply. Principals, coaches, and teacher leaders who wish to nurture collective teacher efficacy in their buildings must clarify the why (the compelling reason for teachers to change practice), the what (research-based strategies to address the why), and the how (clear goals and a system for monitoring progress). Providing teacher teams with this critical information helps to create the foundation for collective efficacy to develop. Leaders who fail to build this foundation jeopardize their efforts to build the collective efficacy of their teacher teams. Whether you are a superintendent, a principal, an instructional coach, or team leader, you will have better success building the collective efficacy of your teams if you take the time to clarify the why, the what, and the how. And whether you are in a school that has not started to implement the PLC process, a school that is midstream in the PLC journey, or a high-performing model PLC school, building this foundation is a vital first step in building the collective efficacy of teacher teams.

In the context of a PLC, the first step to launching the PLC process in a school or district is always to build shared knowledge. DuFour and colleagues (2024) explain, "When all staff members have access to the same information, it increases the likelihood that they will arrive at similar conclusions" (p. 36). The research on collective efficacy reinforces this truth. We must engage staff in learning processes that help them understand why a change is needed, what the change should be, and how we will determine whether or not the change is working and helping us to achieve our goals.

Clarifying the why, the what, and the how is also aligned with the three big ideas of PLCs: (1) our fundamental purpose is to ensure high levels of learning for all students; (2) we must work collaboratively to fulfill our fundamental purpose; and (3) we must have a results orientation and gather evidence every day about how students are learning (DuFour et al., 2016, pp. 18–19). Figure 3.1 shows the alignment of the three big ideas and clarifying the why, what, and how.

The Three Big Ideas of PLCs	CLEAR Process Step 1
Big Idea #1: Our fundamental purpose is to ensure high levels of learning for all students.	**Clarify the Why:** Why are we doing this? We need to implement this task because it will help us to fulfill our fundamental purpose of ensuring high levels of learning for all students.
Big Idea #2: We must work collaboratively to fulfill our fundamental purpose.	**Clarify the What:** What do we need to do to? We need to work collaboratively and implement research-based strategies and practices.
Big Idea #3: We must have a results orientation and gather evidence every day about how students are learning.	**Clarify the How:** How will we know if it is working? We need to set clear goals and monitor progress so that we know what is working and what we must adjust.

Source: Adapted from DuFour et al., 2024.

Figure 3.1: ALIGNMENT OF THE THREE BIG IDEAS OF PLCS AND CLEAR PROCESS STEP 1.

Let's dig deeper into the research about why it is so important for educational leaders and coaches to provide their teams with a strong foundation for their collective efficacy. The following sections detail the research base for each part of step 1 of the CLEAR process.

Clarifying the Why

In step 1 of the CLEAR process, leaders and coaches take the time to clarify why teacher teams must modify their practice. Remember, at its heart, collective teacher efficacy is about teachers believing their collective efforts can positively influence student learning and subsequently seeing evidence that their work is making a difference. Collective teacher efficacy is *always* about student learning. Accordingly, when coaches and leaders start the CLEAR process by clarifying the why, it involves presenting compelling student learning data that show a change is necessary. This compelling why then motivates teachers and teams to be open to change and modifying their practice.

As leaders and coaches begin the CLEAR process by clarifying the why, it is important for them to take note of the current atmosphere in education. Teachers today are being asked to do more than at any other time in history. The avalanche of school, district, state, and federal requirements and expectations is overwhelming. When combined with the unique stresses created in recent years by a global pandemic, it is not surprising that a record number of teachers are leaving the profession and fewer young people are choosing education as their career (Bryner, 2021; Diliberti et al., 2021; Goldhaber & Holden, 2021; Perna, 2024; Pressley, Ha, & Learn, 2021). As a matter of professional respect and practical leadership, we owe teachers a compelling rationale whenever we, as leaders, coaches, or supervisors, require them to add something to their proverbial plate. If we are asking them to do something additional or that requires teachers to change practice, we ought to have a solid data-driven, research-grounded basis for why this change is necessary and why it is worthy of their time and effort. The great majority of teachers and teams are willing to put in extra effort if they know that it will help students learn and help them be more successful (Eaker et al., 2021). When we, as educational leaders, don't take the time to explain the why and simply rely on positional power and the ability to mandate, we will not get maximum effort, we will not build collective efficacy, and we will most likely create confusion and resentment. On the other hand, when we do take the time to clarify the why, we start to build the foundation for the collective efficacy of teacher teams, which has been shown to increase teacher morale and commitment (Donohoo, 2017; Hoogsteen, 2020).

The research on self-efficacy and collective efficacy tells us that, when teachers are presented with a new task, they will draw on their experiences to make a judgment about their ability to complete that task. They will determine their own self-efficacy beliefs and, as a group, their collective efficacy beliefs (Bandura, 1997). Teachers will make judgments about the difficulty of the task, whether or not they have the resources to complete the task, and whether or not they think their school is capable of implementing the task effectively (Goddard et al., 2000). The research also tells us that the sources of self-efficacy beliefs we reviewed in chapter 1—mastery experiences, vicarious experiences, social persuasion, and affective or physiological states (Bandura, 1995) are influential in determining whether the team approaches this new task with a high or low sense of collective efficacy. Finally, the research confirms that a group is more likely to approach a new task with a high sense of efficacy if there is a compelling reason to complete the task (Bandura, 1997; Donohoo, 2017; Hoogsteen, 2020). If we want a group of teachers to build their collective efficacy for a task, it begins with them understanding why they should be doing the task in the first place.

Change is difficult. Anyone who has ever tried to break a bad habit or adopt a new positive practice can attest to this. As humans, we tend to get stuck in our ways and there is comfort in that consistency. In *Atomic Habits*, psychologist James Clear (2018) writes, "Human brains are hardwired to take the path of least resistance and to exert the least energy necessary. That makes the adoption of new habits hard" (p. 44). Brain researchers have found that changing our habits and routines has a neurological origin:

> We naturally resist change because change represents uncertainty—and uncertainty is threatening and painful for a brain that wants to keep us safe and alive. Although many of today's threats are no longer life-or-death situations, our brain still protects us as if they were just that. (Boschi, 2020, p. 2)

Varying from our routine to install a new behavior is hard work, and it takes tons of effort and persistence to achieve sustained growth.

The research on self-efficacy helps us to understand why change is so difficult. When we are asked to change our behavior, we are being asked to perform new tasks—to do something that we haven't done before. If we are being asked to do something that is new and challenging, or something that we have had difficulty with in the past, we are likely to have a physiological response and feel anxious about what we are being asked to do. This can affect our view of the task, our expectations for success, and our willingness to persevere when the task gets difficult (Bandura, 1977). A powerful why is essential in helping people to overcome the negative aspects of implementing change.

When change involves modifying the behaviors and actions of a *group*, instead of just an individual, the challenge for leaders and managers is multiplied. How do we convince a group of unique persons, with different perspectives and needs, that they should invest themselves in learning something new or changing the way they do their work? It is a daunting challenge, yet it is at the core of all personal and organizational progress. It is also the foundation of building the collective efficacy of teacher teams.

Researchers and leaders have published hundreds of books and articles analyzing the best strategies for leading change in an organization. Researcher and author John P. Kotter has studied leadership and change in organizations and written several books on the subject. In *Leading Change*, Kotter (2012) presents an eight-step process for leading others through an organizational change. The first step is to "create urgency." Kotter (2012) explains that leaders must share information that convinces the majority of managers that "the status quo is unacceptable" and the "considerable change is absolutely necessary" (p. 36). Leaders must explain why there needs to be a change.

Jim Collins is a well-known author and researcher who has studied what makes some companies thrive and others fail. In *Good to Great*, a collection of his research on this subject,

Collins (2001) asserts that one of the characteristics of successful companies is the commitment to "confront the brutal facts" (p. 69). When people in an organization are presented with data that show that they are not being successful with their core purpose, it provides momentum and motivation to change practice. When a corporate team is shown evidence that sales are dropping and they are quickly losing market share, workers are more open to change because the mission has become saving the company and protecting their jobs (Collins, 2001). Again, if you want your people to implement change, you must give them a compelling why.

In a school-based PLC, the "brutal facts" are not about sales figures and profit projections. The critical data in a school is about students and their learning.

CLARIFYING THE WHY—HIGH SCHOOL GRADUATION RATES

A high school principal was very concerned about data that showed a high percentage of her incoming twelfth graders were not on track to graduate. She was working to get staff to implement some new strategies to improve these results. During a preservice session, she presented the numerical data she had prepared about the percentage of students in danger of not graduating. She noted a low level of staff engagement. Next, she shared the names of the eighty or so students who would not graduate from high school if they stayed on their current path. The principal noted that seeing the names inspired a higher level of engagement from her teachers. Finally, she displayed a poster that she and her team had created in advance that had photos of the faces of each of the students in danger of not graduating. Every staff member was transfixed by the display. They each saw students they knew, students they had taught, students they had coached. At the end of the meeting, numerous staff members approached the photo display, reviewing the pictures, even touching the faces of the students they knew. The why had become real. The urgency was now personal. Throughout the school year, the principal reminded her teacher teams of the mission to do whatever it took to help all those students graduate successfully at the end of the year. She reinforced the urgency of this mission in staff meetings, sessions with teams, and even informal conversations with individual teachers. This kept teachers and teams thinking about these students and evaluating their own actions: What can I do to help these students? By doing the right preparations, engaging her staff in meaningful sessions, and following through with effective communication, the principal was able to connect her staff to a compelling why.

In a PLC, Big Idea #1 is our why. Our fundamental purpose is to ensure high levels of learning for all students. It is why we exist as a district, school, or teacher team. When we set out to build the collective efficacy of our teacher teams, we remind them of the why—our commitment to student learning. We present compelling student data that show that we are not fully achieving our fundamental purpose—we have some students who are not learning at high levels—and we need to respond. Clarifying the why in step 1 of the CLEAR process reconnects teachers and teams to their fundamental purpose. Reminding teachers of their fundamental purpose helps to set the foundation for building collective efficacy because teachers will see a connection between what they are being asked to do and the higher purpose of ensuring learning for all students.

Even armed with compelling data and an ability to present that data clearly, leading change in a school requires a special set of leadership skills. Anthony Muhammad and Luis F. Cruz are experienced school administrators, authors, and recognized experts on implementing the PLC process in schools. In their excellent book, *Time for Change*, Muhammad and Cruz (2019) assert leaders must create "cognitive investment" in the proposed change. They do this by involving those affected by the change in "examining evidence, weighing options, and engaging in dialogue, both externally and internally" (p. 19). Again, when teachers and teams are given the opportunity to learn and understand the why for a given change, they are more likely to give the change their best effort, and even persevere when implementation is challenging.

Once leaders have established the why, they must help their teachers and teams to understand what they will be doing to address the compelling student need. Once urgency has been established, conscientious teachers will want to know what to do. The second component in step 1 of the CLEAR process is to clarify what we will be changing.

Clarifying the What

The second part of step 1 of the CLEAR process for building the collective efficacy of teacher teams is to clarify the what. Once leaders have presented a compelling case for why teams must change to adjust their practice, they must provide clarity about *what* the teacher teams will be expected to do. Effective leaders work with staff to learn together and identify clear strategies that can be implemented to address the compelling need: What can we do to respond to our students' learning difficulties (our why) and achieve better results? Teachers want and need the details about what they will be expected to do differently. Providing clear information and guidance about the work to be enacted helps teachers to visualize what they must do and makes them more open to the task at hand (Muhammad & Cruz, 2019). In the absence of information about what they will be expected to do, many teachers will try to fill in the blanks themselves and imagine all sorts of difficult tasks they will be assigned, which has a negative effect on their personal self-efficacy and their collective efficacy as a team (Bandura, 1997). DuFour and colleagues (2024) warn that "if uninformed people are asked to make decisions, they will make uninformed decisions. Without access to pertinent information, they resort to debating opinions or retreating to a muddied middle ground" (p. 36). Providing clarity about the new strategies to be implemented is a key step in building the collective efficacy of teacher teams.

Clarifying the what is an important step in leading change in a variety of contexts. Collins (2001) explains how effective businesses adopt the "hedgehog concept" (p. 92). This term goes back to the folktale about a fox and a hedgehog. The fox tries a variety of methods to attack the hedgehog, but he is not successful. The hedgehog's spiny exterior consistently repels the fox's advances. The story teaches us that focusing on one thing and doing it perfectly, like the hedgehog's defense, is more effective than trying to implement a wide variety of practices. Collins found that successful companies identified a specific strategy that they could execute at a high level to achieve their goals, rather than implementing a myriad of plans that will get limited results. In other words, the companies with the greatest and longest-lasting results determined what they were good at and concentrated on doing it better than anyone else. The data showed that these companies had much better outcomes over time than companies that tried to be active in different products and services because that led to a scattered and inconsistent approach that did not result in gains (Collins, 2001).

For leaders in education, Douglas Reeves echoes the importance of focus. He warns that school leaders must be careful to limit the new initiatives that they propose, or *impose*, on staff. Reeves (2021) warns against "initiative fatigue," which occurs when leaders launch so many competing initiatives that the school staff are overwhelmed and ends up not implementing any of the strategies well. I have worked with schools and districts that undermined their own efforts to improve instructional practice by trying to do too many things at the same time. Though their intentions were noble, when you launch multiple new curricula, a new coaching model, new district assessments, new requirements for social-emotional learning, a new teacher evaluations system, and so on in the same year, schools and teachers just don't have the bandwidth for all of it, so often none of it is implemented with quality. Leaders and coaches who will require teachers to change practice must be selective and concentrate all their efforts in a limited number of high-leverage strategies that will get the best results.

When implementing change in a school or district, Muhammad and Cruz (2019) argue that transformational school and district leaders must create "functional investment" (p. 63) with staff. Functional investment happens when teachers and staff understand the strategy that is being implemented to achieve student learning results. Furthermore, they receive guidance, professional development, and support to help them implement the strategy at a high level. Muhammad and Cruz (2019) warn, "Leaders should not assume that people within the organization have the ability to produce a desired outcome simply because they have communicated the outcome to them" (p. 64). Instead, transformational leaders have a concrete plan to build knowledge, and ensure that all staff members "feel equipped to successfully accomplish the task" (Muhammad & Cruz, 2019, p. 65).

In a district or school that is working to implement PLCs, the emphasis is on collaboration. Leaders and coaches work with teams to identify effective strategies to address their students' needs. Then, collaborative teams work together to implement the chosen strategies at a high level. This is encompassed in Big Idea #2.

Big Idea #2 is about *what* we need to do to fulfill our fundamental purpose. To ensure high levels of learning for all students, we must work collaboratively and take collective responsibility for student success. We cannot do this critical work in isolation. The research is clear that student achievement increases when teachers work as high-performing collaborative teams, as opposed to isolated independent contractors (DuFour et al., 2024). As educators in a PLC, we must constantly refine and improve our collaborative processes so that they result in student learning. Clarifying the what in step 1 of the CLEAR process is about identifying what we need to do to address our student achievement needs. Clarifying the what also reminds teacher teams of the value of collaboration. This helps to set the foundation for building collective efficacy because it reinforces the idea that the collective power of the team is greater than the influence of individual teachers. Providing specifics about what the team is expected to do in terms of strategy also helps to increase the team's confidence that they can accomplish what is asked of them.

CLARIFYING THE WHAT—SYSTEMATIC INTERVENTIONS

I worked with an intermediate school during the COVID-19 pandemic in 2020. The school served over six hundred students in grades 4 and 5. The school had a positive culture, hard-working staff, and a supportive community, but the student achievement results were not where the school wanted them to be. In particular, a certain percentage of the student body that consistently failed to meet targets in reading and mathematics was cause for concern. Year after year, the majority of the students performed well on the state tests, but always approximately 30–35 percent of the students were not successful, no matter what the teachers and administration tried. As the school learned more about the PLC process, the four critical questions, and systems of support for students, the administrators and teacher teams became convinced that they could help these students if they revised their processes for providing students with timely interventions. The principal and the guiding coalition clarified the why for teacher teams by sharing data that showed which students were struggling. Next, the guiding coalition built their own shared knowledge about effective systems of intervention by working with coaches and studying research. The guiding coalition then built shared knowledge with the full staff and proposed several options for modifying the master schedule so that students could get the extra help they needed. They took the time to carefully lay out the responsibilities of all staff and answered questions that came up in sessions. They even gave the new system a trial run at the end of one school year before launching it the following fall. This helped all staff to have a clear understanding of the what. They knew what they were expected to do and how it was connected to their why. The principal and guiding coalition communicated consistently about expectations and followed up with teams to make sure that the plan was being implemented. As a result, student achievement on classroom assessments and the state test increased, and the school was recognized as a model PLC school.

When educational leaders work with their teachers and teams to identify a clear strategy for addressing their student data, they add to the foundation that is needed for collective teacher efficacy to develop. Next, leaders and coaches must explain how teams will measure whether the change is working.

Clarifying the How

The third component of step 1 of the CLEAR process is to clarify the how—how will we measure the effectiveness of our strategy? The research tells us that effective leaders working to build the collective efficacy of their teams must provide a clear plan for setting goals and reviewing growth (Bandura, 1995; Donohoo, 2017; Hoogsteen, 2020; Kotter, 2012).

In a corporate setting, Kotter (2012) describes how effective managers who are leading change connect the new practices to be implemented with a goal to be achieved. By "developing a vision and strategy," leaders help their teams to envision how they can work together to achieve the results they want (Kotter, 2012, p. 75). Without this connection, teams lack direction.

In schools, Donohoo (2016) cites "goal consensus" as one of the "six enabling conditions for collective teacher efficacy to flourish" (p. 5). Teachers are more likely to devote themselves to collaborative effort, and thereby develop collective efficacy, if they have a clear picture of what they are trying to accomplish. After all, the essence of collective teacher efficacy is their collective belief that they can work together to have a positive influence on student learning. If they are not setting learning goals and monitoring progress, what evidence will they have that their efforts are making a difference? Plainly stated, you cannot have collective teacher efficacy without clear goals and monitoring of progress. Indeed, Hoogsteen (2020) argues that principals are most effective in promoting collective efficacy in their teacher teams when they use their power as leaders to "set and monitor common goals" (p. 4). Leaders begin the process of building the collective efficacy of their teachers by uniting teams around common goals to improve student learning.

Muhammad and Cruz (2019) explain how shared goals are an important component of establishing a "culture of accountability," which they define as "a professional attitude whereby peers respectfully hold one another accountable for collectively developed and agreed-on actions" (p. 85).

In a PLC setting, this accountability rests on a system that values real data and meaningful response to it—Big Idea #3, a results orientation. We should be hungry every day for evidence about student learning and eager to review information together that tells us if what we are doing is working. If we have a strategy that is positively influencing student learning, let's work to replicate and increase that strategy. If a strategy is not getting results, let's make an adjustment. Clarifying the how in step 1 of the CLEAR process helps to establish the foundation for building the collective efficacy of teams by giving teacher teams clear goals to pursue as well as processes for monitoring progress.

When principals guide their teacher teams to develop learning goals that are specific, measurable, attainable, results-oriented, and timebound (SMART; Conzemius & O'Neill, 2014), they provide a critical foundation for the formation of collective teacher efficacy. When a team of teachers has a clear collective understanding of the specific goals they are trying to achieve for their students, this generates motivation that contributes to their individual self-efficacy as teachers and their collective efficacy as a team. Without a clear goal, a team is less likely to exert full effort and it is less probable that they will demonstrate perseverance when the task becomes challenging or when results appear slowly (Bandura, 1997; Goddard et al., 2004). Having clear shared goals also helps teachers and teams to hold each other accountable for their collective efforts.

In a PLC, the most fundamental goals for a collaborative team in a PLC will always be focused on student learning, but teams can also benefit from discussing, setting, and monitoring goals for improved team *processes and products*. If teams are being asked to implement new practices, it is helpful for them to monitor their implementation and celebrate as they make progress. For example, a team might feel overwhelmed the first time that they are asked to unpack a curriculum standard into student-friendly language and sequential learning targets. Their coach encourages them to set a goal to complete draft learning progressions for all of their essential standards in reading by the end of the school year. As the team continues to work and hammers out new learning progressions as the year goes on, they take note of their progress and celebrate their growth. This can be a big boost to their collective efficacy. I will discuss this in greater detail in chapters 6 and 7.

CLARIFYING THE HOW—MONITORING PROGRESS THROUGH COMMON FORMATIVE ASSESSMENTS (CFAS)

When I was principal at Viers Mill Elementary, our goal setting was focused on students and reading proficiency. Our reading data became the "brutal facts" that drove our PLC effort. I worked with members of my guiding coalition to organize and share the reading data with the full staff. The data were difficult to look at in the beginning. For example, only 9 percent of our students receiving special education services met the standard on the state test in reading. But confronting the data was the starting point for our mission. It wasn't about working harder. It was about changing the way we worked to get better results for our students. The urgency fueled our work and helped us to persevere, even when it was difficult. A big part of this effort was figuring out how to set goals and monitor our progress regularly. If our goal was to make sure that all our students could read at grade level, we couldn't wait until the end-of-the-year state assessment to find out how they were doing. Even waiting until the end of each nine-week marking period seemed too long to check on students and their progress. Through a comprehensive strategy to use frequent CFAs, the teacher teams at Viers Mill learned to check on student reading proficiency on a much more frequent basis. This gave teachers a more accurate picture of individual students' reading performance so that they could be provided supports, if necessary, in a timely fashion. Teachers and teams could see on a weekly basis that they were making progress toward achieving their team and school goals. The staff's efforts gradually resulted in more students reading at grade-level targets and overall reading proficiency increasing. This growth culminated in Viers Mill being named a National Blue Ribbon School of Excellence five years later. While the recognition was nice, the most important thing for the staff at Viers Mill was that we knew we were now sending students to middle school equipped to succeed and even excel. We knew that we had our students on a positive trajectory that would give them many options. This would not have happened if we had not learned how to carefully monitor individual student progress in reading. A strategic how helped us to make a difference in our students' success.

In summary, the research we have reviewed makes it clear that school leaders who are trying to build the collective efficacy of their teacher teams must provide teams with a compelling rationale for why they need to change and take on new tasks (clarify the why), what the tasks and strategies will involve (clarify the what), and how the effectiveness of the new tasks and strategies will be measured (clarify the how). Said another way, understanding the why (the compelling student achievement need), the what (the research-based strategies that will help us to address the need), and the how (our processes for setting goals and monitoring progress) provides teachers and teams with a solid foundation for taking on new tasks. When leaders and coaches provide their teams with this type of clarity, they establish a great environment for collective efficacy to grow. They create the conditions to harness the power of collective teacher efficacy in their schools.

Now, equipped with this research base, let's explore some practical strategies and tools for doing this work with teacher teams.

Making It CLEAR

The practical work of clarifying why there needs to be a change, what the change involves, and how the change will be measured breaks down into three areas for educational leaders: preparation, engagement, and follow-through.

1. **Preparation:** As leaders clarify why, what, and how with their teams, they must begin by doing the necessary preparation and homework to plan how they will lead this initiative. Critical aspects to the planning process must be completed if you are to have a successful launch and build the collective efficacy of your teacher teams. When principals and coaches neglect the advance planning piece, they risk having an ineffective rollout of the initiative, which can dramatically reduce the likelihood that it will be successful. This, in turn, makes it less likely that teacher teams will develop collective efficacy.

2. **Engagement:** Next, principals and coaches must engage their teachers and teams in meaningful collaborative learning experiences. High levels of staff engagement are critical to the work of building collective teacher efficacy. When leaders and coaches facilitate collective learning sessions that are focused on real data and real problems, they will engage the adult learners on their staff. On the other hand, principals and other leaders who try to implement change through top-down proclamations and power-based directives sacrifice their opportunity to build ownership and true collective teacher efficacy.

3. **Follow-through:** Finally, leaders must plan and carry out effective follow-through. Clarifying why there needs to be a change, what the change involves, and how the change will be measured is not a one-shot deal. Effective leaders will have a long-term strategy for how to reinforce the why, what, and how and support their teams as they tackle new tasks. When leaders do not follow up effectively, teacher teams can lose their sense of urgency about the student learning data, their clarity about what to do, and their commitment to achieving goals.

Figure 3.2 provides an overview of how the preparation, engagement, and follow-through apply across clarifying the why, what, and how.

	Clarify the WHY	Clarify the WHAT	Clarify the HOW
	Why do we need to make a change? Why do we need to learn new strategies and tasks? Compelling student learning need	What changes are we implementing? Research-based, high-leverage strategies to improve student learning, including the top ten tasks of teams in a PLC	How will we measure success? How will we know if the change is working? Clear SMART goals, short-term and long-term to monitor progress
Preparation	Ask questions about student learning. Gather data and information about student learning. Identify strengths, needs, trends. Design a plan for engaging staff with student data.	Generate questions about effective strategies. Collect data and information about research-based strategies. Identify possible high-leverage strategies that fit the student need. Design a plan for engaging staff with research-based strategies.	Explore questions about current state and desired state. Gather data to clarify the current state and desired state. Identify possible ranges for school and team goals. Design a plan to engage staff in setting goals.
Engagement	Implement the plan and engage staff in collaborative learning around the student data. Build shared knowledge about the student data, leading to identification of priorities. Identify the highest priority student achievement need as specifically as possible.	Implement the plan and engage staff in collaborative learning around strategies for improvement. Build shared knowledge about research-based strategies, leading to identification of high-leverage strategies to implement. Identify one or two high-leverage instructional or team process strategies to implement and monitor.	Implement the plan and engage staff in collaborative learning around data to set goals. Build shared knowledge about student data, current state, and desired state to establish effective SMART goals. Establish clear school goals and provide guidance for teams to create team goals.
Follow-Through	Reinforce the high priority student need in ongoing communications. Maintain communication with teams to assess needs and provide supports as necessary to maintain focus on student learning need.	Reinforce expectations for implementing the strategies and communicate guidance and support on how to implement. Maintain communication with teams to assess needs and provide supports as necessary to implement chosen strategies.	Reinforce common goals by referring to them, bringing attention to them. Maintain communication with teams to assess needs and provide supports as necessary to keep teams focused on goals and their progress toward achieving them.

Figure 3.2: OVERVIEW OF PREPARATION, ENGAGEMENT, AND FOLLOW-THROUGH IN STEP 1.

In the appendix (page 219), I provide "Coach's Planner for Step 1 of the CLEAR Process: Clarify the Why, the What, and the How," a detailed planner that helps leaders and coaches to plan and execute the key actions for clarifying the why, the what, and the how.

Let's explore what it looks like for leaders and coaches to take the actions to clarify the why, the what, and the how for their teacher teams. A typical scenario for when leaders and coaches are clarifying their school's why, what, and how for teachers and teams is when the staff gathers for meetings at the beginning of the school year during preservice week. Typically, principals have student achievement data to share with staff, so it is an ideal time to review student needs and establish a compelling why. Also, preservice is an appropriate time to clarify instructional expectations and provide training on strategies, so it works as a setting for clarifying the what. Finally, the beginning of the school year is the best time to review progress and establish new goals, so it is a perfect time to clarify the how.

So, to understand the processes that are involved in step 1 of the CLEAR process—clarify the why, the what, and the how—let's imagine a principal and her leadership team as they plan and execute their preservice plan. We will follow their steps as they do the critical work in preparation, engagement, and follow-through. Of course, principals and teacher leaders can introduce and clarify the why, the what, and the how in settings other than preservice, but we will use this scenario to provide an overview.

CLARIFYING THE WHY, WHAT, AND HOW— TWO CONTEXTS

When you think about it, clarifying the why, what, and the how works as a foundation in many contexts to get people to change their behavior. Imagine a doctor who is concerned about one of her patients because he continues to smoke cigarettes every day. She has told him that is not good for his short- and long-term health, but he says he feels fine and argues that "if it ain't broke, don't fix it." Then she presents him with compelling data—x-rays, blood tests, and other evidence—that show how much his heart, blood vessels, and lungs are being harmed by his smoking habit. She explains that the test results indicate his life expectancy is less than two years if he continues smoking. That explanation turns out to be a powerful enough why to get him to be open to changing his behavior. Having been finally convinced that he needs to make a change, the patient now wants to know the best ways to stop smoking—the most effective programs, patches, gums, and other tools, to help him quit once and for all. The doctor provides research-based information, contacts, prescriptions, and support to clarify the what. Next, the doctor explains how they will have follow-up appointments and tests to check on the patient's progress and reexamine his heart and lung function to clarify the how. This combination of a compelling why for the change, a clear what in terms of strategy, and a clear how about goals and how to monitor progress provides the patient with the tools and information to believe he can be successful with this difficult task.

Now imagine an elementary school principal who has discovered that her students' performance in mathematics is falling short of state and district targets and their proficiency levels are significantly lower than comparable schools. Furthermore, she has heard from her middle school colleagues that her students are struggling with middle school mathematics when they move on to sixth grade. To address this need and build the collective efficacy of her teacher teams, she begins by working with her guiding coalition to devise strategies for presenting the compelling student data that need to be addressed (the why) to the full staff. They outline research-based strategies to be implemented and explain how this effort will be supported through training (the what). Next, the principal and teacher leaders work with staff to establish short- and long-term goals for student achievement in mathematics and map out a process for monitoring growth (the how). This foundation provides clarity for the full staff and serves as the launchpad for the rest of the process to ensure student learning and build the collective efficacy of teams.

Preparation for Clarifying the Why, the What, and the How

It is the first week of August and Dr. Connie Wu, principal of Marie Curie Elementary (MCE) is meeting with members of her admin team and several teacher leaders, including instructional coaches and team leaders, to work on the plan for preservice week, scheduled for two weeks from now. Dr. Wu always tries to involve teacher leaders in planning and decision making at her school. She has gathered the group together so that they can prepare a plan for engaging all Curie's teachers and teams in review of compelling student data (the why), research-based strategies to address the why (the what), and discussions about setting goals and monitoring progress (the how). She explains her goals for the day to her team:

> Our goal for today is to work together to develop the plan for preservice week. Our goal for preservice week is to make sure that all teachers and teams at Curie finish the week with (1) a clear understanding of our students' learning data and the most urgent needs for us to address (the why), (2) a clear understanding of how we will address our student learning needs through instructional strategies and collaborative team practices (the what), (3) and a clear understanding of our school goals and how those lead to team goals (the how). To make the best preparations, we need to engage with information and each other so that we are ready to lead the rest of the staff in their learning.

Over the next seven hours (with a nice break for lunch), Dr. Wu works through a sequence of activities with her team. They generate questions about their student learning data. What do they want to know about how their students are performing? They gather all the available information from reports that Dr. Wu provided and from their own records of student progress. They analyze the data together and identify strengths, needs, and trends. The amount of data, from graduation rates, course failures, report card grades, advanced placement tests, state tests, district assessments, and so on, is a little overwhelming. The team decides to look for strengths, needs, and trends that really stand out. The writing target data get the attention of several teacher leaders. Across several assessments and multiple grade levels, students are really struggling. Their scores in several areas are well below the state average. The team identifies student writing as a critical learning need. They work together on a plan for having staff engage with the data themselves. Dr. Wu suggests a few ideas about how to organize the data exploration. The mathematics department chair shares a strategy that everyone thinks will work well. Dr. Wu and her team have prepared a plan for clarifying the why.

Dr. Wu and her teacher leaders then generate questions about strategies and practices that can help them to address their students' needs in writing. What are the best instructional strategies? How do effective teams support student learning in writing? They break up into groups and research the questions online and through contacting colleagues. The reading coach shares a few websites with good information. They share their findings and decide together that they have a good chance of improving student performance in writing if they implement student writing conferences, a research-based approach to improving student writing by listening to students talk about their writing and providing meaningful feedback. They all agree that this approach could make a difference in the amount of writing students will do and the quality of the writing as well. Further, they decide that it would be helpful if each grade-level team agreed on common writing prompts and scoring tools for their students' work. Having identified two promising strategies, the planning team works on strategies for engaging teachers and teams during in-service with activities that will help them to understand the key components of effective student writing conferences and the importance of feedback in the writing process. In addition, they plan to provide guidance for developing common writing prompts and scoring tools. One of the coaches reminds everyone that they are planning sessions for adult learners, so the group works hard to make sure that this is not a "sit and get" session but rather professional learning marked by active involvement, time to discuss with peers, and time for practice and reflection. They have prepared a plan for clarifying the what.

Next, Dr. Wu and the teacher leaders review the school goals and team goals they set the previous year. As they gather the information, they have to admit that very few people on the staff had paid much attention to the school and team goals during the year. They had been mostly forgotten about by the third week of school. The team reviews the previous goals and the student achievement data they had studied earlier in the day. They brainstorm together what appropriate school goals would look like. They talk through how to make it a stretch goal while still making it reachable. They agree together on school goals for writing. Then, they plan an activity to explain the new school goals to teachers and teams. The school counselor volunteers to lead the discussion of goals. In addition, Dr. Wu and her leaders develop a plan for teams to learn about the monitoring system and calendar that will be used to make sure everyone is thinking about these important goals. This learning session ends with giving teams instructions about how to develop their own team-level goals. Dr. Wu and her team have developed a plan for clarifying the how.

It has been a long and fairly intense day, but Dr. Wu and her team now have a clear understanding of the why, the what, and the how that will drive their school this year—and they have a cohesive plan for engaging all teachers and teams in building shared knowledge about their school priorities. The next step is to actually put the plan into action.

The story of Dr. Wu working with her team in preparation for clarifying the why, what, and how illustrates how this work can happen in a real school setting. Let's review the critical steps involved in preparation for step 1 of the CLEAR process.

Whether leaders and coaches are preparing to clarify the why, the what, or the how, the important steps are similar. The key components of the preparation work are (1) asking questions, (2) gathering information, (3) reviewing and analyzing the information, and (4) preparing the plan for sharing the information with teachers and teams.

Leaders and coaches begin their preparation for clarifying the why, what, and how by asking questions about their students' current learning levels and needs (the why), possible strategies to address the needs (the what), and the current states of goals and monitoring at their school (the how).

Next, they collect all the information they can to answer the questions they have generated. They accumulate all the data and information they need to have a comprehensive picture of their students and their learning (the why), current practices and opportunities for improvement (the what), and how they have set goals and monitored progress (the how).

They conduct an analysis of the data and research, hopefully in tandem with their teacher leaders or guiding coalition. They identify strengths, needs, trends, and patterns in the data, which leads to focusing on a particular student learning need. They examine the research and identify key high-leverage strategies they can use to address their student learning need, and they start to develop draft goals and plans for a monitoring system.

Their final step in the preparation phase is to develop a plan for engaging teachers and teams in examination of the student learning data, exploration of the research-based strategies, and review of the draft goals and monitoring plan. Leaders and coaches will work to develop cohesive training plans that will work for adult learners. Whether they are engaging their teachers and teams with student achievement data (the why), a new instructional strategy (the what), or information to help in setting goals (the how), they want to engage teachers and teams in collaborative activities that build shared knowledge and give teacher and teams time to practice, ask questions, and reflect.

In a PLC where a guiding coalition has been established, it is critical for the members of the guiding coalition to be involved in the review of student data, research about effective strategies, and the planning for staff engagement. Including representatives from teams in this work helps to ensure that the needs of all teams will be addressed and also empowers members of the guiding coalition to lead a critical process. Teachers and teams need to know this is not just a top-down project from the principal or admin team.

The reproducible "Coach's Planner for Step 1 of the CLEAR Process: Clarify the Why, the What, and the How" in the appendix (page 219) provides guidance for leaders and coaches to understand the preparation work for clarifying the why, what, and how, and to take actions for their teachers and teams. In addition, the appendix (page 215) provides a variety of print and online references to assist with all aspects of clarifying the why, the what, and the how.

Once leaders and coaches have completed the critical preparation work for clarifying the why, the what, and the how, they move on to active engagement with their teams.

Engagement With Teams to Clarify the Why, the What, and the How

It is the second day of preservice week, and Dr. Wu and her teacher-leader team are ready. Shortly, all the MCE teachers and teams will enter the cafeteria for a day of meetings. Yesterday, the first day back, Dr. Wu provided a nice breakfast and let all teachers work in their classrooms and with their teams all day. It was much appreciated. Now, on day 2, it is time to set some priorities and hopefully generate some excitement about the upcoming school year. Throughout the day, Dr. Wu and her team execute their plan for engaging all staff in the why, the what, and the how.

Dr. Wu does a brief presentation on student learning data, pointing out celebrations, strengths, and positive trends. She also presents the "brutal facts" about the areas in which student performance is not where it needs to be, especially in writing. Then, teams are given time to explore data reports on their own, working with their teammates to discuss and share what they notice in the data. By the end of the session, it is clear to everyone in the room that they need to do something right away about helping their students to write more proficiently.

Dr. Wu shares comments as they complete the clarifying the why portion of the day:

> Let's summarize what we have learned through exploring our student data together this morning. When we look at our students' writing performance across the grade levels, as reflected on the state writing assessment, our students are not hitting the proficiency targets. Overall, 45 percent of our students demonstrated proficiency, which is short of our state goal of 70 percent. When we looked closer at the data, we found that our students are relatively strong in writing narrative pieces, with their scores at or above the state average. However, when we looked at the scores for writing argumentative/persuasive pieces and writing informational essays, our students' scores were considerably below the average scores in the state. We discussed how our fundamental purpose as a school is to ensure that all students learn at high levels, and right now, we are not achieving that when it comes to our students and their writing. We agreed that it is essential for all our students to be able to write proficiently in all areas because of how it will affect their ability to be successful in future grades in school, in college, and in the world of work. We see student writing as a critical student learning need that requires our attention and a collaborative effort to help all students improve their performance. We need to do whatever we can to support our students' achievement in writing.

For the next portion of the preservice day at MCE, Dr. Wu hands the facilitating duties over to the instructional coaches. The two coaches lead activities that engage staff in reviewing strategies that are shown to improve writing proficiency with elementary students, especially student writing conferences. Teachers have time to review information from the research and then discuss it with their team. The coaches also use several videos to clarify the research and use Padlet so that teachers could comment and ask questions during the presentation by typing them into their own devices. By the end of the session, teachers are buzzing with ideas about working with students and providing feedback about their writing. There is also interest in and questions about how teachers could coordinate their efforts by using common writing prompts and scoring tools.

Dr. Wu concludes the clarifying the what portion of the day by sharing comments:

> I want to thank everyone for your participation and contributions today. I also want to thank Ms. Newton and Mr. Galileo for their expertise in helping us all learn together. Earlier today, we reviewed the data about our students and their learning, and it was clear that we wanted to focus on their performance in writing. So, in the

session we just finished, we shared some success stories, reviewed the current state of writing instruction, and explored two high-leverage strategies that could help us make a difference in how well our students write—student writing conferences and common prompts and scoring rubrics. Today we had an introduction, but we will continue to learn and work on this together throughout the year. We will follow up today's training by supporting you in your team meetings as you work on how to integrate these strategies into your team planning and instruction. We will also have reference materials, articles, samples, and videotapes available on our staff learning hub. You can review these individually or as a team, whenever you feel the need. No one is expected to implement these new strategies perfectly tomorrow or next week in your classroom. We will keep learning together, we will ask questions, we will research together and come up with answers together. In our next session, we will look at setting some goals for the improvement we want to see in our students' writing.

In the next portion of the preservice day, several teacher team leaders take the lead in helping all teachers and teams understand the overall school goals for the school year. They present data and show what previous goals looked like. They explain the process that the leadership team used to establish goals. They give teachers time to review the goals and ask questions. Then, another team leader describes the process and tools that teams will use to establish their own team goals over the next two weeks.

Dr. Wu wraps up the day by helping everyone review what they have done and what they learned together.

On behalf of the teacher leaders and guiding coalition members who worked hard to establish our school goals, I want to thank everyone for your input and insight today. Through our sessions, we have established our why—we need to improve our students' performance in writing, because it is a critical skill for them to have in their current grade, in future grades, and in life beyond school. We then established what we would do together to try to improve our instruction and support so that student writing will improve. By clarifying our what, we know the strategies that we are implementing, and we have committed ourselves to ongoing training and carrying out the work in our classrooms. Having clarified our why and our what, this afternoon we established the how. How will we know if this is working? We confirmed our schoolwide goal to improve student writing performance, as measured by the state test, by at least 15%—from 45% to at least 60% by the end of the year. We will monitor student growth in writing by implementing student writing conferences and establishing common writing rubrics across grade levels and departments. Plus, we will collaboratively review student writing samples as teams at least once a month. We will be following up with you in your teams to help you set team-specific goals over the next few weeks. If you have any questions, please feel free to ask me or any one of the teacher leaders who presented today. Thanks for all you do every day.

The description of Dr. Wu and her team engaging with their teachers and teams to clarify the why, what, and how illustrates how important it is to plan and execute effective engagement with staff to build shared knowledge. Let's review the key components of the engagement work for step 1 of the CLEAR process.

Whether leaders and coaches are engaging with teacher teams to clarify the why, the what, or the how, the work is very similar. The key components of the engagement work are (1) bring teams together in a setting that supports learning, (2) facilitate professional learning activities that work for adult learners so that all teams build shared knowledge, and (3) confirm the schoolwide commitment to the why, the what, and the how.

Coaches and leaders bring their teacher teams together and execute the plan they developed during the preparation phase. They implement strategies that are appropriate for adult learners, such as the following (Aguilar, 2016).

- Coaches involve teachers and teams in active review of student data, giving them time to examine information in teams, rather than just presenting the data for teams to consume. This helps in building shared knowledge and confirming *why* we need to change practice.

- Coaches engage teachers and teams in active discussion and role plays about instructional strategies and how they would work for students, rather than just presenting a slide deck for teachers to sit and take in passively. This helps to build shared understanding and establish *what* we will do to address our student learning needs.

- Coaches engage teachers and teams in examining past goals and active discussion to establish new goals and develop a plan for monitoring growth, rather than just presenting goal information. This helps to build shared knowledge and clarify *how* we will measure success.

Leaders and coaches use these strategies to engage their teachers and teams and to build shared knowledge about the why, what, and how. As a result of this collaborative learning, leaders and coaches are able to confirm why there needs to be a change in practice (our compelling student learning needs), what the change involves (the strategies and practices we will be using to address student learning), and how we will measure success (our school goals and monitoring system).

In a PLC, empowering guiding coalition members to lead these sessions also does a tremendous job of building individual capacity and self-efficacy. Teachers who are new to the role of guiding coalition member may resist the suggestion to lead a presentation, but effective principals can express confidence, help them prepare, and praise their efforts afterward. The payoff for the school, the principal, and the guiding coalition member is always worth the effort.

The reproducible "Coach's Planner for Step 1 of the CLEAR Process: Clarify the Why, the What, and the How" in the appendix (page 219) provides guidance for leaders and coaches to understand the engagement work for clarifying the why, what, and how, and take actions for their teachers and teams.

Once the engagement tasks are done, the work is not over. Leaders and coaches who are working to build the collective efficacy of their teacher teams must commit to effective follow-through. Clear and consistent follow-through is critical to clarifying the why, what, and how, and establishing the foundation for collective teacher efficacy to grow.

Follow-Through to Clarify the Why, the What, and the How

It is the third day of preservice week, and Dr. Wu is meeting with her leadership team to debrief the full staff day devoted to the why, what, and how. The team debriefs how the day went, and overall, they are very happy with how engaged teachers and teams were and how they were able to deliver clear messages about why they needed to change practice, what the change would involve, and how they would measure success and monitor progress. After a few minutes of celebrating that success, the team turns its attention to follow-through. How would they make sure that all teachers and teams keep the urgency about student learning in writing at the front of their mind? How would they follow up decisions about high-priority instructional strategies and collaborative team practices to make sure that teams were implementing the selected strategies? How would they make sure that all teams had the ongoing support and job-embedded training they need to be successful? And most immediately, how would they provide guidance and support so that they could establish SMART team goals that were aligned with the school targets? They discuss formal and informal communication strategies, including staff meetings and the staff bulletin. They finalize the one-sheeter that they will share with all staff that day to reinforce the why, what, and how commitments (figure 3.3).

Marie Curie Elementary School, 2024–2025		
Our Why	Our What	Our How
Our fundamental purpose is to ensure high levels of learning for all students. Currently, 45 percent of Curie students are demonstrating proficiency on the state test in writing. We are fully committed this year to do whatever it takes to have at least 60 percent of our students demonstrate proficiency on this year's test.	To address our students' learning needs, we are committed to implementing research-based instructional strategies and collaborative practices to improve our instruction and ensure student learning. This school year, we are focused on building student writing skills through consistently implementing student writing conferences. In addition, grade-level teams will develop and implement common writing prompts and scoring tools for their students.	We are committed to increasing student learning through improving our practice. This year, our schoolwide goal is to improve student writing performance. At least 60 percent of students will demonstrate proficiency on the state test in writing. In addition, students will demonstrate growth throughout the year on grade-level writing assessments.

Figure 3.3: SAMPLE OF SCHOOL'S ONE-SHEETER TO REINFORCE THE WHY, WHAT, AND HOW.

They also developed a second one-sheeter that shows their school mission, vision, collective commitments, and shared goals (figure 3.4).

Marie Curie Elementary School, 2024-2025			
Our Mission	**Our Vision**	**Our Collective Commitments**	**Our Shared Goals**
We work together every day to ensure high levels of learning for every child.	We strive to develop each student's gifts to prepare them to be successful in pursuing their dreams.	1. We will work in collaborative teams to meet the needs of every learner. 2. We will use data and review of student work to make the best decisions for each learner. 3. We will always work in the best interest of our students.	By the end of the 2024–2025 school year, our students' reading proficiency will increase at least 15 percent to at least 60 percent.
Our Why		**Our What**	**Our How**
Our fundamental purpose is to ensure high levels of learning for all students. Currently, 45 percent of Curie students are demonstrating proficiency on the state test in reading. We are fully committed this year to do whatever it takes to have at least 60 percent of our students demonstrate proficiency on this year's test.		To address our students' learning needs, we are committed to implementing research-based instructional strategies and collaborative practices to improve our instruction and ensure student learning. This school year, we are focused on building student writing skills through consistently implementing student writing conferences. In addition, grade-level teams will develop and implement common writing prompts and scoring tools for their students.	We are committed to increasing student learning through improving our practice. This year, our schoolwide goal is to increase students' reading and writing skills and be able to link those changes to changes in our practice—in our how.

Figure 3.4: SAMPLE OF SCHOOL'S ONE-SHEETER TO REINFORCE THE WHY, WHAT, AND HOW IN RELATION TO THE FOUNDATIONAL PLC PILLARS.

They talked about their plan to establish a learning hub where teachers and teams could find videos, materials, and resources to help them with implementation of strategies. Dr. Wu reminded each member of the leadership team that they had an important responsibility to be a spokesperson and even champion for the why, what, and how with their teams. They would need to support, encourage, and maybe prod their teams into doing the critical work and encourage them when the work was difficult. The leadership team members were satisfied with how their first day of communication and training had gone, but they knew that their work was not done, and they needed to provide effective follow-through for the next ten months.

The description of Dr. Wu and her team providing ongoing and thoughtful follow-through to reinforce their school's why, what, and how, illustrates how important it is for leaders and coaches to see clarifying the why, what, and how as long-term work that requires commitment and consistency. Let's review the key components of effective follow-through for step 1 of the CLEAR process.

Whether leaders and coaches are following through to clarify the why, the what, or the how, the tasks are very similar. The key components of the follow-through work are (1) reinforce decisions and commitments through various forms of ongoing communication, and (2) provide all the ongoing guidance, support, and job-embedded professional development that teams will need to effectively implement strategies to support the why, the what, and the how. This also includes help with establishing team goals.

As we saw in chapter 2 (page 33), transformation efforts often fail due to a lack of follow-up communication and support from leaders (Kotter, 2005). Leaders and coaches must commit to ongoing communication, both formal and informal, to reinforce the school's why, what, and how. The goal is to ensure that all teachers and teams know the why, what, and how and incorporate that knowledge into their daily work. Through formal communications (staff bulletin, emails to all staff) and informal communications (conversations with teams during collaborative team time, chats with individual teachers), leaders and coaches reinforce the why, the what, and the how. They ask teachers and teams what they need to get started and follow through to provide supports. They check in with teams and answer any questions they have as they work to try new techniques. Leaders and coaches praise teachers and teams who take a risk and try out the new strategies and help them to reflect and debrief about what to do next.

In PLC schools where a guiding coalition has been established, its members play a critical role in the ongoing communication to support a schoolwide effort. Effective guiding coalitions will have discussions in their meetings about how to reinforce school expectations and support implementation by teams.

Leaders and coaches should strive to practice reciprocal accountability, an idea promoted by Richard Elmore, school improvement expert (2002). Reciprocal responsibility requires that, whenever a leader is requiring a new unit of accountability from teams (like implementing new practices), she should make sure to also provide a unit of capacity. In other words, if we are holding teachers accountable for new practice, we have the obligation to build their capacity as well. This includes providing formal professional development, providing teachers and teams with tools and resources they can refer to and use as appropriate, and effective response when a team is struggling and needs guidance or support. When leaders don't provide this type of information and ongoing support, teams are likely to lose focus and revert to the way they were doing things previously, since this is more familiar and comfortable.

An important part of follow-through for clarifying the how involves helping teacher teams translate school goals into team goals. Leaders and coaches should guide teams to establish team goals that are aligned with the school-level goals. This alignment supports school focus and makes it possible to target professional development to support team and school efforts. Figure 3.5 shows how this alignment works in a school.

	WHY	WHAT	HOW
School level	Overall school data and overall student needs	Overall, global school strategies to address the why	School goals for overall student performance
	↓	↓	↓
Team level	Team-level data and specific student needs	School strategies implemented, as appropriate for the grade level or content area	Team-level goals that support the school-level goals

Figure 3.5: ALIGNMENT OF SCHOOL AND TEAM GOALS.

Clarifying why a change needs to happen, what the change entails, and how the change will be measured is critical work that demands careful preparation, engagement of staff, and follow-through by leaders and coaches. This is demanding work, but if leaders and coaches do the things that are required to clarify the why, the what, and the how, they establish a strong foundation for building the collective efficacy of their teacher teams.

The reproducible "Coach's Planner for Step 1 of the CLEAR Process: Clarify the Why, the What, and the How" in the appendix (page 219), provides guidance for leaders and coaches to understand the follow-through work for clarifying the why, what, and how, and take actions for their teachers and teams.

Clarifying the why, what, and how involves effective preparation, engagement, and follow-through, regardless of a coach's role. As I previously mentioned, the CLEAR process can be implemented by folks who are working as the principal of a school, as an instructional coach, in a department chair role, or serving as a teacher team leader. Leaders in all these roles can implement the CLEAR process and have a significant impact on the collective teacher efficacy of their teacher teams. The overall process is the same for each role, but there are some differences in specific aspects of implementing the steps of the process. These differences have special impact at the beginning of the CLEAR process when leaders and coaches are clarifying the why, the what, and the how.

- When implementing step 1 of the CLEAR process, a school principal will have more position power and overall influence as she leads the process than someone in a team leader position. The principal has more opportunities to direct staff attention to a compelling student need (the why), to require implementation of a strategy or practice (the what), and to establish school goals that all staff are expected to achieve (the how). Effective principals will work with their guiding coalitions (or teacher leaders if a guiding coalition has not been established yet) to explore the data and research to identify critical student needs, research-based strategies, and school goals. The guiding coalition also plays a critical role in working with the full staff to build shared knowledge about the school's why, what, and how. In a high-performing PLC, the principal will delegate various tasks to guiding coalition members and share leadership for processes related to examining student data (the why), effective strategies (the what), and shared goals (the how). This accomplishes two purposes: (1) the principal builds leadership capacity within her staff, and (2) the staff sees the why, the what, and the how as a collaborative staff venture, rather than a top-down decree from the principal. In a school that has not begun the PLC journey, the principal should still endeavor to involve teacher leaders in clarifying the why, the what, and the how for the whole staff. Otherwise, teachers are likely to view the initiative as something the principal wants to do, rather than a compelling mission that they all must accomplish together.

- Instructional coaches have a critical role in schools, but there are limits to what they can do in terms of clarifying the why, what, and how. Instructional coaches can influence the school's review of data, selection of instructional strategies, and the range of school goals, but compared to principals, they have limited position power and will align their work to the why, what, and how that the school has established. Instructional coaches implement step 1 by helping the teams they work with to personalize the school's why, what, and how, supporting their efforts to enact new practices while simultaneously building their collective efficacy. For example, a school might determine that their compelling student need (the why) is student performance in mathematics, that the most promising strategy involves effective small-group instruction during mathematics classes, and that the common school goal (the how) is to increase student achievement by at least 10 percent as measured by the state mathematics test. While this is a common mission for the school, implementation of the strategy will look slightly different in each grade: small-group instruction in kindergarten is different than small-group instruction in grade 5. In addition, coaches can help teams to translate the schoolwide goals into team goals.

- The next group that may be charged with clarifying the why, what, and how is department chairs and team leaders. These leaders have less formal position power, and they likely have somewhat limited influence over whole-school decisions, but they can have a tremendous impact on their team and the team's collective efficacy. Department chairs and team leaders work on a daily basis to help their teams understand the school's why, what, and how and guide their teammates to implement practices that support school and team goals. As the teams and departments work through their teaching tasks, these leaders can reinforce key messages and provide the guidance and direction that teams need.

Through their regular support of their colleagues and partners, they build the collective efficacy of their teams.

Each leader, regardless of their position or title, can implement the steps of the CLEAR process and play a powerful role in building the collective efficacy of their teams.

An important note about ongoing follow-through and support of teams: While clarifying the why, what, and how is the first step in the CLEAR process, it is critical to remember that, to build the collective efficacy of teams, school leaders will need to repeat and reinforce the why, what, and how as the teams implement new practices. It is not enough to clarify the why, what, and how at one meeting during preservice week and then never refer to it again. I have worked with many principals who express frustration when their teachers, halfway through the school year, say, "Why are we even doing this?" The principals know that they devoted substantial time at the beginning of the year to explaining the critical need for these practices, but reinforcement is key.

In a school setting, principals and members of the guiding coalition must use every opportunity to engage teacher teams in examining data and information that reminds them of the critical student learning need. In addition, they must consistently reinforce the vision for how teams will work to achieve the vision. In a PLC, the principal must demonstrate all the positive attributes of true collaboration and the guiding coalition must serve as a model for all collaborative teams.

If a principal presents data during preservice that show a critical student learning need, but then never mentions it again, what kind of urgency does he expect teachers to have? But if the principal and the guiding coalition provide regular updates and fresh data about student performance through staff meetings and team sessions, the need to address the student data will stay "top of mind" and be a priority for teachers. In the same way, if the principal announces that teams should function as high-performing collaborative teams, but then does nothing to reinforce the expectation or hold teams accountable, how can he be surprised when teams revert to their past practice? If, however, staff meetings are transformed into team learning sessions and collaborative practices are reinforced and celebrated, there is a much better chance that teams will modify their practice. If a principal makes a big deal about setting goals during preservice week, but then never updates staff on progress toward the goals or requires teams to monitor progress on their own goals, do we really think busy teachers will devote time to goal setting and progress review? Leaders must help staff embrace the foundation of why, what, and how, and then follow up in meaningful ways if they expect their teams to develop high levels of collective teacher efficacy.

Let's look at how clarifying the why, what, and how might work in two different situations. In our first scenario, Ms. Carson is a middle school principal launching a PLC initiative in her school (figure 3.6) with the support of a guiding coalition ("GC" in the figure).

In the second scenario, Ms. Goodall is an elementary instructional coach working to support the implementation of strategies to teach academic vocabulary (see figure 3.7, page 84).

Implementing Step 1 of the CLEAR Process as a Principal		
Clarify the WHY	**Clarify the WHAT**	**Clarify the HOW**
Why do we need to make a change? Why do we need to learn new strategies and tasks? Compelling student learning need	What changes are we implementing? Research-based, high-leverage strategies to improve student learning, including the top ten tasks of teams in a PLC	How will we measure success? How will we know if the change is working? Clear SMART goals, short-term and long-term to monitor progress

	Clarify the WHY	Clarify the WHAT	Clarify the HOW
Preparation	Ms. Carson asks questions about how her students are performing on state and district tests. With her guiding coalition (GC), she accumulates data to answer their questions. Their analysis shows student performance in reading is not meeting targets and compares unfavorably to similar schools.	Ms. Carson and the GC ask research questions, seeking answers for their students' reading issues. Ms. Carson and the GC compile the research and data on effective strategies. Ms. Carson and the GC decide that enhancing team use of CFAs will help to address student reading.	Ms. Carson and the GC ask questions about student performance in reading and the trends in the data. They accumulate all the pertinent data for review. They determine a draft SMART goal for student performance in reading—a 10% increase in proficiency in all grades on the state test.
Engagement	Ms. Carson and the GC brainstorm ideas for presenting the reading data to staff. They plan and hold a session that engages teachers in looking at the overall school data and the scores for their own students. Ms. Carson and the GC lead processes that engage teachers in asking questions about the data and building understanding. Ms. Carson and the GC lead teachers to reach consensus about the need to address student achievement in reading.	Ms. Carson and the GC brainstorm ideas for presenting research about CFA techniques to staff. They plan and hold a session that explains how teacher teams use CFAs and review of student work to improve reading performance. Ms. Carson and the GC lead processes to engage teachers in reviewing the use of CFAs and understanding how they will use them. Ms. Carson and the GC confirm that, as a school, they will use regular CFAs to monitor student performance in reading.	Ms. Carson and the GC brainstorm ideas for engaging staff in reviewing draft goals. Ms. Carson and the GC hold a session, present the draft goals, and allow time for questions and discussion. Ms. Carson and the GC lead processes to engage teachers and teams in review of the draft goals. After discussion and review of cohort data, Ms. Carson, the GC, and the staff agree that the school goal will be to increase student proficiency by 8%.
Follow-Through	Ms. Carson and the GC develop communications to establish the school focus on reading and school efforts to improve performance. Ms. Carson and the GC commit to working with teams to provide the guidance and training they will need to support their schoolwide effort to improve student reading proficiency.	Ms. Carson and the GC develop communication strategies to reinforce the expectations around use of CFAs in reading. Ms. Carson and the GC plan regular job-embedded professional development for teams to help them implement CFAs with their students and continually refine their practices.	Ms. Carson and the GC develop communication strategies to reinforce the school goal and to guide teams to set their team-level goals. Ms. Carson and the GC develop and implement a calendar for reviewing data and progress toward the school goal in reading, recognizing teams that show progress, and supporting teams in need.

Figure 3.6: CLARIFYING THE WHY, WHAT, AND HOW—PRINCIPAL.

Clarifying the Why, What, and How as an Instructional Coach		
Clarify the WHY	**Clarify the WHAT**	**Clarify the HOW**
Why do we need to make a change? Why do we need to learn new strategies and tasks? Compelling student learning need	What changes are we implementing? Research-based, high-leverage strategies to improve student learning, including the top ten tasks of teams in a PLC	How will we measure success? How will we know if the change is working? Clear SMART goals, short-term and long-term to monitor progress
Preparation Ms. Goodall asks questions about the performance of students in grades 3–5 in reading.	Ms. Goodall conducts research and consults with colleagues to find strategies for addressing student vocabulary needs.	Ms. Goodall asks questions about trends in student reading performance.
Ms. Goodall accumulates the data from the most recent state test and district benchmarks.	Ms. Goodall accumulates the data and reviews possible approaches.	Ms. Goodall accumulates the data for each team, noting details and trends.
The data show student performance in vocabulary is low across all three grade levels. Ms. Goodall consults with the principal about addressing this need.	Ms. Goodall determines that Marzano's six steps for building academic vocabulary is a research-based process that could help the students at her school.	Ms. Goodall conducts an analysis of the student data and a review of the school goals for reading performance and determines what a draft goal might look like for each team.
Ms. Goodall brainstorms strategies about how to engage her teacher teams to review the data.	Ms. Goodall brainstorms strategies for sharing the Marzano strategy with her teams.	Ms. Goodall brainstorms ideas about how to lead the goal-setting discussion with her teams.
Engagement Ms. Goodall brings teams together and provides the data for them to review, using a notice and wonder approach.	Ms. Goodall meets with each team and shares her findings about research-based approaches to teaching vocabulary.	Ms. Goodall establishes with her teams that they will work on goals in their next session.
Teachers note the low scores in vocabulary and how they appear in each grade level.	Ms. Goodall leads an activity that engages teachers in using the Marzano approach, thus building their familiarity with it.	Ms. Goodall shares the data and engages the teams in discussing what team SMART goals might look like.
Ms. Goodall confirms with the teams that academic vocabulary is an area of concern that they should study.	Ms. Goodall gains consensus from the teams that they will try some Marzano strategies for six weeks and then check on progress.	Ms. Goodall guides her teams to reach consensus on a clear SMART goal. The goals vary slightly by team, but all teams agree to aim for increasing student proficiency from 40% in September to 75% in May.
Follow-Through Ms. Goodall communicates this in messages and conversations with teams.	Ms. Goodall reinforces this team decision in her messages with her teachers and conversations with teams.	Ms. Goodall reminds teams of their goals and offers support through messages and conversations.

Figure 3.7: CLARIFYING THE WHY, WHAT, AND HOW—INSTRUCTIONAL COACH.

As figures 3.6 (page 83) and 3.7 show, clarifying the why, what, and how is a critical step for leaders and coaches who are working to build the collective efficacy of their teachers, regardless of their specific position. Both principals and instructional coaches (and team leaders, and superintendents) can use the CLEAR process to improve their teams, and they start by clarifying the why, the what, and the how. Whatever your role is, you begin the process of strategically building your teams' collective efficacy by giving them the foundation to build it on.

Team Update

At Einstein High School, the last staff meeting of the year has just concluded, and the room is full of smiling faces and positive energy. Dr. Brown devoted the full meeting time to having collaborative teams share their processes, progress, and celebrations with each other. This is something he would not have done at the beginning of the school year, but over time, he reflected on his practices and realized that his teachers and teams would be more successful if he was clear about why they needed to work in collaborative teams, what true collaboration would look like, and how they would measure and enhance collaboration within teams. This change of mind made a big difference in Dr. Brown's leadership moves and had a huge impact on his teacher teams.

At this last staff meeting, the history department described their journey through the year. They admitted that heading into the school year, they were confused about why they were being told to collaborate across multiple grade levels and courses. They also didn't understand what this collaboration would look like or how it was supposed to help teachers or students. They recalled how it made more sense in August when Dr. Brown and several department heads shared data that showed that 45 percent of Einstein students were not meeting the standard on the state tests in reading, mathematics, and science. In addition, student survey data indicated that the majority of students (68 percent) did not feel that instruction at Einstein was engaging, and 50 percent of the students reported that they did not feel challenged in their classes. This combination of data was a big wake-up call for the whole staff. They needed to work collaboratively to improve instruction and get better student results. Dr. Brown and the department chairs led sessions to teach teams how to collaborate and provided ongoing support when teams struggled. Everyone agreed to an ambitious school goal to increase student proficiency in reading by at least 25 percent (from 45 percent to 70 percent). Each department worked on establishing a team goal that would support the overall school effort. Having the rationale for the change, more information about what collaboration would look like, and a clear goal for student learning provided the foundation for teams to try new practices. This led to the celebrations they were now enjoying. The history team shared that as they started to meet regularly in the collaborative team time established in the new master schedule, they gradually saw how regular collaboration gave them the chance to learn from each other, and that helped them to achieve higher levels of learning for their students. They used the weekly team time to develop a common rubric for evaluating student essays. As they reviewed student writing together, they shared ideas for framing writing assignments and for providing students with meaningful feedback about their writing. The other teams were very impressed with what they had done and applauded at the end of their mini session. The Career Technology and Education (CTE) team also shared about their journey as a collaborative team. They were candid about the struggles at the beginning of the year, when it was really difficult to see why they should collaborate across courses as different as agriculture, foundations of business, home design, and carpentry. But thanks to the time that they had to meet and the guidance they received, they realized that a common theme across their courses was communication, especially in terms of giving and receiving feedback. They developed common expectations about how students would verbally provide feedback to another student after a presentation. In addition, they clarified expectations for how students would respond to feedback from a peer. The other departments commented on how the CTE team was reinforcing a critical skill for all students. Over the course of the school year, the staff as a whole had grown in their understanding of why collaboration was such a critical and valuable aspect of working as a teacher. As they started to see some payoff for their collaborative efforts, their collective belief in what they could accomplish together increased dramatically. Now, as they finish the school year, they are celebrating their growth and looking forward to doing even better next school year.

CLEAR Thoughts and Next Steps

As we finish our discussion of step 1 of the CLEAR process, let's summarize, identify key takeaways, reflect, and plan the next step.

Leaders at every level of school structure and administration and at every point of the PLC journey can work intentionally and strategically to ensure high levels of student learning by building the collective efficacy of the teachers and teams they supervise, coach, or support. The critical first step of this work, as reflected in the CLEAR process graphic (chapter 2, page 33), is to build a strong foundation for collective efficacy to grow—a clear understanding of the compelling student learning needs that must be addressed (the why), a firm grasp of the specific strategies that teams will be implementing to address the student need (the what), and a solid commitment to shared goals that will mark the teams' growth and inform their efforts (the how).

While establishing this foundation is not an easy task, it can be accomplished by committed leaders who invest energy in the right types of preparation of information and plans, engagement of staff in collective learning, and dynamic follow-through that reinforces the common commitment to students and their learning. It is a process that is worth the effort.

Let's review critical takeaways.

- When asking teachers and teams to make a change in practice, leaders must clarify *why* there needs to be a change, *what* the change will involve, and *how* the change will be monitored and measured. The why, the what, and the how form the foundation for collective efficacy to develop.

- Effective educational leaders clarify the why by presenting compelling student achievement data that create urgency and motivates teachers and teams to act.

- Effective educational leaders clarify the what by working with staff to identify research-based, high-leverage strategies for addressing the student achievement need.

- Effective educational leaders clarify the how by engaging teachers and teams in setting shared goals that measure progress and inform efforts.

- To effectively clarify the why, what, and how for teacher teams, leaders and coaches must do the necessary preparation of information and activities, engage staff in collective learning and building shared knowledge, and follow through to reinforce implementation of the plan through regular communication and support.

- Clarifying the why, what, and how is a critical step for all types of leaders (principals, instructional coaches, team leaders, and so on) and for schools at all points of the PLC journey (initiating, implementing, or sustaining).

Let's reflect on the content from this chapter.

1. As a leader or coach, when you reflect on the work that you have done with teacher teams, have you consistently clarified why you were asking them to implement practices or take certain actions? If you have, what effect did that have on the teams? If you haven't, what difference could that have made in your work with them?

2. As a leader or coach, when you reflect on the work that you have done with teacher teams, have you consistently clarified what you were asking them to do? If you have, what effect did that have on the teams? If you haven't, what difference could that have made in your work with them?

3. As a leader or coach, when you reflect on the work that you have done with teacher teams, have you consistently clarified how you would measure success? If you have, what effect did that have on the teams? If you haven't, what difference could that have made in your work with them?

4. Of clarifying the why, clarifying the what, and clarifying the how, which do you think is the most difficult for leaders and coaches? Which do *you* find to be the most challenging?

Let's plan an action step.

The next time that you work with a team, take a few minutes at the beginning of the session to introduce the why, the what, and the how into the conversation. Ask, "So if I were to ask you, why are we doing this, what would you say?" Do the same for the what and the how. Notice how the discussion of this foundation affects teacher and team clarity.

_____

_____

_____

_____

_____

_____

_____

_____

_____

_____

_____

_____

CHAPTER FOUR

Step 2 of the CLEAR Process:

*Listen to Teachers' Fears, Anxieties,
Questions, and Concerns*

FOR LEADERS AND coaches working to build the collective teacher efficacy of collaborative teams, the second step is to listen to teachers' fears, anxieties, questions, and concerns. Even after leaders and coaches have done a thorough job of clarifying why there needs to be a change, what the change involves, and how the change will be measured (step 1), many teachers will still feel stressed by the new tasks. If leaders and coaches fail to address this anxiety, it can undermine their efforts to build the collective efficacy of their teams. That's why step 2 of the CLEAR process is to *listen to teachers' fears, anxieties, questions, and concerns.*

In this chapter, I explore the research behind affective states and efficacy beliefs and explain why it is so important for leaders to recognize the impact of teachers' emotions and anxiety as they work to build the collective efficacy of their teams. I also share the research that shows that when leaders do not create a space for questions, concerns, and anxieties to be shared, the result is an organizational culture where people do not feel safe and, as a result, are limited in their performance. Next, I share practical strategies for carrying out step 2 of the CLEAR process, which involves preparing a clear plan for inviting and hearing teacher concerns, engaging with staff to demonstrate openness, and following through on concerns to build trust and a supportive environment for collective teacher efficacy. And I share real-world-inspired scenarios showing leaders and teams doing this work. At the end of the chapter, we summarize, review key takeaways, reflect, and plan an action step in the CLEAR Thoughts and Next Steps section.

Now, let's visit a scenario where a middle school principal is working to implement changes in practice with her teams.

Meet the Team

It's the last day of preservice week, and the grade 8 science team at Mary Shelley Middle School is feeling anxious. Principal Poe started off day one of preservice week with her welcome-back-to-school address. Accompanied by members of the school's guiding coalition, she shared data that showed that students at Shelley were not doing well in terms of reading performance. Shelley students' reading scores did not meet the state or district targets. In addition, students in comparable schools in the district were scoring significantly higher than Shelley. It was clear that the faculty needed to do something to address the scores. Dr. Poe and the guiding coalition outlined their draft plan for addressing reading performance. This plan involved new expectations for collaborative teams. She explained all teams would be expected to use CFAs this year. Furthermore, she described how teams will be given time to meet and review CFA results as a team. Principal Poe enthusiastically asserted that when teams of teachers review student assessments together, it provides a great opportunity for teachers to learn from each other. The research shows, she said, that when teachers collaborate around student work, student achievement increases. In ensuing sessions, Dr. Poe and members of the school's guiding coalition provided more details about what teams would be expected to do. They explained the expectations for teams and their use of common assessments as well as the supports that teams would receive. There were also sessions to engage teams in learning about CFAs together. As a result, teams gained a greater understanding about how to develop assessments and use the data. Finally, Dr. Poe and the team leaders also explained the overall goals for implementing this initiative. The theory of action was that using CFAs consistently would help to raise student reading scores by at least 10 percent.

Now, as the eighth-grade science team teachers meet for their department time at the end of preservice week, they are feeling stressed. They understand why they must make a change. The student results that Dr. Poe shared were not acceptable and there was a clear rationale for trying some new strategies so that students do better on the tests. They also understand what they are expected to do—the preservice sessions have given them a chance to build their shared knowledge about using common assessments. It makes sense that teachers who are teaching the same subject should use common tools to assess student learning and progress. They also understand how this new initiative will be measured and how they will know if it is working. Dr. Poe and the school's reading coach explained how student reading skills would be monitored throughout the school year to make sure that they were on track to meet the new school goals for student performance. So, the science team has a good understanding of the why (compelling data about poor student reading achievement), the what (using a research-based practice—CFA—to address student needs), and the how (regular monitoring of student reading levels to mark progress toward a school goal of increasing overall student reading achievement by at least 10 percent by the end of the school year).

But they are still nervous. It's the sharing of student results that's making them anxious. The thought of bringing their students' scores to a team meeting and laying them on the table for all to see is very stressful. They ask themselves many anxiety- and fear-fueled questions: *What if my students bomb the test? What if my students do poorly compared to my teammates? That could be embarrassing and scary. How will the results be used? If my scores are not as good as other teachers' data, will I be in trouble with the principal? Will this affect my standing as a teacher?* They feel uneasy about what they are being asked to do, and it is affecting their attention to all aspects of their teaching.

Principal Poe is making a common leadership mistake that makes it difficult to build the collective efficacy of teacher teams. While she has taken the time to explain the why, the what, and the how around this change in practice, she has not yet created the space for teachers to share their questions, concerns, and, yes, even fears and anxieties, about the new expectations. As a result, teachers are left feeling stressed and confused. The research on self-efficacy and collective efficacy tells us that affective states are a significant source of efficacy beliefs: furthermore, if teachers' affective states and emotional responses are not addressed, self-efficacy and collective efficacy growth can be undermined (Bandura, 1997). To build the collective efficacy of teacher teams in a PLC, leaders must listen to teachers' fears, anxieties, questions, and concerns.

As in step 1, preparation, engagement, and follow-through are also critical in step 2. As I mentioned earlier, even when leaders and coaches do a great job of completing step 1 of the process, there will still be many teachers and teams that have questions, concerns, fears, and anxieties about the change in practice. If these concerns are not discussed and addressed, they can stifle the whole effort to build the collective efficacy of teams. Some leaders will think that they can address questions and concerns when they explain the why, what, and how and, therefore, do not need to have a separate step to delve into teacher affective states. This often leads to giving this critical aspect of building collective efficacy a passing glance rather than a deep exploration. If a principal or coach presents tons of information about student learning needs, a new strategy to implement, and new targets, and then asks at the end, "Any questions?" he will not do much to create an environment of safety and trust, even if he demonstrates wait time before moving on to the next agenda item. If, however, the principal follows the download of new information by introducing an ongoing process to hear teacher feedback and questions, there will be a different feeling in the room. Following through on that ongoing process will go a long way toward establishing a safe environment and building the collective efficacy of teacher teams.

Let's explore the research about affective states, organizational culture, and collective efficacy.

What the Research Says

Step 2 of the CLEAR process is based on research around the role of affective states in collective efficacy. As we will see, if leaders and coaches have a deep understanding of how affective states affect their teachers and teams, it can make a substantial difference in their work with the team and their efforts to build collective efficacy with their teacher teams.

So, what do we mean by affective states? The research shows that when people are presented with a new task or challenge, they will interpret their ability to successfully complete that challenge based on their past experiences. Individuals will also have a physiological response to this new task (Bandura, 1997). The introduction of the task produces energy and a reaction that can be felt in the body. Bandura found that if individuals have had negative experiences with this task in the past, they will interpret their reaction as anxiety and fear of failure. The natural response then is to try to avoid the task, if possible. If avoiding the task altogether is not an option, individuals will attempt the task, but they will not give full effort, and they will abandon the task as soon as they can (Bandura, 1997). In schools, if teachers have unshared or unaddressed stress about a task, they will sometimes act on this stress by consciously or unconsciously avoiding the task. They may "go through the motions," but they will not exert a full effort. The root of this inaction is fear. So many times, when a teacher or team seems to be resistant to a task, it is not that they are just trying to be difficult or oppositional. Very often, they are afraid of failing at the new task, so they avoid it any way they can.

Here is an example of how affective states can affect a teacher's stress level, instructional decisions, and work performance. At Viers Mill Elementary, when we were implementing our efforts to improve student achievement in reading, we established expectations about reading instruction in all classrooms. Guided by the research, we expected all teachers to use a portion of their reading block every day to meet students in small groups to provide differentiated support. As I visited classrooms, I would see teachers implementing this aspect of our schoolwide strategy across all grade levels. But there was one teacher who never seemed to be meeting students in small groups. Every time I visited, the teacher was delivering whole-group instruction. When I followed up with the teacher, after a candid conversation, it became clear that she was avoiding meeting with students in small groups because she was afraid that the rest of the students would misbehave while she was having small-group time and that she would lose control of her classroom. She shared that she had some previous experiences of difficulty with student behavior and the idea of releasing some control in order to meet with small groups was terrifying. Her anxiety about classroom management was getting in the way of her implementing a schoolwide strategy to meet student needs through research-based small-group instruction. Once she had a chance to share this anxiety, we were able to address it and provide her with the necessary supports, including coaching, targeted training, and opportunities to observe other teachers. Over time, she became an expert in small-group instruction and even served as a model for other teachers. If I had not taken the time to hear her anxieties, she would have continued in her previous practice and not achieved a breakthrough in her self-efficacy for instruction.

Affective states also play into the collective efficacy of a group. If a team is presented with a task, they will individually and collectively reflect on how they have done with this task, or similar challenges, in the past and this will inform their level of collective efficacy. They will also consider the difficulty of the task and judge whether they think their team, and the school as a whole, is capable of completing the task effectively (Goddard et al., 2000).

Stanford professors and authors Jeffrey Pfeffer and Robert I. Sutton (2000) identified what they called "the knowing-doing gap" as they studied how successful companies were able to turn institutional knowledge into observable action. They examined the frustrating reality that sometimes the individuals within a company knew what to do—but it did not translate into action and results. They found that there were a number of factors that caused this "knowing-doing gap" including internal competition, ineffective leadership, and fear (Pfeffer & Sutton, 2000, p. 245). Pfeffer and Sutton's work reminds us it is not enough to just communicate information and knowledge to our staff members. We must create a culture where people feel safe and empowered to do their work at the highest level.

When we apply Pfeffer and Sutton's research to building the collective efficacy of teachers and teams in schools, we begin to understand that it is not enough for a principal or coach to provide a clear explanation of the why, what, and how. You also must develop a culture based on safety and empowerment, thereby creating a space for teachers and teams to share their questions, concerns, fears, and anxieties. Harvard professor and author Amy C. Edmondson (2018) argues that organizational leaders should strive to provide "psychological safety" — an environment where [people] can speak up, offer ideas, and ask questions without fear of being punished or embarrassed" (p. 15). Edmondson also notes that leaders in any organization play a key role in whether the environment is psychologically safe:

> Psychological safety is a key factor in healthy teams. A leader's job— whether at the top of an organization or somewhere in the middle—is to create a safe space for people to speak up, make mistakes, and bring their full selves to work. (Edmondson, 2022)

In schools, principals, administrators, and teacher leaders all have a role to play in creating and sustaining a psychologically safe environment that builds trust, productivity, and collective efficacy. When school leaders make time for step 2 of the CLEAR process, seeking out and listening to teachers' fears, anxieties, questions, and concerns, they are taking action to create a safe culture that will support building the collective efficacy of teacher teams. When school leaders do not make time to truly hear teachers' concerns, it sends a clear message that their concerns do not really matter. The result is a culture where teachers and teams are afraid to ask questions or share concerns because they fear that they will be labeled as negative, uncooperative, or even not committed to their students.

There is a clear connection between Bandura's research on the sources of efficacy beliefs, Pfeffer and Sutton's knowing-doing gap, and Edmondson's work on psychological safety. When the individuals in a business or school know the actions to take, know the right things to do, and still do not take those actions, something is getting in the way. Bandura's research shines a light on the role that fear and anxiety play in this situation. If an individual or team is presented with a task, even if they are given all the information and knowledge necessary to complete it, they may still fear that they will fail. If they work in a school that is not psychologically safe, they may worry that they will be punished if they are not successful. Their affective states kick in and they consciously or subconsciously decide it is better to avoid doing the task rather than risking failure. They may go through the motions and appear to carry out some of the tasks, but closer examination reveals that they have not given the task the effort it needs (Bandura, 1995).

In *Deep Change Leadership*, Douglas Reeves (2021) makes the point that people in organizations do not see change as just an annoyance or inconvenience, but as true psychological, and even physical, pain. Change brings uncertainty and fear. Major change, Reeves (2021) explains, expands the opportunities for "catastrophic thinking" (p. 29). Major change can lead people to imagine the worst possible impacts and outcomes before the initiative has even started. Leaders must demonstrate compassion and understanding as they lead their staffs through change. Again, this aligns very well with the research on efficacy beliefs. A leader or coach who hopes to build the collective efficacy of teacher teams needs to consider teachers' affective states during the change process. That is why the CLEAR process for building the collective efficacy of teacher teams in a PLC or without includes a specific, and critical, step to address teacher fears and anxieties.

Let's look at some practical strategies and tools for doing this work.

Making It CLEAR

Leaders who want to build the collective efficacy of their teams and have their staff members implement their plans at the highest level must have a plan for hearing and addressing staff concerns, questions, fears, and anxieties. Coaches who are committed to creating a culture that supports collective teacher efficacy must be strategic and thoughtful in how they address teacher affective states. As we saw in step 1, this work involves careful preparation and planning, meaningful engagement with staff, and, most importantly for this step, thoughtful follow-through and support.

- **Preparation:** Leaders and coaches implementing step 2 of the CLEAR process must devote time to planning deliberate actions for carrying out this part of the process. It is not enough to casually adopt a mindset of "I will do more to listen to my teachers." Effective leaders develop a strategic plan for hearing teachers' concerns and responding in a meaningful way. This includes planning for multiple methods of collecting input, including face-to-face meetings, surveys, and comment walls.

- **Engagement:** Leaders and coaches implementing step 2 of the CLEAR process effectively will engage with their teachers and teams in a variety of settings (whole staff, team meetings, one-on-one with teachers) to promote, build, and sustain a culture of psychological safety.

- **Follow-through:** Leaders and coaches implementing step 2 will be deliberate and strategic in their follow-through with staff after gathering their feedback. They will work to honor teacher and team input and sharing by putting energy into thoughtful responses and ongoing dialogue. Because step 2 of the CLEAR process involves asking teachers to be vulnerable and transparent, effective follow-through that is prompt, empathetic, and clear is essential.

Figure 4.1 provides an overview of the preparation, engagement, and follow-through work involved in carrying out step 2 of the CLEAR process.

	Meetings	Surveys	Comment Boards and Suggestion Boxes
Preparation	Leaders and coaches plan and deliver communication to staff explaining why and how they will be collecting staff input on fears, anxieties, questions, and concerns.		
	Leaders and coaches develop a strategic plan for using different types of meetings (full staff, team meetings, individual conferences) to gather input and perspective.	Leaders and coaches develop survey instruments and methods of distribution to collect input and perspectives from staff.	Leaders and coaches develop plans for using staff comment boards and suggestion boxes to gather staff input.
Engagement	Leaders and coaches meet face-to-face with staff in various settings to explain the need to address stressors and to have an open discussion.	Leaders and coaches distribute surveys and communicate desire to staff to have full input—that their voice is valued.	Leaders and coaches make comment boards and suggestion box tools available to staff and encourage input.
Follow-Through	Leaders and coaches review the data collected through meetings, surveys, comment boards, and suggestion boxes. They analyze the data to identify trends and patterns. Next, they communicate with staff about the trends and needs and explain how questions and concerns will be addressed, while maintaining commitment to the why, what, and how.		

Figure 4.1: OVERVIEW OF PREPARATION, ENGAGEMENT, AND FOLLOW-THROUGH FOR STEP 2.

In the reproducible "Coach's Planner for Step 2 of the CLEAR Process: Listen to Teachers' Fears, Anxieties, Questions, and Concerns" in the appendix (page 222), I provide a detailed planner for leaders and coaches to use in implementing this part of the CLEAR process.

Let's look at some practical tips and tools for leaders and coaches to use in preparation, engagement, and follow-through of step 2.

Preparation for Listening to Teachers' Fears, Anxieties, Questions, and Concerns

To launch step 2 of the CLEAR process, leaders and coaches must intentionally communicate to their teacher teams that their next step, after clarifying the why, what, and how, is to purposefully listen to teachers' fears, anxieties, questions, and concerns. They establish that it will be a normal part of business to devote time to helping teachers and teams express and work through their worries and stresses. Leaders should consider the best timing and setting for their first delivery of this message. Ideally, leaders should deliver a clear message about wanting to hear teachers' fears, anxieties, questions, and concerns as soon as possible after the why, what, and how have been established. In this way, leaders and coaches acknowledge that the work ahead is challenging and begin to address those concerns immediately, rather than sending overwhelmed teachers off to stress about what they have heard. For example, a principal may make a clear connection between step 1 and step 2 with comments like these:

> *I want to thank everyone for your participation and input during our recent staff meetings as we reviewed our students' learning data, identified strengths and needs, learned together about research-based strategies, and established goals for student performance. We have identified a critical student learning need (our why), a powerful strategy that we will all be implementing to address this need (our how), and shared goals and a monitoring system to help us measure how our work is impacting students (our how).*
>
> *I know that this is a lot to take in and many of you probably have additional questions about all of this. You might even be feeling a bit of stress or anxiety about what we will try to do together. I want you to know that I understand that this can be a little scary sometimes and that changes like this can feel overwhelming. Sometimes, it is overwhelming for me, too. We all want to do great things for our students and the work to be done is a lot. So, I want to give you and us a chance to talk those things through. I will be meeting with every team over the next two weeks to review our why, what, and how and to hear any questions you have about the work we have to do. I want you to feel comfortable sharing your questions, concerns, and, yes, even your fears and anxieties about our why, what, and how, because I believe that will help us to do the work effectively. When we get our concerns out in the open, then we can address them and have a plan for working through them. There is important work we have to do for our students, and I want every teacher and every team to feel empowered and supported in that work. I will send every team an email following this meeting to begin the process of setting up our sessions to meet together. I look forward to meeting with you.*

The prospect of deliberately asking teachers to share their fears and anxieties is, ironically, very *scary* for some leaders and coaches. Many administrators will worry (again, ironic) that if they open the door to hearing teacher concerns, they may lose control of the whole initiative. What if there is a critical mass of teachers who share that they are completely stressed out and can't see implementing the why, what, and how at all? This is why the CLEAR process starts with a strong establishment of why there needs to be a change (students' learning and their future success depends on it), what the change will be (students will benefit from us implementing these strong new research-based practices), and how we will measure success (shared goals that we have for our students' growth). As Edmondson (2022) explains, the goal is to create a balance between accountability for the why, what, and how, while also fostering a safe environment for learning and productive work:

> If you are ONLY creating psychological safety, then you are creating a comfort zone. And if you are ONLY talking about accountability for excellence, then you are creating an anxiety zone where people are less likely to do their best work. But if you are able to simultaneously create psychological safety and drive motivation, you can get people into the learning zone, which also happens to be the high-performance zone (Edmondson, 2022, p. 2).

When a leader or coach implementing the CLEAR process listens to teachers' fears, anxieties, questions, and concerns, the purpose is to identify stressors to be aware of. All teachers and teams will be expected to follow through on the common mission, but step 2 of the CLEAR process recognizes that the reality of a new mission can be overwhelming and cause stress. By providing a space for teachers and teams to share their concerns, leaders can help to address, or minimize the stress, and build a culture of trust at the same time.

After leaders have communicated to staff that they want to hear teacher and team input, they need to determine how they will collect that input. They must develop a strategic plan for inviting, welcoming, and collecting teacher reactions, thoughts, and feelings about the why, what, and how in a variety of settings and through a range of tools. The plan should include opportunities for teachers to personally share their fears, anxieties, questions, and concerns in a safe environment as well as avenues for teachers to share their thoughts and feelings anonymously.

Leaders and coaches can use the "Coach's Planning Tool for Step 2 of the CLEAR Process: Listen to Teachers' Fears, Anxieties, Questions, and Concerns" in the appendix (page 222) to organize their thoughts and their plan for listening to teachers' fears, anxieties, questions, and concerns.

Engagement for Listening to Teachers' Fears, Anxieties, Questions, and Concerns

When leaders and coaches begin listening to teachers' fears and anxieties, they must be strategic and intentional. How will they get the most complete and most accurate feedback and input from teachers? How can they gather data in different ways? The following strategies touch on three areas: (1), meetings, (2) surveys, and (3) suggestion boxes and comment walls.

Meetings

One excellent way for leaders to demonstrate to the full staff that they are serious about hearing from teachers about their anxieties, questions, and concerns is to devote all or part of a whole staff meeting to the effort. My recommendation is for leaders to be upfront about inviting teachers to share about what stresses them and how this process is linked to building the collective efficacy of teacher teams. Leaders should at least explain that they are devoting time to this activity because research shows if we get these worries out in the open, we can address them, and it will put us in a better place to move forward. For example, leaders might say:

> In today's staff meeting, we will take some time to identify the questions, concerns, fears, and anxieties that we have about the work involved in following through on our why, our what, and our how. The research shows that it is natural for people to feel some stress and anxiety when confronted with new tasks. I know that I sometimes feel like there is too much to learn and too much to do. The research also shows that we are more likely to be successful with these tasks if we identify any stressors, get them on the table, and then work together to address them. Today, we will do an activity that helps us to name any fears and anxieties we have so we can create a plan for

dealing with them. When we do this together, it helps to build our collective efficacy because together, we know we can accomplish great things for our students.

After explaining the rationale, leaders also must explain in advance how the input will be used. Some teachers might worry that, if they are candid and share their concerns, that it will somehow by used against them. Edmondson (2018) reminds us that some team members may have the perception that there will be "punitive" consequences for "asking for help or admitting a failure" (p. 15). Leaders must assure teachers that the goal is to hear candid input from teachers and teams about what is stressing them about the why, the what, and the how, and that there will be no negative repercussions for any questions or comments. It is also very helpful for teacher leaders and members of the guiding coalition to reinforce this message so that all teachers will feel more comfortable sharing their input.

Next, principals and teacher leaders facilitate a collaborative process to ask questions and invite teacher responses. It is best to use a process that gives teachers a chance to talk in small groups and then share group thoughts, rather than putting individual teachers on the spot. Then, all group thoughts are collected and grouped so that everyone has the same view of staff fears, anxieties, questions, and concerns. Leaders might also choose to invite teachers to share what is making them feel positive or optimistic so that there is a balance to the activity.

Leaders should conclude this activity by thanking teachers and teams for their candid input, summarizing the key information, and committing to follow up with action steps within a week.

The following shows two versions of a seven-step protocol that leaders can use to collect input from their teacher teams. Version one concentrates fully on stressors and concerns, while version two supports a wider discussion that includes sharing excitement and ideas. This is a process that leaders can use after they have established the why, what, and how in step 1 of the CLEAR process.

The goals of this process are as follows.

- Establish and reinforce that our school is a place where it is OK for teachers and staff to be candid about their questions and concerns.

- Gather meaningful data about the current state of teacher fears, anxieties, questions, and concerns as they relate to the why, what, and how that we will be implementing.

The steps for the process are as follows.

1. Briefly review why the school is making a change (the compelling student learning need), what the change will involve (the strategies or processes that all teams will be implementing), and how the changes will be evaluated and monitored (our shared goals for student learning).

2. Acknowledge that changes like this can produce stress and anxiety. Explain that the staff will be engaging in a collaborative process to try to identify the stressors and concerns that teachers have.

3. Explain that teachers will work in small groups to discuss their fears, anxieties, questions, and concerns and that all input will be collected and reviewed so that everyone has a clear picture of the issues to be addressed.

4. Divide teachers into random groups of four to six and provide each group with sticky notes and a four-frame sheet labeled: 1. Fears—I'm a little scared by . . . , 2. Anxieties—I'm a little stressed about . . . , 3. Questions—I have a question about . . . , and 4. Concerns—I'm a little worried about . . . . Invite teacher groups to have an open conversation and capture their group input on their chart. This version of the chart allows staff to think through and capture the aspects of the why, what, and how that create stress. Providing this opportunity to staff reinforces the message that leaders and coaches genuinely want to identify and address the stress that teachers and teams are feeling. A second version of the four-square activity varies the prompts to provide participants with the opportunity to express the positive feelings they are having about the why, what, and how. In this second version, the prompts are: 1. I am feeling excited about . . . , 2. I am feeling anxious or concerned about . . . , 3. I have questions about . . . , and 4. I have ideas about . . . . This second version collects staff fears and anxieties while also giving teachers the opportunity to share what they feel positive about. Either version will help leaders and coaches to collect important input. Leaders and coaches can decide which version of the four-frame will work best for their teachers, team, and situation. In general, the first four-frame works best if the leaders want to reinforce their openness to teacher concerns, while the second version works better to gather a wider range of teacher sentiments. Figures 4.2 and 4.3 (page 100) capture the types of feedback that teachers may offer through this activity with each version of the four-square chart.

   Note: *This portion of the activity can be facilitated by using an app like Padlet or Jamboard, which allows participants to type in input that is displayed on a screen that all participants can see, without directly connecting the input to the person who typed it in.*

5. After teams have had a chance to share their thoughts and complete their sticky notes, the facilitator invites groups to post their notes on a larger chart that also has four sections. Teams can do this at the same time with some music playing so little attention is paid to who is posting which notes.

6. The facilitators lead a discussion of the notes that are in each portion of the chart and help the staff identify any patterns or repeated concerns. The leader asks clarifying questions and invites participants to share their comments. For example, if one of the themes that is reflected in the chart is concerns about professional development to support the why, what, and how, the leader might say: *There seem to be a number of concerns about training support for the work we will do. It looks like a fair number of teachers are worried that they will not have ongoing guidance and training to carry out the work. Would anyone like to comment on that? Would it help if we provided a detailed calendar of how training sessions will be provided throughout the year?* The leaders close the activity by explaining how all the data will be shared with the staff and how the school leaders will follow up on the issues raised.

7. Within two to three days, or a week at most, the school leaders share their analysis of all the teacher input that was collected and explain the first steps that they will take to address the concerns that were raised.

When I think about our school's why, what, and how:	
I am feeling scared about: The amount of time it might take to learn the new strategies What happens if it doesn't work? Achieving our goals and how things like student attendance and motivation affect their performance	**I am feeling anxious about:** What happens if we do all this work and student scores don't go up? Repercussions for me if my students' performance doesn't improve
I have questions about: When will we receive professional development to help us with this? Who do we go to if we have questions about how to implement this?	**I am feeling concerned about:** How will I implement new strategies in my classroom?

Figure 4.2: VERSION ONE OF FOUR-SQUARE ACTIVITY TO GATHER STAFF REACTION TO THE WHY, WHAT, AND HOW.

Visit **go.SolutionTree.com/PLCbooks** *for a free reproducible version of this figure.*

When I think about our school's why, what, and how:	
I am feeling excited or positive about: Having a clear goal and plan for the whole school Clarity about what we are trying to do and why Getting to work with my team on implementing these strategies	**I am feeling anxious or concerned about:** The amount of time it might take to learn the new strategies What happens if it doesn't work? Achieving our goals and how things like student attendance and motivation affect their performance
I have questions about: What kinds of ongoing professional development and support we will get to support implementation If our staff meetings will now focus on the why, what, and how or other information	**I have ideas about:** Creating a teacher shared folder where we could keep all our plans, goals, and data Interventions that might help students to reach their goals

Figure 4.3: VERSION TWO OF FOUR-SQUARE ACTIVITY TO GATHER STAFF REACTION TO THE WHY, WHAT, AND HOW.

Visit **go.SolutionTree.com/PLCbooks** *for a free reproducible version of this figure.*

Through leading the four-square activity with the full staff, leaders and coaches demonstrate publicly that they are interested in teacher and team input about the why, what, and how and the stress the new initiatives may cause. Then, when leaders and coaches follow up by identifying the stressors and explaining how they will be addressed, they communicate respect and understanding. These leader behaviors help to reduce the negative effects of affective states and clear the way for collective efficacy to develop.

Some teachers may feel more comfortable sharing their fears and anxieties in a smaller team-meeting setting, as opposed to a whole staff gathering. Principals or teacher coaches can initiate an open conversation with a team, or the team may request to meet. Again, the leader should explain the purpose of hearing teachers' concerns—that we want to have a clear understanding of the stresses that teachers are feeling so that we can plan for how to address them and help everyone on the staff to feel safe and empowered to do the necessary work to implement the why, the what, and the how. Coaches and team leaders, by virtue of their positions, are more likely to engage with their clients at the team level, as opposed to the whole staff. Effective coaches can use this smaller setting to provide their teams with a high level of attention and responsiveness.

A teacher team may have specific questions or concerns that are related to the unique circumstances of their team. For example, a team with several new teachers might have different concerns than a team of experienced educators. Later in this chapter, I provide quadrant tools (page 106) that help leaders to anticipate concerns that different teams might have and respond to the teams' fears and anxieties.

Beyond whole staff meetings and team-level sessions, some teachers may want to meet privately with the principal or teacher leader to share fears, anxieties, questions, or concerns that they do not feel comfortable sharing with other people. For example, teachers may be stressed about their own personal ability to implement part of the schoolwide or team plan, or they might have a concern about how their team or a particular teammate will be able to handle elements of the plan. Leaders, of course, should be open to this input and demonstrate openness and support, while still reinforcing the school's commitment to student learning, trying new strategies, and pursuing ambitious goals. Leaders will also want to carefully protect the confidentiality of information that they hear from individual teachers, unless the teacher gives permission to share their input. Leaders should take the input from individual teachers and fold it into the overall input from the staff.

In any of these settings—whole staff, team-level, or one-to-one conferences—leaders and coaches can accomplish two important goals: (1) they demonstrate to staff that they, as leaders, empathize with teachers and teams and want to hear their concerns, and (2) they gather critical information about how their teachers and teams are feeling about the school's why, what, and how—information that they should use as they plan follow-through.

Surveys

Electronic surveys are an efficient and effective way to gather staff input in addition to the information gathered face-to-face in staff, team, and individual meetings. Surveys can be emailed to teachers, and they can enter their responses anonymously. Leaders and coaches should stress that the survey responses are anonymous and will not be traced back to any individual and that, of course, there will be no negative repercussions for survey responses.

Surveys should be efficient and user-friendly. The best surveys will anticipate possible responses and have those preloaded into the survey document, while also allowing responders to add their own unique thoughts. For example, the teacher and team survey shown in figure 4.4 (page 102) offers five possible sources of stress that respondents can rate (anxiety about time, fear that they will not be successful, etc.), but also invites them to add any other stressors that are not listed.

We also see how leaders and coaches might fill out the top section of the teacher and team survey to make it specific for their school and the why, what, and how they have established.

As a staff, we have established our why, what, and how for this school year.

Why do we need to make a change?

(Example) We need to make a change because the data from our state test, our district benchmarks, and our own common assessments shows that our students are not currently meeting targets for reading proficiency.

What is involved in the change we are making?

(Example) In order to address our why, teachers and teams will institute research-based collaborative team practices that are aligned with increasing student learning, including identifying essential standards, planning instructional units that support learning of the essential standards, and using CFAs in reading.

How will we know if it is working?

(Example) We will monitor progress toward our shared goals by setting and monitoring goals for student reading performance. Our school SMART goal is: The percentage of students in grades 3–10 scoring at the Ready and/or Exceeding level on the state test in reading will increase from 45% in 2023 to at least 65% in 2024.

The purpose of this survey is to gauge the current stress and anxiety levels about our work moving forward. We will use a scale from 0 (*No stress at all*) to 10 (*A high level of stress*).

Please answer each question as candidly as you can and feel free to add comments. All responses are anonymous and will not be attached to any staff member. Overall results of this survey will be shared with the full staff within two weeks.

When you reflect on our why, what, and how, which point on the following scales best represents how you are currently feeling?

1. Stress about how much time it will take to learn and implement new practices

   0 —— 1 —— 2 —— 3 —— 4 —— 5 —— 6 —— 7 —— 8 —— 9 —— 10

   No stress at all　　　　**Moderate level of stress**　　　　**A high level of stress**

2. Stress that I will struggle to implement the new strategies effectively or that I will fail

   0 —— 1 —— 2 —— 3 —— 4 —— 5 —— 6 —— 7 —— 8 —— 9 —— 10

3. Stress that I will struggle, and it will affect my standing as a teacher

   0 —— 1 —— 2 —— 3 —— 4 —— 5 —— 6 —— 7 —— 8 —— 9 —— 10

4. Stress about what happens if we work hard to implement changes and it doesn't work

   0 —— 1 —— 2 —— 3 —— 4 —— 5 —— 6 —— 7 —— 8 —— 9 —— 10

5. Stress that implementing the new practices will cause friction on my team or on the staff

   0 —— 1 —— 2 —— 3 —— 4 —— 5 —— 6 —— 7 —— 8 —— 9 —— 10

Are there any other aspects of our why, what, and how that are causing you stress or making you anxious? Please feel free to add those in the space below:

_____

Are there any other aspects of our why, what, and how that are making members of your team anxious? Please feel free to add those in the space below.

_____

What questions do you have about implementing our why, what, and how?

_____

Please feel free to add any other comments:

_____

Figure 4.4: EXAMPLE OF TEACHER AND TEAM SURVEY WITH TOP SECTION COMPLETED.

Visit **go.SolutionTree.com/PLCbooks** *for a free reproducible version of this figure.*

One of the main drawbacks or dangers with surveys is the possibility that you may get a low response rate. Leaders and coaches want the survey data to reflect the thoughts and feelings of the full staff, so ideally, we would want 100 percent of the surveys to be returned. This is a lofty goal that is rarely reached with any type of survey, so a leader should not be disappointed if some surveys are not returned. If, however, only 20 to 25 percent of the surveys are returned, the data reflect a fairly limited sample, which makes the data less powerful. To increase the chances of a healthy survey return, leaders should follow the advice provided in the preceding paragraphs: (1) assure staff that the survey is anonymous and will not be used against any staff member, and (2) make the survey as user-friendly and efficient as possible.

Leaders and coaches can provide secure surveys to teachers and teams through Google Forms, Survey Monkey, Jotform, Questionpro, or other tools, which will also help them to compile and analyze the results.

Leaders should also use the survey document as an opportunity to reiterate the rationale for the school's why, what, and how. In the example survey (figure 4.4), the leader summarizes the rationale for why there needs to be a change, what the change is, and how the change will be measured in the top section. This helps to keep survey responses focused specifically on the school's initiatives.

When surveys are used effectively, leaders and coaches can gather a great deal of actionable data in a short amount of time and with a limited amount of effort. When leaders combine the survey data with the input gathered in the meeting settings described earlier, they have a detailed representation of where their staff are in terms of the why, what, and how.

Suggestion Boxes and Comment Walls

In addition to electronic surveys, leaders and coaches can provide teachers and teams with other ways to provide anonymous input. Again, this is intended to demonstrate to teachers that all input is valued and that leaders do not want important questions, concerns, or ideas to be missed because staff are afraid to speak publicly. Two options are suggestion boxes and comment walls. The office or school suggestion box is an old-fashioned idea, but it can also be an effective way to gather staff input. Boxes are placed in common locations, and staff members are invited to jot down their thoughts regarding the why, what, and how, and then place their input in the boxes.

When I was a principal, we were implementing a lot of new practices, and we wanted to provide a way for teachers to share questions and concerns without taking the risk of speaking up at a staff meeting or knocking on the principal's door. We put out two boxes in the teacher workroom, one labeled "clarify" and the other "simplify." The clarify box was for any questions about the new strategies we were implementing and the expectations for teachers and teams. When an issue was raised through the clarify box, I made a point of addressing it in the staff bulletin, with team leaders, and directly with teams to make sure everyone was clear. The simplify box was for suggestions about how to take all the things we were doing and simplify some processes. Sometimes, these were suggestions about how to improve communication or reduce the steps in a process. Simplify material was reviewed by the guiding coalition, which worked to implement process improvements that were suggested through the simplify box.

Principals and teacher leaders who are implementing the CLEAR process can also use a comment wall approach. In this strategy, leaders place a display that summarizes the why, what, and how and posts it in the staff workroom or lounge area. Teachers and teams are invited to write questions or comments on Post-it notes and then attach them to the display or write directly on a whiteboard. This approach provides the same anonymity as the suggestion box but puts the input where any staff member can see it. The comment wall can be left up for a week or two to give all staff the opportunity to post their input and also see other staff members' thoughts. Figure 4.5 shows what a comment wall might look like.

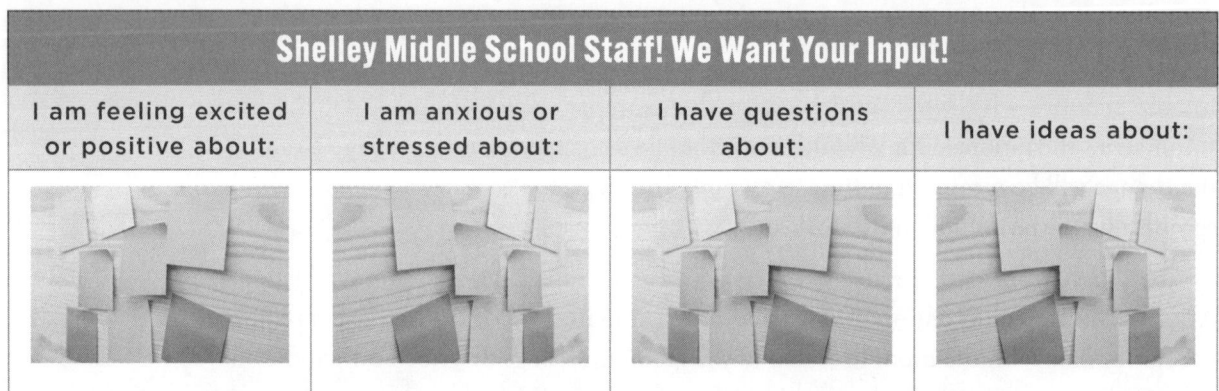

Shelley Middle School Staff! We Want Your Input!			
I am feeling excited or positive about:	I am anxious or stressed about:	I have questions about:	I have ideas about:

Figure 4.5: SAMPLE COMMENT WALL FOR STEP 2 OF THE CLEAR PROCESS.

Suggestion boxes and comment walls, when combined with in-person meetings and survey strategies, provide useful information to leaders and coaches about how their teachers and teams are thinking and feeling about the why, what, and how that they have outlined for their staff. Collecting these data in several forms also sends that message "We really want to hear what you have to say." The next, and most critical piece in step 2, is to honor that data by following through in meaningful ways.

Follow-Through for Listening to Teachers' Fears, Anxieties, Questions, and Concerns

After engaging with staff in these settings and through these methods, principals and leaders will have a sizable amount of data to review. Their next step is to analyze the data and follow through on teacher and team input. Leaders and coaches also must communicate *how* they are following through. This is the most critical aspect of step 2. If a leader goes through the motions of collecting teacher input, particularly candid feedback about their fears and anxieties, and then does nothing to act on their concerns and questions, it sends a clear message that the teachers' feelings were not valued in the first place. This can be even more destructive than failing to solicit teacher input at all. Teachers will be frustrated and hurt that they were vulnerable and shared their fears and anxieties, only to have leadership ignore what they said. If, however, leaders carefully review the data, identify key themes, and then clearly communicate to teachers what they will do to respond, it sends a message that leadership really was interested in teachers' thoughts. Next, the leader or coach needs to follow through and take concrete action to respond to the fears, anxieties, questions, and concerns that teachers shared. It is important to communicate this effectively to staff and keep them apprised of the ongoing efforts to create and sustain a psychologically safe work environment. This, in turn, will support effective implementation of the why, what, and how. Leaders and coaches can use the "Coach's Planner for Step 2 of the CLEAR Process: Listen to Teachers' Fears, Anxieties, Questions, and Concerns" in the appendix (page 222) to plan and execute this part of the CLEAR process.

It is important to note before turning to specific methods that completing the follow-through phase of step 2 does not end with the leaders' response to the first collection of teacher input. While it is critical to address teachers' affective states after clarifying the why, what, and how, teachers and teams may experience stress and worry at any point during implementation of the process. Remember our CLEAR process graphic (figure 2.1, page 36) from chapter 2—the step 2 portion of the process stretches throughout all five steps of the process. For example, in step 4 of the CLEAR process—activate new learning through coaching, practice, and implementation—leaders and coaches guide teams as they adapt the models they explored in step 3. This is demanding work that can cause stress for even the most confident teams. Leaders and coaches must monitor the stress level of teacher teams throughout all steps of the CLEAR process. Effective leaders will "take the temperature" of their teacher teams as they coach and work to build their collective efficacy. If some signs of stress are noticed, the coach should call attention to it, invite a candid discussion about what is happening, and then take steps to address it. This will help to ensure that teams stay on track as they implement effective strategies and build their collective efficacy.

As leaders and coaches engage collaborative teams in why there needs to be a change, what the change entails, and how the change will be measured, they must pay attention to how each team, and the individuals on the team, are reacting to this new information. Like a good teacher who monitors how students respond to new content in the classroom, leaders must "read the room" to assess how the new content is being received.

Are teachers and teams agitated by the compelling student data behind why a change is needed? Or are they displaying passion and a firm resolve to make a difference in the data that have been shared? Consider the following.

- Do any of the teams seemed overwhelmed by the prospect of changing practice? Or do teams demonstrate a high level of interest in learning what to do to implement strategies that will work?

- Do teams or team members express a sense of hopelessness when the staff are discussing ambitious goals for student learning? Or are teams optimistic about their ability to achieve significant growth for students?

Leaders and coaches are likely to see many different reactions—different variations and combinations occur when leading change with any group of people. In implementing the CLEAR process, leaders who are working on step 1 must already have an eye on step 2. As they engage teachers and teams in building shared knowledge about the why, the what, and the how, they must be monitoring initial reactions and planning for longer-term work to respond to each team's fears, anxieties, questions, and concerns.

Numerous researchers and authors have used quadrant or matrix tools as a visual representation of the interplay of different factors in the workplace to better understand the dynamics at hand and to plan how to respond, including Hersey and Blanchard's skill-and-will matrix (Hersey, Blanchard, & Johnson, 2012). In a school setting, Anthony Muhammad and Sharroky Hollie (2012), in their book on transforming school culture, apply a version of the Hersey-Blanchard version of the matrix to capture the interplay of skill and will in how educators operate in schools in terms of their belief systems (Muhammad & Hollie, 2012). For leaders who are specifically working to create collective teacher efficacy, Navo and Savage, whom I cited in chapter 1, offer quadrant tools that help coaches to assess where teams are and plan interventions to help them be successful (Navo & Savage, 2021).

These tools are always designed to help managers and leaders to analyze their situation, organize their thinking, and plan actions for working with their teams. For leaders working to build the collective efficacy of their teacher teams, it is useful to have a tool that helps us think through the work we are doing with our teams and how they are reacting to it. This is especially true when we are implementing the first two steps of the CLEAR process. In step 1, we clarify the why, what, and how and thereby outline the work that teachers and teams will be expected to do. In step 2, we create the space to hear teachers' questions, concerns, fears, and anxieties about that work. At this point in the process, it can be very helpful for coaches to analyze and reflect on how each team is responding to the why, the what, and the how.

To support leaders and coaches who are implementing the CLEAR process, I have built on the previous work of Hersey and Blanchard, Muhammad and Hollie, and Navo and Savage to create a set of tools that are specifically designed to help leaders assess teams' reactions to the why, what, and how and to help them implement step 2—listen to teachers fears, anxieties, questions, and concerns, as effectively as possible. The matrix in figure 4.6 captures the interplay between two factors that are critical to implementing the CLEAR process: (1) teachers' reactions to the change that is being presented and (2) their perception of whether their team can accomplish the change.

Figure 4.6: STEP 2 MATRIX TOOL.

In essence, the CLEAR process step 2 matrix asks the following questions.

1. First, it looks at how teachers or teams react to the why, what, and how. How strong is their embrace of the rationale, the change, and the targets? Do they accept there is a need for change? Are they open to implementing the new strategy? Do they see value in the new goals? Or does the team question the why, disagree with the strategy, and reject the goals? What is their level of embrace of the why, what, how? The x-axis in the CLEAR step 2 matrix captures a team's embrace of the why, what, how from low to high. To help support our work with the matrix, we will apply an identifying term to the teams that are accepting and eager about the why, what, and how. For our purposes, we will call them "embracers." We will also use a term to refer to teams that are not enthusiastic about the why, what, and how and who resist the new initiatives—we will refer to them as "resisters." Before going any further, let me acknowledge that sometimes there are good reasons for a teacher or team to be "resisters" and push back against an initiative—for example, the initiative has no clear rationale, it has no support, there are too many new projects at the same time, and so on. I do not pass judgment on teams who do not immediately go along with new practice. I just want to understand what they are thinking, why they are thinking that, and how to respond effectively as a coach or leader.

2. Next, the matrix looks at what a team's level of collective efficacy is when they consider implementing the why, what, and how. When they review why there needs to be a change (compelling student data), what the change will be (new strategy or practice to be implemented), and how the change will be measured (shared goals, monitoring system), do they believe that their team has the capabilities to implement these changes effectively? Or do they have serious doubts about their team's ability to be successful? What is their perceived collective teacher efficacy for this specific why, what, and how? The y-axis on the CLEAR step 2 matrix captures a team's sense of collective teacher efficacy for the why, what, and how from low to high. As we did with the x-axis, we will use identifiers for the teams at the different ends of the spectrum in terms of their collective efficacy. Since a key aspect of collective efficacy is collective confidence, we will refer to those who have a high level of belief in the team as "confident", while teams with a lower level of collective efficacy will be referred to as "insecure." Again, no judgment here. There are many understandable reasons that a teacher team might be "insecure" in their collective confidence. For example, a team made up of first-year teachers working together for the first time naturally will start the year with a lower level of collective efficacy because they are new to the role, and they haven't had the opportunity to build mastery experiences together. So, again, I am not trying to pass judgment, but rather trying to understand why a team feels the way they do and then planning an effective response to meet them where they are.

Using these descriptors for the different levels of embrace of the why, what, and how and the collective belief in the team, our matrix shows that our teams can be perceived as "confident embracers," "confident resisters," "insecure resisters," and "insecure embracers." Figure 4.7 shows how these four situations are reflected in the matrix.

Insecure Embracers High embrace of the why, what, how Low confidence in the team	**Confident Embracers** High embrace of the why, what, how High confidence in the team
Insecure Resisters Low embrace of the why, what, how Low confidence in the team	**Confident Resisters** Low embrace of the why, what, how High confidence in the team

Figure 4.7: MATRIX TOOL: TEAM RESPONSES TO THE WHY, WHAT, AND HOW.

Using the matrix and these descriptors as a launch pad, let's look at each of the quadrants and try to understand indicators of where a teacher team is on the matrix, possible explanations for how or why the team is in a particular quadrant, and advice for leaders and coaches who want to help these teams to be successful and build their collective efficacy.

In figure 4.8 we look more closely at a teacher team that the matrix defines as *insecure resisters*—a team that is struggling with both a low sense of collective efficacy as well as resistance to the school's why, what, and how.

High embrace of the why, what, how Low confidence in the team	High embrace of the why, what, how High confidence in the team
Insecure Resisters Low embrace of the why, what, how Low confidence in the team	Low embrace of the why, what, how High confidence in the team

Insecure Resisters: Low Embrace of the Why, What, and How; Low Confidence in Team

Teams in this quadrant are not embracing why they need to change, what they are expected to do, and how it is being measured.

Teams in this quadrant also have a low level of confidence in their team's ability to meet the challenges presented by the compelling student data (the why), research-based strategies (the what), and shared goals (the how).

Possible indicators that a team is in this quadrant:

The team expresses resistance to or lack of interest in the why (they don't see the urgency in the student data), the what (they are resistant to new strategies or initiatives), and the how (they are not enthusiastic about the school or team goals).

The team is slow to complete tasks related to the why, what, or how or they may not complete them at all.

Members of the team or the team as a whole express doubt that they can complete what they are being asked to do. They may cite different reasons why it is difficult or impossible for the team to do what leaders and coaches are asking.

Possible reasons a team might end up in this quadrant:

A team that is currently insecure and resisting may have tried to implement changes before without success, so they are hesitant to put themselves "out there" and try again. They fear failure or negative consequences of failing. They may mask their fear of failure in active resistance to any new task.

What teams in this quadrant need from their leader or coach:

A team in this quadrant needs the highest level of care, support, and guidance. As leaders and coaches implement step 2 of the CLEAR process, they need to carefully listen to this team's fears, anxieties, questions, and concerns. Leaders will have to be strategic and perseverant as they reinforce the case for the why, what, how while simultaneously providing guidance and encouragement to help the team believe in themselves. Coaches should be especially watchful for evidence that the team is making progress and use that to reinforce mastery experiences and build the team's collective efficacy.

Figure 4.8: COACH'S SUMMARY—TEAMS IN THE INSECURE RESISTERS QUADRANT.

While insecure resisters have both a low level of collective efficacy and a resistance to the school initiative, other teams may have enthusiasm about the why, what, and how, but lack confidence that their team can do the work at a high level. The matrix identifies these teams as *insecure embracers*. In figure 4.9, we look more closely at these teams and how to support them.

Insecure Embracers High embrace of the why, what, how Low confidence in the team	High embrace of the why, what, how High confidence in the team
Low embrace of the why, what, how Low confidence in the team	Low embrace of the why, what, how High confidence in the team

Insecure Embracers: High Embrace of the Why, What, and How; Low Confidence in Team

Teams in this quadrant are embracing why they need to change, what they are expected to do, and how it is being measured.

However, teams in this quadrant have a low level of confidence in their team's ability to meet the challenges presented by the compelling student data (the why), research-based strategies (the what), and shared goals (the how).

Possible indicators that a team is in this quadrant:

The team expresses enthusiasm and a high level of interest in the why (they see the urgency in the student data), the what (they are open to new strategies or initiatives), and the how (they are enthusiastic about the school or team goals).

Although the team believes in the why, what, and how, when it comes down to doing the work, they may hesitate or falter, because they don't have a high level of confidence in themselves as a team.

Members of the team or the team as a whole express doubt that they can complete what they are being asked to do. They may cite different reasons why it is difficult for them.

Possible reasons a team might end up in this quadrant:

One common reason for a team to find itself in this quadrant is a lack of experience that leads to a low sense of collective efficacy. It may be that the team has several new teachers, that teachers on the team are teaching a new grade level or course for the first time, or it is the first time that a group of teachers is working together as a team. In any of these cases, the teachers and team have not had the opportunity, yet, to build their collective efficacy. This can change quickly if the team is given adequate support that helps them to achieve early wins. If teachers on the team are enthusiastic about the school's why, what, and how, and then they are successful in implementing strategies that get results, their collective efficacy will increase rapidly.

What teams in this quadrant need from their leader or coach:

A team in this quadrant needs a coach who can build on their enthusiasm and eagerness and help them to achieve mastery experiences that will build their collective efficacy. They need expert coaching, feedback, and encouragement so that they maintain their enthusiasm while building their collective efficacy. In chapter 6, we will explore social persuasion and effective coaching in our look at step 4 of the CLEAR process. Teams in the "Insecure Embracers" quadrant need patient, empathetic, and targeted coaching.

Figure 4.9: COACH'S SUMMARY—TEAMS IN THE INSECURE EMBRACERS QUADRANT.

While insecure embracers require supportive coaching to help the teams believe in themselves, the next type of teacher team presents a different coaching challenge. In figure 4.10, we examine teams we might call *confident resisters*—teacher teams that profess a high level of confidence in their ability to implement change, but who are resistant to the why, what, and how that have been established at their school.

High embrace of the why, what, how Low confidence in the team	High embrace of the why, what, how High confidence in the team
Low embrace of the why, what, how Low confidence in the team	**Confident Resisters** Low embrace of the why, what, how High confidence in the team

Confident Resisters: Low Embrace of the Why, What, and How; High Confidence in Team

Teams in this quadrant are not embracing why they need to change, what they are expected to do, and how it is being measured.

However, teams in this quadrant express a high level of confidence in their team's ability to meet the challenges presented by the compelling student data (the why), research-based strategies (the what), and shared goals (the how).

Possible indicators that a team is in this quadrant:

The team expresses resistance to or lack of interest in the why (they don't see the urgency in the student data), the what (they are resistant to new strategies or initiatives), and the how (they are not enthusiastic about the school or team goals). The team may express that they are doing fine, the students are doing fine, and there is no reason to change.

The team is slow to complete tasks related to the why, what, or how or they may not complete them at all.

Members of the team or the team as a whole express resistance to what they are being asked to do. They may cite different reasons why it is difficult or impossible for the team to do what leaders and coaches are asking. They reiterate that they do not feel the changes are necessary.

Possible reasons a team might end up in this quadrant:

A team that is resisting the why, what, and how while expressing confidence in their ability might be a truly successful team (there are clear data that show that they are consistently producing student learning) that believes they have a legitimate reason to resist the why, what, and how (lack of clarity, lack of resources, overwhelm, etc.). In these cases, the leader needs to meet with the team, hear their questions, and work to help them see the importance of the school initiatives. It is also possible that a team in this quadrant may have grown complacent about their student data. If the evidence shows that their students are not making adequate progress, leaders and coaches should review the data with them and help them to see the urgency in the data. Skilled efficacy builders will help a team in the "confident resisters" quadrant to get excited about what they can accomplish as a team and provide the supports they need to be truly successful.

What teams in this quadrant need from their leader or coach:

A team in this quadrant needs skilled coaching to help them build on the positive perception that they have of themselves and use that to benefit students and their learning. If the coach is working with a successful team (there evidence of student learning) and they are resisting the why, what, and how because they have concerns about lack of clarity, lack of resources, too many initiatives, etc., coaches should meet with the teams to hear their input. Coaches can remind these teams of how they have been successful previously and encourage them to continue to do high-level work that benefits them as a team and their students as learners. Sometimes, members of this team just want leadership to listen to their concerns and empathize with the load they are carrying. Coaches should check in with these teams frequently to check how things are going and offer support. If the confident resisters team has not demonstrated success in student learning, coaches may need to skillfully address their complacency and misguided sense of confidence. This involves exploring the evidence of student learning and, sometimes, confronting the brutal facts about how students are achieving. Coaches should lead teams to discover that learning results must improve, while simultaneously expressing confidence in the team and the value of the school's why, what, and how. The goal is to move this team from "confident resistance" to "confident embrace of the why, what, and how" that benefits both the team and their students.

Figure 4.10: COACH'S SUMMARY—TEAMS IN THE CONFIDENT RESISTERS QUADRANT.

Confident resisters can be a challenge for leaders and coaches who are working to build the collective efficacy of their teacher teams. With the right coaching and guidance, these teams can embrace the research-based why, what, and how and develop true collective efficacy that is based on increases in student learning.

In figure 4.11, we examine teams we might call *confident embracers*—teacher teams that profess a high level of confidence in their ability to implement change, and who embrace the why, what, and how that have been established at their school. While it is the goal of leaders and coaches to have all teams thrive in the confident embracers quadrant, this does not mean that teams do not still need coaching and support once they arrive in that quadrant.

	Confident Embracers
High embrace of the why, what, how Low confidence in the team	High embrace of the why, what, how High confidence in the team
Low embrace of the why, what, how Low confidence in the team	Low embrace of the why, what, how High confidence in the team

Confident Embracers: High Embrace of the Why, What, and How; High Confidence in Team

Teams in this quadrant are embracing why they need to change, what they are expected to do, and how it is being measured.

Teams in this quadrant have a high level of confidence in their team's ability to meet the challenges presented by the compelling student data (the why), research-based strategies (the what), and shared goals (the how).

Possible indicators that a team is in this quadrant:

The team expresses enthusiasm and a high level of interest in the why (they see the urgency in the student data), the what (they are open to new strategies or initiatives), and the how (they are enthusiastic about the school or team goals).

The team is eager to complete tasks related to the why, what, or how. They complete tasks on time and may even go above and beyond expectations in the work they do.

Members of the team or the team of the team as a whole express confidence that they will be able to complete what they are being asked to do. They take the new tasks on as a challenge and jump in to see what they must do and how they can do it well.

Possible reasons a team might end up in this quadrant:

A team that is confident and embracing the why, what, and how has probably had numerous experiences where their collaborative work as a team has been successful. They have also probably had success implementing new strategies or pursuing new goals. They draw on these experiences as they face new challenges.

Teams in this quadrant often include teachers with significant experience and repeated success in their teaching role.

What teams in this quadrant need from their leader or coach:

A team in this quadrant is performing at a high level, but leaders and coaches should still be diligent in providing guidance and support. Leaders should not make the mistake of thinking that this team does not need any attention. A team in the confident embracers quadrant will still need encouragement and coaching. Coaches and leaders should make sure to provide teams in this quadrant with specific feedback to help them recognize their growth and mastery experiences. Coaches and leaders should help teams in this quadrant to carefully monitor their data and engage in deep reflection when their efforts positively influence student learning.

Figure 4.11: COACH'S SUMMARY—TEAMS IN THE CONFIDENT EMBRACERS QUADRANT.

Leaders and coaches who are working diligently to build the collective efficacy of their teacher teams must be sensitive to how different teams might react to the school's why, what, and how. Skilled efficacy builders will be aware of affective states and how they might influence a team's embrace of the school efforts and the confidence they have in their ability to get the work done. The matrix tools above are designed to provide some insight into what teams might be thinking and feeling and provide some guidance on how leaders and coaches can respond and effectively implement step 2 of the CLEAR process.

Team Update

It is the last collaborative team meeting before winter break, and the science department at Shelley Middle School is feeling empowered. They have just finished sharing their students' results on the latest common summative assessment—a unit test on energy and matter. The results are excellent! The students did really well on a pretty demanding unit test, and they demonstrated a grasp of concepts across the board. These results were far better than the scores on the CFAs that the team administered at the beginning and midpoints of the unit. On those assessments, some students did well, but a lot of them missed the boat and did not demonstrate proficiency. But when the teachers met as a team, they all noticed that one member of the team had student results that were far better than the rest of the team. Rather than feeling threatened, the teammates asked questions and tried to identify the instructional strategies that were working in their colleagues' classes. She shared ideas about how she helped students to remember content and a system she had put in place to have students give each other feedback as they worked on writing assignments in her class. She explained her strategies and offered to share her materials. Her teammates then took what they had learned and applied it in their classrooms. The results were very encouraging on the next CFA, and now the unit test showed even greater growth. The team had used CFA data to learn from each other so that, in turn, their students could learn at high levels. This might not have ever happened if they hadn't had a candid conversation with principal Poe back in September. When the principal first shared the expectation about reviewing CFA data together, some members of the team were anxious. They worried about what would happen if their students did not do well. They were scared that they would be embarrassed in front of colleagues or that the principal would use the results to "write them up." No one seemed to care that they were really stressed about this! Principal Poe, for her part, was hearing that teacher teams were feeling stressed. As she met with teams, she noticed an underlying anxiety whenever the subject of common assessment came up. She decided to address the stress levels openly with the whole staff and developed a plan for gathering candid input. Principal Poe devoted part of a staff meeting to gathering input from all teams about the new CFA initiative. Teams were invited to share their hopes, their fears, and their questions. By the end of the activity, everyone had a better picture of what was causing anxiety. Principal Poe addressed the stressors and calmed some fears. For example, she publicly stated that formative assessments were for supporting learning and that teachers would not be penalized for their CFA results. The only negative consequence would be for refusing to participate in the CFA process with one's team. Principal Poe also sent out a follow-up survey that teachers could fill out anonymously, shared those results, and explained how she would respond. As a result, the science team felt more comfortable trying the full CFA process, including sharing results with each other. When they shared the first results, the student scores were not great, but everyone had room for improvement. And as they looked at the errors that students made, they started to talk about different ways to present content and review key concepts. They actually picked up useful teaching ideas from each other by talking about student work! Over time, they became even more comfortable and looked forward to meeting and learning from each other. Being allowed to share their fears in a safe place helped them to open up to a powerful collaborative team experience.

CLEAR Thoughts and Next Steps

Leaders and coaches who are trying to harness the power of collective teacher efficacy in their schools or districts must pay attention to affective states and the impact they can have on efficacy beliefs. Skilled efficacy builders will devote time and energy to step 2 of the CLEAR process and listen to teachers' fears, anxieties, questions, and concerns. By doing so, they work to create a culture of psychological safety, which has been shown to improve workplace climate and productivity. As we conclude our look at step 2, let's review some critical takeaways, reflect on the implications for our work, and plan a next step.

Let's review critical takeaways.

- Affective states or emotional or physiological arousal can have a major impact on individual self-efficacy beliefs and the collective efficacy of a group or team.

- The introduction of a new task will cause a physiological reaction. If a person has a low sense of self-efficacy for a task because of past experiences, the person will interpret the arousal in negative terms—stress, worry, anxiety. This is also true of groups. If, however, the person has a higher level of self-efficacy for the task, the person is more likely to interpret the arousal as excitement or enthusiasm for the task. This is also true of teams.

- Leaders who create spaces for teachers to share their fears, anxieties, questions, and concerns help to build a climate of psychological safety in their schools. Creating and sustaining a culture of psychological safety will reduce the impact of the "knowing-doing gap" and help to build a trusting environment that is an ideal for supporting collective teacher efficacy.

- Leaders listen to teachers by strategically creating spaces for teachers to safely share their concerns and offering multiple methods for teachers to share their thoughts and ask questions. Effective leaders address teacher concerns in settings with the whole staff, particular teams, and individual teachers, as appropriate.

- Leaders can gather meaningful staff input through face-to-face meetings in different settings (whole staff, team meetings, individual conferences) and remote/anonymous methods (electronic surveys, suggestion boxes, comment walls).

- It is critical for leaders to follow through after they have gathered staff input. This will help to build trust. Failure to follow through and communicate can cause more damage than not collecting input in the first place.

- Leaders who skip step 2 of the CLEAR process or do not give it the attention it needs run the risk of undermining their own work to build collective efficacy.

Let's reflect on the content from this chapter.

1. In your professional or personal life, do you have tasks that instantly create anxiety, dread, or resistance? Are there tasks, that when they are presented to you, create a sensation in the pit of your stomach, causing you to avoid the ask, if possible? Why do you think you feel that way? What is behind the stress that you feel? Was there a past failure or embarrassment? What is the baggage you are carrying?

2. In your leading and coaching, have you ever encountered a teacher or team that simply won't follow through on what they have been asked to do? Have you been frustrated by teachers or teams who do not complete the required tasks even though they have received frequent reminders and the support they need to do the work? What have you attributed this to?

3. Now that you have reviewed the research about self-efficacy, collective efficacy, affective states, stress, and psychological safety, will you view resistant or insecure teachers and teams differently? How will you change your approach?

4. As a coach, are you worried about the idea of deliberately inviting teacher teams to identify and name their stressors, fears, and anxieties? What are you worried could happen? How can you plan to invite staff to share their concerns, while maintaining the commitment to your school's why, what, and how?

Let's plan an action step.

The next time you work with a team, pay extra attention to how they react to the introduction of a task or the mention of work to be done. Do you sense some anxiety or stress? Point out that it is normal to feel stress when you are doing new things. Invite the team to share by using the four-square activity (figure 4.2, page 100). Notice how the team responds to this invitation and then notice how you react to their sharing.

_____

_____

_____

_____

_____

_____

_____

_____

_____

_____

CHAPTER FIVE

Step 3 of the CLEAR Process:

Explore Examples, Models, Best Practices, and Proven Processes

FOR LEADERS AND coaches working to build the collective teacher efficacy of collaborative teams, the third step is to lead teams to explore examples, models, best practices, and proven processes. At this point in the CLEAR process, leaders and coaches have done a thorough job of clarifying why there needs to be a change, what the change involves, and how the change will be measured (step 1), and also listened to teachers' fears, anxieties, questions, and concerns (step 2). Now teacher teams are ready to get down to the hands-on work of implementing new strategies and processes.

It is critical for leaders and coaches to provide their teams with vicarious experiences—powerful models and examples of how successful teams have accomplished this work. Studying successful teams and their practices can be a powerful boost to the collective efficacy of a teacher team. That's why step 3 of the CLEAR process is to *explore examples, models, best practices, and proven processes*.

In this chapter, I explain the research concerning how vicarious experiences can have a positive effect on individual and collective efficacy beliefs. Next, I outline three different methods for providing collaborative teacher teams with vicarious experiences to boost their collective confidence to complete critical tasks. Finally, I provide tools, strategies, and sources that assist leaders and coaches with providing high-quality examples and models to their teams as well as a real-world-inspired scenario to help readers see examples of a leader and team doing this work. At the end of the chapter, we will review key points, reflect, and plan action steps in the CLEAR Thoughts and Next Steps section.

Now, let's imagine a scenario where a fourth-grade team of teachers is challenged by a new initiative.

Meet the Team

It is the second collaborative team meeting of the school year, and the fourth-grade team at Frank Lloyd Wright Elementary School is confused. Their school has embraced a new practice of establishing essential standards. This process involves having teams review district and state curriculum objectives and then use criteria to identify the most critical standards for students to learn in each grade level and for each subject. The team understands why they are being asked to do this. In fact, they embrace the idea because they have struggled for years to teach all the standards. Most years they don't get to some of them, and some years they race to finish all of them, but they've never felt that they are taking the time to make sure their students have a deep understanding, so the thought of working to identify the critical learning in each grade makes sense. They also understand what is expected. Teams are provided with tools for examining curriculum standards and determining which are essential for the students in their grade level. All teams are expected to turn in their draft list of essential standards for reading by the end of the month. By teaching the essential standards at a deeper level, the staff hope this higher level of learning will be reflected in student performance on school-based assessments and the state test in the spring. The grade 4 team has a clear understanding of the why, the what, and the how.

In addition to being guided in developing a clear understanding of the reasons for the change in their practice, the fourth-grade team has also been given an opportunity to share their fears, anxieties, questions, and concerns—their principal and the school's instructional coach led a session to address teachers' questions during preservice week, and the team members took an anonymous survey, which provided an additional opportunity to share their worries about the new practice privately.

So, the fourth-grade team approaches the new task with clarity and a sense that they are and will be listened to. Still, they are a little confused as they sit to do the work together. They have never done work like this before, and though there have been some professional development sessions during preservice, they are having a hard time getting started. It seems like a big task, and they can't even imagine what a completed list of essential standards would look like, let alone unpacking and breaking them down into learning targets and progressions. They wish they could see some examples of how this has been done or talk to other teachers who have already faced this challenge. Just then, the instructional coach joins their meeting and says, "I have some resources and examples that I think will help you with this work on your essential standards."

The fourth-grade team at FLW Elementary is facing a common challenge connected to implementing new strategies or practices. They understand why there needs to be a change, what the change will entail, and how the change will be measured, and they have had an opportunity to share their questions and concerns, but they are getting stuck as they start to take the steps to implement the new practice. The new task still seems a bit overwhelming and confusing. This is where the research on self-efficacy and collective efficacy beliefs points out the need for *vicarious experiences* or powerful models and examples (Anderson, Summers, Kopatich, & Dwyer, 2023; Bandura, 1997; Li, Jia, Cai, Kwan, & You, 2020; Wilde & Hsu, 2019; Zhu, Law, Sun, & Yang, 2019).

Let's take a further look at what the research says about vicarious experiences and efficacy beliefs.

What the Research Says

The research base for step 3 of the CLEAR process is found in the studies conducted by Bandura and others that show that people can increase their levels of self-efficacy and collective efficacy through vicarious experiences. (Bandura, 1997; de Carvalho, Durksen, & Beswick, 2023; Li et al., 2020; Mather & Visone, 2024). The word *vicarious* comes from a Latin term for *substitute*. Merriam-Webster defines "vicarious" as "experienced or realized through imaginative or sympathetic participation in the experience of another" (Merriam-Webster, n.d.). As we discovered in chapter 1, the most powerful influence on self-efficacy is mastery experiences (Bandura, 1997). In other words, when someone successfully completes a task, that experience is likely to increase their self-efficacy beliefs for that task in the future. Bandura also found, however, that a person can experience an increase in self-efficacy simply by observing another person complete the task. In fact, he argues that these vicarious experiences are second only to personal mastery experiences in their influence on self-efficacy beliefs (Bandura, 1997). When we see someone comparable to ourselves performing a task successfully, it increases our belief that we can also be successful. In other words, "If they can do it, we can do it!"—like when a child sees his siblings riding bikes without training wheels, and it strengthens his belief that he can do that too.

The power of vicarious experiences extends across many fields. Researchers find that vicarious experiences like observing others have a positive effect in athletics, creative arts, and business, for example (Bruton, Mellalieu, & Shearer, 2016; Dampérat, Jeannot, Jongmans, & Jolibert, 2016; Fransen et al., 2012; Li et al., 2020; Wilde & Hsu, 2019). Studies in sports physiology find that athletes who observe teammates performing tasks increase their collective efficacy (Bruton et al., 2016); There is also a clear neurological aspect to this finding—when we observe others' actions and emotions, our brain activates as though we were experiencing those actions and emotions ourselves (Gatti, Tettamanti, Gough, Riboldi, Marinoni, & Buccino, 2013).

In educational settings, studies have found that vicarious experiences can increase teacher self-efficacy and performance. This is particularly true when the vicarious experience is observation of another teacher (Pearson, 2016). For example, researchers determined that providing primary teachers in Australia with vicarious experiences (modeling) in literacy and mathematics increased the learning teacher's implementation of targeted instructional strategies (Ryan & Hendry, 2023; de Carvalho et al., 2023). Mather and Visone (2024) conclude that collegial visits (observations of peers in practice) fostered higher levels of teacher self-efficacy. Numerous studies find that vicarious experiences are valuable for novice and preservice teachers (Atasoy & Çakıroğlu, 2020; Clark & Newberry, 2019; Nikoçeviq-Kurti, 2021; Pfitzner-Eden, 2016). Nikoçeviq-Kurti finds that "mentor teachers can contribute to the development of student teachers' self-efficacy in teaching through modeling student engagement activities, behavior modification techniques, and teacher qualities" (Nikoçeviq-Kurti, 2021, p. 146). Because novice teachers have relatively few mastery experiences due to lack of experience in teaching, vicarious experiences of observing other teachers demonstrating mastery with challenging teaching tasks can be particularly powerful (Clark & Newberry, 2019).

Vicarious experiences can play a critical role in building the collective efficacy of teacher teams. While the research into how vicarious experiences directly impact collective teacher efficacy is limited, studies find that when groups of teachers have shared learning experiences, collective efficacy is enhanced. Loughland and Nguyen (2020) find that teachers and teams had increases in their sense of collective teacher efficacy when they had an opportunity to observe each other teaching. They also explain how teachers and teams could have valuable vicarious experiences through collaborative planning, job-embedded mentoring, and reflective discussions (Loughland & Nguyen, 2020).

Leaders and coaches working to build the collective efficacy of their teacher teams will get better results if they harness the power of vicarious experiences. In the next section, let's examine practical strategies for getting this done.

Making It CLEAR

Vicarious experiences are a powerful tool for building the collective efficacy of teacher teams. Skilled efficacy builders will provide their teams with a variety of vicarious experiences that will help them to gain confidence with the specific tasks they are working on. This is accomplished through leading teachers and teams through exploring examples, models, best practices, and proven processes. As we have seen in previous steps of the CLEAR process, this work requires coaches and leaders to be deliberate in their preparation, engagement with staff, and follow-through.

- **Preparation:** To effectively implement step 3, coaches and leaders must complete detailed work in advance. To maximize the power of vicarious experiences, coaches must identify the needs of the team, find appropriate models to address the team's needs, and make a plan for how to share those models with their teams.

- **Engagement:** Carrying out step 3 involves engaging teacher teams in exploring models, best practices, and proven processes. Effective coaches will plan this engagement so that teams get the most benefit through reviewing examples and proven practice. As we will see in the next section of this chapter, vicarious experiences can take place on several levels, from reviewing the work products of effective teams, to consulting with experts, to actually observing efficacious teams as they perform specific tasks.

- **Follow-through:** When implementing step 3 of the process, effective follow-through involves guiding teams to reflect on the models and examples they have observed or reviewed. The goal is to help teams get the greatest amount of benefit from the vicarious experiences they are having.

Before going into the details of preparation, engagement, and follow-through for step 3, let's take a closer look at the different levels of vicarious experience.

For leaders working with teachers, vicarious experiences generally fall into three levels of intensity.

1. Reviewing other educators' work products

2. Consulting about the work with others who have been successful

3. Observing other educators completing the task

Each succeeding level offers a greater level of benefit to a team, but also requires a higher degree of preparation and implementation by leaders and coaches.

The most powerful vicarious experience—which has the greatest impact on the collective efficacy of a team—is *observing* a comparable team execute the actions that are necessary to complete the task. Direct observation of a similar team successfully carrying out challenging team tasks delivers the message, "This is a doable task. We can do this!" For example, if a high school mathematics department is having difficulty unpacking essential standards and planning effective units, being able to observe another secondary mathematics team work through the unpacking and planning process is extremely helpful. Direct observation takes away the mystery of how to complete the task and helps the observing team to believe they can do it. However, an in-person observation can be difficult to arrange, especially if the team to be observed is located in another district or even another state. In such cases, reviewing a videotape of the team doing similar work successfully can be extremely informative as well—the team's collective efficacy is still boosted by this more remote vicarious experience.

Another option for boosting the team's collective efficacy for a task is offering them an opportunity to *consult* with others who have successfully done the work. Having the chance to talk with another team and ask questions about how they approach the work is very helpful. Although this is not a direct observation of the team completing a task, there are still vicarious benefits. Speaking to another team about the task to be completed helps the learning team feel more confident about their chances of success. If a team of middle school mathematics teachers is having difficulty developing CFAs, it is beneficial to be able to talk with another similar team that is further along in this work.

Lastly, a teacher team can get a boost in their collective efficacy for a task simply by *reviewing* work products from a successful team. When it is not possible or feasible to observe another team, either in person or through video, or to consult with them directly, reviewing their high-quality work products can still increase a team's collective efficacy through a vicarious experience of the successful team's efforts. Reviewing a similar team's unit plans, assessments, intervention plans, meeting agendas, and so on, helps the learning team to gain confidence that they could produce similar work. A second-grade team that is developing a learning progression for the first time might feel overwhelmed by the task, but if they have a chance to review learning progressions that have been developed by other successful second-grade teams, it usually reduces their anxiety and increases their collective belief that they can complete the task.

While the direct observation of another team completing a task is the most powerful of the three types of vicarious experiences, followed by consultation, and then review of work products, all three levels can be valuable, and each experience has the potential to significantly increase the collective efficacy of teacher teams.

Figure 5.1 captures the alignment of the coach's tasks in step 3 of the CLEAR process through the preparation, engagement, and follow-through phases. In the sections that follow, we take a deep look at the work involved in step 3 of the CLEAR process and explore several tools that will help leaders and coaches as they work to build collective efficacy through providing vicarious experiences.

	Coach's Task	Reviewing the Work of a Model Team	Consulting With a Model Team	Observing a Model Team
Preparation	The coach helps the learning team to identify their area of need or interest.	Through discussion and coaching with the learning team, the coach helps the team to identify areas or tasks where they would like to improve their practice.		
	The coach identifies examples, models, best practices to share with the learning team.	The coach searches for team products and examples that fit with the team's needs.	The coach researches and reaches out to identify possible model teams for consultation or observation.	
	The coach gathers examples and contacts the model teams.	The coach collects appropriate work products from available sources.	The coach contacts the model team or teams through appropriate channels to inquire about consulting or observing.	
	The coach plans logistics and processes for the learning team to interact with the models or examples.	The coach develops a training plan for having the learning team review the examples and models.	The coach coordinates the logistics for the consultation session with the model team.	The coach coordinates the logistics for the observation session with the model team.
Engagement	The coach facilitates the interaction between the learning team and the model team.	The coach works directly with the learning team, guiding exploration of the model work products.	The coach facilitates the consultation session.	The coach facilitates the observation session.
Follow-Through	The coach debriefs with the learning team to make sure they get the full benefit of the vicarious experience.	The coach helps teams to decide how they will use the information from the work products they have reviewed.	The coach leads the learning team in reflection on the consultation and establishes next steps.	The coach leads the learning team in reflection on the observation and establishes next steps.
	The coach follows up to support implementation of the learned strategies.		The coach sends thank you and acknowledgment messages to the model team.	

Figure 5.1: OVERVIEW OF PREPARATION, ENGAGEMENT, AND FOLLOW-THROUGH FOR STEP 3.

In the reproducible "Coach's Planner for Step 3 of the CLEAR Process: Explore Examples, Models, Best Practices, and Proven Processes" in the appendix (page 224), I provide a detailed planner for leaders and coaches to use in implementing this part of the CLEAR process.

Preparation for Exploring Examples, Models, Best Practices, and Proven Processes

To implement step 3 of the CLEAR process, coaches must invest time in effective preparation. In the preparation phase of step 3, it is critical for leaders and coaches to do the following.

- Help the team to identify their areas of need and interest—this helps to clarify which examples and models would be most valuable for the team.

- Search for and find models and examples that meet the needs of the team. For reviewing work and products, this involves collecting examples to share with the learning team. For consultations and observations, the coach needs to identify model teams.

- Gather and organize the identified models for the team. For reviewing work, the coach organizes the examples so that they will be clear and accessible to the team they are coaching. For consultations and observations, this is where the coach actually makes contact with model teams to arrange for the consultation or observation.

- Plan for engagement, including logistics. Here the coach plans for how she will present the work of model teams to her learning teams. She thinks through the best processes and protocols to use to engage her teams. For consultations and observations, this involves working with the consulting or model team to plan for an effective session and to work out all logistics in advance.

Successful completion of this preparation work sets the table for effective engagement with teams.

Let's take a deeper look at the preparation work that coaches must do for step 3 in the three focus areas of vicarious experiences.

Reviewing Examples and Models of Successful Teams

The preparation work for reviewing models and examples involves identifying a focus area, collecting models from various sources, organizing the artifacts so that they can be used effectively with the teams, and creating a plan for sharing.

Identifying a Focus

Coaches who want to build the collective efficacy of their teacher teams through sharing examples of work done by successful teams begin by helping their teams to identify their area of need. This will help to focus the work and aid in identifying models. A team may have lots of questions and needs, but if a coach buries the team in dozens of examples representing many different aspects of collaborative teamwork, it can be overwhelming and frustrating. Teams will get the most benefit if their review of models is focused on one or two areas.

Coaches can use the Top Ten Tasks of Teams in a PLC Reflection Tool in figure 5.2 to help teams identify their greatest need. This will help narrow the search for effective examples and models. In the sample reflection in figure 5.2, the team identifies determining proficiency standards as an area of need. Thus, their coach would be able to focus their review of model items on proficiency scales completes by successful teams.

Task	Current Practice and Questions
1. Establishing and using team norms	We have established norms, and we refer to them regularly.
2. Establishing and using clear team SMART goals	We established SMART goals at the beginning of the year, and we have been monitoring progress.
3. Identifying and focusing on a limited number of essential standards—guaranteed and viable curriculum	This is an area of strength for us. We have gotten really good at clarifying what is essential for students to learn.
4. Determining proficiency expectations for students on essential standards	This is an area of need for us. While we are clear on our essentials, we haven't really gotten to the point where we have exactly the same expectations for student work.
5. Planning units of instruction to ensure learning of essential standards	We are doing well with our unit plans. We work collaboratively to plan the learning targets, the pacing, the materials, and the timing of assessments.
6. Developing common assessments (both formative and summative)	We are getting better at developing assessments together. We are still working on being clear about what we expect all students to be able to do on the assessment.
7. Reviewing common assessments to inform instruction and teaching practice	We have gotten better at sharing instructional ideas as we review assessment data and look for strategies that are working.
8. Reviewing common assessments to identify students for support and extensions	Because we are not completely clear on our expectations for proficiency, we run into problems when we score our CFAs together.
9. Planning and delivering interventions and extensions	Our schoolwide system of interventions is working well and moving student data.
10. Measuring, evaluating, modifying interventions and extensions	We are still working on refining our processes for evaluating our interventions and extensions.

Summary: It would be very helpful if we could learn more about how effective teams decide together on proficiency standards and then incorporate that into their assessments. It would be helpful to see the work products of an effective team (proficiency scales, common assessments). It would be even more helpful to consult with a successful team to ask them questions about these tasks. It would be especially helpful if we could observe a successful team discussing proficiency and creating proficiency scales or watching a model teams review CFA data.

Figure 5.2: THE TOP TEN TASKS OF TEAMS IN A PLC—TEAM REFLECTION TOOL.

Visit **go.SolutionTree.com/PLCbooks** *for a free reproducible version of this figure.*

An important caveat: The vicarious experience of reviewing expert work completed by successful teams can boost the collective efficacy of teams at all levels, but coaches must have a clear understanding of their teams and where they are functioning as they plan for work product review. Research has shown that vicarious experiences are most powerful for teams and individuals who already have some self-efficacy for the task (Wilde & Hsu, 2019). In other words, teams with some experience and success with the task are best positioned to take new ideas and apply them to their own work. You might hear responses such as, "That's a cool way of doing that! Let's figure out how to integrate that into what we do!" The danger with beginning teams, or teams with low collective efficacy, is that they may see the work of expert teams as beyond their ability. If a team with no experience developing unit plans is presented with the meticulously detailed unit plans of an expert team, they might feel overwhelmed and incapable of producing such work (Wilde & Hsu, 2019). Coaches must choose examples carefully and plan for incremental growth so that teams can gradually build collective efficacy as they complete steps in the process.

Identifying Models

All coaches and leaders who are committed to building the collective efficacy of their teacher teams will need to collect and organize a variety of examples and models for their teacher teams because these items will be critical in providing a base level of vicarious experience for their teams. Where can leaders and coaches find examples and models to share with their teams? The following list offers some sources for examples of high-quality collaborative team-work products.

- **AllThingsPLC.info:** This website features the stories of schools throughout the United States that have implemented effective practices and increased student achievement consistently. Many of the schools share their work products. Leaders and coaches can search for examples of work products and then share them with their teams.

- *The Big Book of Tools for Collaborative Teams in a PLC at Work* (Ferriter, 2020): This book contains dozens of helpful tools for collaborative teamwork and is a user-friendly collection of examples and models. There are also many samples of completed tools, including sample SMART goal worksheets.

- **Online resources:** There are numerous websites that are affiliated with educational journals, educational foundations, and educational organizations that can be searched for examples of high-quality work completed by teacher teams, including the following.

  ▸ www.edutopia.org

  ▸ learningforward.org

  ▸ www.edweek.org/teaching-learning

  ▸ www.educationworld.com

As we have seen, many print and online resources can provide coaches with the examples and models they need to build collective efficacy through the vicarious experience of reviewing the work of successful teams. In addition, as coaches are providing these experiences, the teams they are working with will grow in skill and eventually produce examples that can then be used in inspiring and informing other teams. Effective efficacy builders make a habit of collecting artifacts and tools from their teams and organizing these artifacts so that they can be accessed when working with new clients. Coaches can organize Google folders where they keep photos and PDFs of model tools organized by task (norms, essential standards, rubrics, etc.). I have found that teams are very open to trying a new tool if the coach can say, "Here is an example of how a team I worked with last year approached this task."

Having a robust library of model tools, processes, and products helps coaches to be prepared to build the collective efficacy of teams through reviewing models and examples.

Planning for Engagement

Once leaders and coaches have gathered the appropriate models and examples for their teams to review, they should develop a plan for engaging their teams in purposeful examination of the products. The goal of these sessions is to give teams the opportunity to review a high-level work product, examine it closely enough to understand why it is a high-quality product, and then establish next steps to use the example of this work to enhance and improve their own work. The guiding questions for this preparation are:

1. What have we identified as the focus area for the team?

2. What examples and models have I identified and collected?

3. When do I have an opportunity to share the models with the team?

4. How will I help the team to get the most out of examining these examples?

5. How do I make sure not to overwhelm the team with too many models or work that is way beyond their capacity right now?

Later in this chapter, we will look at specific protocols and tools in the engagement section for reviewing model team products.

Let's look at the preparation work for arranging a consultation or observation.

Consulting and Observing Model Teams

While reviewing the products of successful teams is a powerful efficacy-building experience, it can be even more impactful to consult with a model team (ask questions and seek advice) or conduct an observation (see the team demonstrating mastery of a critical task). In this section, we will examine the preparation work that is necessary for facilitating a consultation or observation. We will look at these two options together since there is a lot of overlap between the two. For example, whether a coach is preparing a consultation or observation for his team, he will need to identify a model team and organize the logistics for the session. There are some differences in setting up a consultation or observation, and I will point them out in this section.

The key preparation work when coaches are arranging a consultation or observation are similar to the steps we saw in the section on reviewing team products. Coaches must help teams identify their areas of need and focus and the appropriate model (the team to consult or observe), they must organize the models and prepare them for sharing with their team (make contact and start to plan logistics with the model teams), and they must plan how to engage with the models (develop an agenda and training plan for the consultation or observation). Let's look closer at each of these steps and some tools that can help coaches to do the work.

Identifying a Focus

Coaches will help their teams to identify areas of need using the same tools described earlier. Teams can complete the Top Ten Tasks of Teams in a PLC Reflection Tool (figure 5.2, page 124) to focus on the area of their consultation and observation. Coaches must be open to the team's reflections while also guiding them to the experience that fits best with their current level of work and need.

Identifying a clear focus area is especially important when arranging a consultation or observation with another team. When consulting with or observing a model team, the time available will likely be limited. Teachers everywhere are very busy. Even the most generous model teams will have limited time to connect with the learning team that is seeking their support. We do not want the "ask" of the model team to be "Please tell us about how you function as a collaborative team and complete all of the required tasks." This would be overwhelming for the model team, and covering such a broad question would likely take more time than is available. Instead, the learning team should conduct the self-assessment outlined above and make a more targeted request. Consider these examples.

- We are working on how to use our collaborative team time more effectively. Can you teach us or model for us how you plan and implement your collaborative team meetings so that they are focused on student learning and productive for your team?

- We are just learning how to develop CFAs. Could you walk us through (or demonstrate) the process you use to develop an efficient, high-quality, rigorous assessment?

- We are working to build our skills in analyzing data. Could you tell us about (or demonstrate) your processes for gathering student learning data, analyzing the information, and using it to inform instruction and identify students for intervention and extension?

A more focused request of the model team is more likely to produce usable information that the learning team can apply.

Identifying the Model Team

Once the team's area of interest or need has been established, the leader or coach must help the team identify a successful team to contact. The process of identifying a model team for consulting or observation should start at the closest proximity and then branch out. In other words, is there another team in the same school that is having some success with a particular task? It is not unusual for different teams in the same school to progress at different rates when it comes to implementing the critical tasks of collaborative teams. If a team in the same school is having some success, the leader or coach should try to take advantage of this and facilitate an opportunity for teams to learn from each other. As the saying goes in educational settings: sometimes the best professional development is the teacher (or team) down the hall.

In this situation, it is important for the leader or coach to frame the consultation or observation so that it is not perceived as "good team, bad team." The coach should reiterate that, in a PLC, we all learn from one another. Just as we expect teachers within a collaborative team to be open to learning from each other, we should expect teams to be willing to learn from each other. A skilled coach will manage this opportunity so that there are no hurt feelings, bruised egos, or feelings of inadequacy. One way to do this is to be diligent and strategic in finding opportunities to have all teams serve as consultants to others.

If there is no team within the school that could serve as effective consultants or models for the particular tasks the learning team is working on, find out if there is such a team within the district. Perhaps a third-grade team or a high school science department at another district school is having some success with their collaborative work. This brings up a new challenge—how will principals and coaches become aware of teams in other schools that are having success?

This is where implementing PLCs at a district level can pay such dividends. Imagine that the leaders of a school district publicly commit to the PLC process and work to build knowledge and support implementation. One aspect of this work would be to recognize and celebrate teams and schools that are demonstrating deep collaborative practice and increased student learning. In such an environment, principals and coaches would have regular professional meetings and conversations, so they would know about teams at other schools that are thriving. They would also know who to contact to ask for consultation and advice. This is the ideal scenario for identifying model teams within a school district.

If PLC implementation is not supported throughout the district, principals and coaches can identify possible model teams by reaching out to other principals and coaches to ask about teams that are demonstrating success. Leaders and coaches should ask some pertinent questions to ensure that a potential consulting team is a match for the learning team's needs.

Note that while most principals and coaches will be happy to spotlight their effective teams, they will also be protective of their time. Wise leaders and coaches want their teams to share, but they do not want to overwork them in the process. This is another reason why defining focus areas, as we discussed earlier, is a critical step in asking for guidance and advice.

If neither the school nor the district has an appropriate team to consult or observe, leaders and coaches can expand the search to include the state or province or neighboring geographic areas. If the principal or coach looking for a model team does not have any contacts beyond their district, they could reach out to district-level staff, who might have colleagues in other districts or at the state level. Leaders and coaches can also take advantage of opportunities to attend state, regional, and national education conferences. These conferences often feature schools and teams that are implementing excellent practices and achieving impressive student learning results. The goal in all these searches is to identify a high-performing team that could serve as an effective model for the learning team.

For schools on the PLC journey, there is a specific online resource that can be helpful when searching for a model school, team, or department. Leaders and coaches can visit allthingsplc.info and use the "PLC Locator" tool to identify similar schools in other states that have achieved National Model PLC status. Leaders and coaches can do an initial search, identify possible matches, and then reach out via phone or email.

In summary, leaders and coaches who are working to build the collective efficacy of their teacher teams through providing the vicarious experience of consulting with or observing successful teams should start locally and then expand their search to the national level, using all available contacts, venues, and tools to identify possible consulting teams.

Contacting the Model Team for Support

Once a potential model team has been identified, the appropriate coach or school administrator reaches out via email to make an inquiry and to provide some details about what the learning team is hoping to gain. If the host school or team is open to the possibility, coaches can then set up a phone conversation or virtual session to discuss more details.

Leaders and coaches can use the Planning Call with a Model Team, School, or District Tool (figure 5.3) to organize their thoughts for the call and to take notes about the plans.

Greeting

State the purpose of the call:

I have heard wonderful things about the work that is happening at your school and that you have several collaborative teams that are working at a high level.

My collaborative teams are working hard to implement best practices, but most of them are very new to these tasks.

I am contacting you because I would love to explore the possibility of having some of my teams learn from your teams.

Ideally, this could involve giving my teams an opportunity to actually see your teams in action. I know my teams would learn a lot by observing your teams at work.

If that is not manageable at this time, I would love to arrange a video conference so that my team could ask your team some questions about how they work at such a high level.

I am particularly thinking about one of my teams that is just learning to _____ (fill in a specific collaborative team task). Do you have any teams that are doing advanced level work in this area? Could we arrange for a visit or video conference?

I will handle all logistics.

Following the observation or consultation, I will write letters of appreciation for all the teachers involved.

Figure 5.3: PLANNING CALL TEMPLATE WITH A MODEL TEAM, SCHOOL, OR DISTRICT.

Planning the Logistics of the Consultation or Observation

For a successful consultation or observation to take place, the necessary logistics must be planned and confirmed in advance. Nothing ruins a potentially powerful learning session faster than a glitchy internet connection, a misunderstanding about who is supposed to participate, or miscommunication about the materials needed for the session. Coaches of the learning team must take the lion's share of responsibility for this, since the consulting team or school is already going out of their way to help. The Coach's Planner for a Consulting or Observation Session (figure 5.4) provides a guide for making sure that the appropriate details have been clarified and confirmed.

Date	
Time	
Location	
Contact Persons	Team 1 (Learning Team)-
	Team 2 (Sharing Team)-
Internet Connection (if meeting virtually)	Zoom link: Microsoft teams link:
Participants and Roles	Team 1 (Learning Team)-
	Team 2 (Sharing Team)-
Outcomes	What are the primary learning outcomes for the learning team?
Agenda	1. Introductions 2. Norms 3. Review of outcomes and agenda 4. Consultation/Observation 5. Questions and Answers 6. Action Steps
Materials Needed	

Figure 5.4: COACH'S PLANNER FOR ORGANIZING A CONSULTING OR OBSERVATION SESSION.

Visit **go.SolutionTree.com/PLCbooks** *for a free reproducible version of this figure.*

Working out the nitty-gritty details can feel tedious sometimes, but attention to these items helps to ensure that the consulting or observation experience will be pleasant for the model team and valuable for the learning team.

Engagement for Exploring Examples, Models, Best Practices, and Proven Processes

Once leaders and coaches have completed the preparation work for step 3 of the CLEAR process, they move on to actually engaging their teams with the models they have identified, whether these are work products of a successful team or opportunities to consult with or observe a model team. Let's look closer at engagement strategies for providing teams with powerful vicarious experiences to build their collective efficacy.

Reviewing Examples and Models of Successful Teams

The goal of engaging teams in reviewing the work products of successful team is threefold: (1) to show the learning team that the task can be completed ("This is doable!"), (2) to build the learning team's understanding of the task and how to complete it, and (3) to jumpstart their efforts to create their own tools and processes. The coach might use a protocol like this.

1. The coach reminds the team of the specific task(s) they have identified as a need or interest.

2. The coach asks the team to brainstorm or review the main questions about implementing this practice.

3. The coach shares one work product example and gives the team a chance to review and ask questions such as these.

   a. What do you notice about this example?

   b. What surprises you?

   c. What questions do you have?

4. The coach leads a collaborative discussion about what the team sees in the example and how they could take what they have learned by reviewing this product and apply it to the work they are doing.

   a. How does this example help you understand how successful teams do this work?

   b. What do you see in this model that could be applied to the work you are doing as a team?

   c. How would you modify this model so it fits better with your team and your circumstances?

5. The coach and team agree on action steps, a timeline for implementation, and a date to review progress.

Effective coaches will use a protocol like the one above or a similar process to engage their teams in a vicarious experience that builds their collective efficacy. Teams come out of a session like this with a clearer understanding of the task, a heightened confidence in their ability to complete the task, and a plan for moving forward.

Later in this chapter, we explore the important follow-through work that coaches must do to make sure that their teams' review of examples results in improved team performance.

Next, we will look at the engagement phase of providing teams with consultation or observation experiences.

Consultations and Observations of Model Teams Within the Same School

As I discussed in the preparation section of this chapter, leaders and coaches should start the search for model teams within their own school. When handled skillfully, peer observations and team observations can be a powerful vicarious experience, and, thus, a boost to collective efficacy. One technique that leaders and coaches can use to help teams learn from each other is the *fishbowl* approach. Using this approach, the leader or coach arranges for a team or teams to demonstrate how they complete a particular task (breaking down a standard, for example), while other teams observe. The leaders can then facilitate a discussion using a simple protocol (see figure 5.5). The protocol clarifies in advance what the observers will be looking for, key aspects of the observed task, and allows for follow-up questions for the demonstrating team.

1. Arrange the training space so that the model team is seated in a circle in the center of the room. The observers are seated around the outside of the model team so that they have a clear view of the team as they are demonstrating their processes.
2. The facilitator explains the purpose of the fishbowl observation, which is to give the observers an opportunity to see how another team carries out a critical team practice.
3. The facilitator explains which practice the team will be demonstrating. The facilitator also explains that the team will be demonstrating and working through the full process without interruption. Observers should take notes and make note of questions that they want to ask at the end of the demonstration time.
4. The model team introduces themselves and explains the collaborative team process that they will be demonstrating.
5. The model team demonstrates the practice, working just as they would if they were not being observed. Observers take notes and write down questions.
6. When the model team is done with their demonstration, they announce that this concludes the demonstration.
7. The facilitator gives observers a few minutes to review their notes and organize their questions.
8. The facilitator invites observers to ask their questions and invites members of the model team to respond to questions. The facilitator encourages everyone to maximize the efficient use of time by listening to other's questions so that questions are not repeated.
9. The observers ask questions, and the model team members respond. The facilitator may write key topics on a chart that all can see as the discussion continues.
10. When the time for questions and answers is done, the facilitator leads a discussion to identify key learnings and helps observing teams to begin planning their action steps.
11. The facilitator thanks the model team and the observing teams and adjourns the session.

Figure 5.5: PROTOCOL FOR FISHBOWL OBSERVATION.

A less-threatening version of the fishbowl approach is to devote a staff meeting to all teams sharing a strategy, tool, or process that is helping them to do the work. Leaders and coaches can "prime the pump" for this type of sharing by pointing out when a team is implementing an effective practice and saying, "That's a great strategy!" "You should share that at the next team sharing time."

I have seen these types of sharing meetings dozens of times in all kinds of schools and districts, and I always come away with the same conclusion: teachers love learning from each other, and they are eager to pick up proven tools, strategies, and ideas from their colleagues if they are given the opportunity in the right environment.

The emphasis in either of these school-based approaches is to maximize professional learning. The same is true when engaging teacher teams in consulting with or observing teams from another school or district.

Consultations With Model Teams

After leaders and coaches have completed the necessary preparation work to set up a consultation with a model team, the next step is effective engagement to produce professional learning. When it is time to hold the call or Zoom session for a virtual consultation, coaches should plan to kick off the meeting by establishing norms, clarifying outcomes, and reviewing the agenda. Coaches can use the Sample Consulting Agenda (figure 5.6) to focus the meeting. Sample norms for virtual coaching sessions can be found in figure 5.7 (page 134).

Outcomes: By the end of the consulting session between the mathematics department at Washington High School and the mathematics department at Jefferson High School on October 4, 2024, we will have:

Reviewed norms for our meeting

Identified selected best practices of collaborative teacher teams

Shared opening questions about the selected best practice

Heard expert advice from teaching team

Reviewed sample materials and processes provided by teaching team

Reviewed key points and action steps

Time (minutes)	Content	Lead
5	Welcome, introductions, review norms, review outcomes	Two School Leads
5	Identify the selected best practices for the consultation Discuss key aspects of the best practice	Two School Leads
15	Consulting team presentation and comments about the selected best practice	Teaching Team
20	Questions from learning team and responses from consulting team	Learning Team Teaching Team
10	Review of key learning and discussion of action steps	School Leads/Teams
5	Thank yous, recognition, adjournment	Two School Leads

Figure 5.6: COMPLETED SAMPLE CONSULTING AGENDA.

Our Norms: During our virtual coaching sessions, we will:
Stay focused on learning
Honor the questions, insights, and statements of others
Minimize sidebar conversations
Take risks and ask questions when something is not clear
Demonstrate professional courtesy and respect
Honor time limits that have been established

Figure 5.7: SAMPLE TEAM NORMS FOR COACHING SESSIONS.

Coaches should serve as the facilitators of the consulting session, keeping the focus on the identified areas, asking questions to get discussions going, posing follow-up questions to gain clarity, and checking with the learning team to make sure they are getting the information they need. If there is a lull in the conversation, coaches should be prepared to ask pertinent questions to get the discussion back on track. Coaches also serve as the timekeeper and ensure that the session does not last beyond the time that was agreed to. Coaches should signal the end of the session is approaching and wrap up the meeting by reviewing actions steps and thanking the consulting team for their time and help.

Observations of Model Teams

When coaches have arranged for an observation of another team, they should plan to kick off the session by establishing some norms, clarifying outcomes, and reviewing the agenda. Coaches can use the sample observation agenda (figure 5.8) to focus the meeting. Sample norms for observation sessions can be found in figure 5.9.

As we saw in consultation experiences, coaches, in conjunction with the lead for the model school, should serve as the facilitators of the session. In an observation setting, it is especially important for the facilitator to establish the norms and ground rules. For example, in most cases, it is best to hold questions until after the modeling team has completed their task, rather than interrupting the flow with questions. Coaches and leaders also want to maximize

Outcomes: By the end of the observation session between the sixth-grade team at Madison Middle School and the sixth-grade team at Monroe Middle School on October 10, 2024, we will have:

Reviewed norms for our meeting

Identified selected best practices of collaborative teacher teams

Shared opening questions about the selected best practice

Observed the teaching team completing the task

Engaged in questions and answers regarding the model team's actions

Reviewed key points and action steps

Time (minutes)	Content	Lead
5	Welcome, introductions, review norms, review outcomes	Two School Leads
5	Identify the selected best practices for the observation Discuss key aspects of the best practice	Two School Leads
5	Teaching team's introductory comments regarding the selected best practices to be modeled	Teaching Team
25	Teaching team demonstrates the identified practice Learning team observes and takes notes	Learning Team Teaching Team
15	Teaching team answers questions from learning team	Learning Team Teaching Team
5	Review of key learning and discussion of action steps	School Leads/Teams
5	Thank yous, recognition, adjournment	Two School Leads

Figure 5.8: COMPLETED SAMPLE OBSERVATION AGENDA.

Our Norms: During our observation sessions, we will:
Stay focused on learning
Honor the team process being modeled—wait until after the observation to ask questions
Minimize sidebar conversations
Take risks and ask questions when something is not clear
Demonstrate professional courtesy and respect
Honor time limits that have been established

Figure 5.9: SAMPLE TEAM NORMS FOR OBSERVATION SESSIONS.

the impact of the question and answer (Q&A) period following the observation. One way to do this is to ask the observing teachers to write their comments and questions on Post-it notes during the observation. These are then collected and quickly sorted by the coach. The coach then can start the Q&A by saying, "There are several notes and questions about how you (the model team) decided on the proficiency criteria for the rubric you were developing. Can you walk us through the steps you use?" This helps all questions to be addressed in the limited time available. Through effective facilitation, leaders and coaches help their teams to be engaged and benefit from the observation.

In implementing step 3 of the CLEAR process, skilled efficacy builders engage their teams in learning through reviewing exemplary products, consulting with successful teams, and observing model processes. The coaches work, however, does not end with engagement. For teams to have the most valuable vicarious experiences, coaches and leaders must be strategic and consistent in their follow-through. Let's examine the critical follow-through strategies for coaches who are working to build the collective efficacy of their teacher teams.

Follow-Through for Exploring Examples, Models, Best Practices, and Proven Processes

After engaging their teams in vicarious experiences, coaches and leaders must follow through to deepen and sustain the learning that takes place. Let's look at some key strategies.

Reviewing Examples and Models of Successful Teams

After reviewing the work products of successful teams, the learning team, led by their coach, will identify specific tools or processes that they will work on. Coaches should follow up by communicating with the team. Coaches should remind the team of the strategy or process that was selected, review guidance for implementing the strategy, and offer to answer any questions the team might have. After the team has had time to implement the tool or process, coaches should follow up to ask how implementation is going and offer assistance. In the ongoing work with the team, the coach should help teams to analyze their work, identify successes and areas for growth, and help the team to modify the tools and strategies to fit their own work and situation.

Consulting and Observing Model Teams

After a consultation/observation is completed, coaches have the responsibility of making sure that their teams absorb and retain as much useful information as possible. It is very helpful to schedule time for the team to have at least a short reflection and debriefing time immediately after the consultation or observation ends. This helps teams to digest key learning and clarify next steps while the information is still fresh in their minds. Coaches can use a reflection form or activity like the one in figure 5.10.

Sample Debrief and Action Planning Protocol
Coach begins the debrief by asking team members to do some quiet individual reflection: 1. What did you learn today as a result of this experience?   2. What was the most compelling aspect of our learning today?   3. What surprised you most?   4. What questions do you still have?
Coach invites team members to share and write comments on a chart.
Coach invites team members to review the charted comments and look for patterns.
Coach asks team, "Based on your comments, what is one action that you could take, as a team, in the next two weeks, that would support your growth as a team and your students' learning?   Coach asks team, "Based on your comments, what is one action that you could take long-term to support your growth as a team and your students' learning?"

Figure 5.10: SAMPLE DEBRIEF AND ACTION PLANNING PROTOCOL.

This will help learning team members to identify the key pieces they learned and compare notes with each other about how to move forward. If the team is not given guided time to reflect, each member may walk away with different perceptions about what they heard and how to follow up. Effective coaches can help to ensure that all the effort that went into setting up the consultation or observation experiences pays off in terms of high levels of professional learning and team practice.

Leaders and coaches who are working to build the collective efficacy of their teacher teams are wise to harness the power of vicarious experiences. These powerful experiences, whether it is reviewing high-quality work, consulting with an expert team, or seeing a model team in action, provides a substantial boost to a team's collective belief in themselves.

Team Update

At the fifth collaborative team meeting of the school year, the fourth-grade team at Wright Elementary School is feeling accomplished. Two weeks ago, they were feeling stuck because they were overwhelmed by the task of identifying essential standards in reading for their fourth-grade students. They understand the why, what, and how, and they had been given the opportunity to share their questions and concerns, but they were still having trouble getting their minds around the task at hand. Then, Ms. Hadid, the literacy coach, visited their team meeting with some examples of essential standards lists that had been completed by another school in the district. Ms. Hadid explained that, in her role as an instructional coach, she also supports the fourth-grade team across town at Pei Elementary. The team at Pei started the work of identifying essential standards the previous school year. Ms. Hadid asks the Pei team if she could share their work with the team at Wright, and they agree. Ms. Hadid shows the Wright team some of the documents and plans the other team created, including a shared Google Drive where they keep their essential standard information and tools for easy retrieval. It is so helpful to see quality work completed by another fourth-grade team working on the same task. Reviewing this work makes it much easier for the Wright team to visualize how to do the work and to be successful with the task. Their confidence grows even more when Ms. Hadid organizes for the Wright team to have a Zoom session with the team at Pei. During the Zoom, they ask questions about how the team does the work. After the Zoom session, Ms. Hadid helps the Wright team debrief what they learned, and they immediately apply it to working on their essential standards. As they start their fifth meeting of the year, they have a clear listing of essential standards and a clear understanding of how they will use this document to guide their planning, inform their instruction, and ensure that all students at Wright learn the essential skills for fourth-grade students in reading.

CLEAR Thoughts and Next Steps

The different types of vicarious experiences are powerful tools in the toolbox of effective coaches and leaders. Skilled efficacy builders use step 3 of the CLEAR process to build the collective efficacy of their teacher teams through guided review of examples, consultation with experienced teams, and observations of highly successful peers. As we conclude our look at step 3, let's review some critical takeaways, reflect on the implications for our work, and plan a next step.

Let's review critical takeaways.

- Providing teams with examples of others' success with critical team tasks helps to build collective teacher efficacy through "vicarious experiences," which Bandura identified as the second-most-powerful source of efficacy beliefs.

- Providing vicarious experiences in working with teacher teams can happen at three levels.

  a. sharing team products and examples of their work

  b. communicating directly with successful teams about their work

  c. observing successful teams as they conduct their processes

- Vicarious experiences are most powerful when the team being observed or studied is perceived as similar to the observing team

- There are many excellent resources for finding and reviewing model team products and teacher processes, including Solution Tree resources such as AllThingsPLC.info, Global PD Teams, and Avanti.

- For teams to get the most out of observing another team, consulting with colleagues, or reviewing the work of peers, coaches and leaders must plan and lead effective debriefing sessions that lead to clear action planning.

Let's reflect on the content from this chapter.

1. Vicarious experiences can be a powerful source of self-efficacy and collective efficacy. Can you think of a time in your work as a teacher or leader that having a vicarious experience—the opportunity to observe someone completing a task—helped to build your own self-efficacy? What was the situation? How did the vicarious experience affect your self-efficacy?

2. In your coaching and leadership, have you been able to provide vicarious experiences to your teachers and teams? What were the circumstances? What worked? What didn't work? What did teams learn? What could you have done differently?

3. As you think about your next steps for implementing the CLEAR process and working to build the collective efficacy of your teacher teams through providing vicarious experiences, what do you see as the most critical actions to take? What can you do in the next week, month, or year to build the collective efficacy of your teacher teams through vicarious experiences?

4. When you think about your actions steps for providing your teams with vicarious experiences, what do you see as the most complex, demanding, or difficult steps? How will you approach these challenges and overcome them?

Let's plan an action step.

The next time you work with a team, have them think about a time that they learned to do something by watching someone else do it. Have them share those experiences. Then, ask them what they would like to learn to do as a team. Confirm their answers and commit to bringing them a wonderful work sample or a video of a team doing that work for your next session with the team.

_____

_____

_____

_____

_____

_____

_____

_____

_____

_____

CHAPTER SIX

Step 4 of the CLEAR Process:

Activate New Learning Through Coaching,
Practice, and Implementation

FOR LEADERS AND coaches working to build the collective efficacy of their teacher teams, the next step in the CLEAR process is to activate new learning through coaching, practice, and implementation. After coaches have clarified the why, what, and how, listened to teacher's fears and anxieties, and explored models and best practices, teams will need high-quality coaching to apply what they have learned to their own practice. Coaches who provide this differentiated, ongoing support, which the efficacy research refers to as *social persuasion*, give a powerful boost to the collective efficacy of the team. That's why step 4 of the CLEAR process is to *activate new learning through coaching, practice, and implementation*.

In this chapter, we explore the research behind social persuasion and its impact on collective efficacy. We also examine the wealth of research concerning effective professional development, characteristics of excellent coaches, and aspects of high-quality coaching. I provide practical advice on how to build the collective efficacy of teams through effective social persuasion. I also share tools and resources to help coaches and leaders do this work and a real-world inspired scenario of a leader and team doing this work. At the end of the chapter, we review key points, reflect, and plan action steps in the CLEAR Thoughts and Next Steps section.

Now, let's visit a middle school mathematics team as they struggle to implement new practices.

Meet the Team

It is the Wednesday before winter break, and the sixth-grade mathematics team at John Wooden Middle School is stumped. In their weekly collaborative team meeting, they are trying to figure out how to plan and implement effective Tier 2 interventions for their students. Tier 2 has been an emphasis at John Wooden since preservice. Principal Lombardi and some teacher leaders, including the school's interventionist, Ms. Summit, led training sessions on effective intervention strategies and how to implement them. The team understands the why—effective interventions that are targeted and timely are one of the most powerful influences on student learning. It was definitely worth investing time and effort into how to make their interventions effective. They also understand the what. Principal Lombardi and Ms. Summit provided an overview of the school's systematic approach to interventions for students, including a protected block for Tier 1 instruction, identified times for Tier 2 intervention, and strategies for providing Tier 3 support to students with foundational skill needs. The six-grade mathematics team understands their role and their responsibilities within the overall system at Wooden. They also understand how the work will be evaluated. Principal Lombardi and Ms. Summit explained the system for collecting data and monitoring the progress of individual students. The team has been a little nervous about the progress-monitoring piece, but they feel better after meeting with the interventionist to discuss their questions and concerns. They also appreciated when the interventionist connected them with another middle school mathematics team on the other side of the district that has been implementing effective Tier 2 interventions for several years. In October, they had a Zoom session with the other team. It was so helpful to hear about how they do the work and to ask them questions about nitty-gritty implementation with real sixth-grade students.

The six-grade mathematics team has a good grasp of the why, the what, and the how, their questions and concerns have been addressed, and they were able to consult with a teaching team about this specific work. Still, as they meet to plan their next unit, they are a little stumped about what to do. They have been implementing Tier 2 interventions during the identified WIN (what-I-need) time between third and fourth periods four days per week. They tried to use the most recent student achievement data to identify students who need help and to target intervention plans so that they are as specific as possible. And they used tools provided by the school to monitor student progress as they provided interventions. But they just are not seeing the results they want. Some students are making minor progress, but overall, the results are flat. They are disappointed that all the effort that is going into the WIN block is not producing the student gains they hoped for. They feel like they are doing everything right, but it just isn't working. They are beginning to feel like they are a failure as a team.

The six-grade mathematics team at Wooden has been provided with a lot of information, guidance, and support as they work to ensure high levels of learning for all their students. Their principal and teacher leaders have explained the why, the what, and the how of providing high-quality interventions to students (step 1 of the CLEAR process). They have had the chance to discuss their fears, anxieties, questions, and concerns (step 2), and they even got to consult with a more experienced team about their successful strategies (step 3). Still, they have hit a rough spot where they are not sure what to do, and they are beginning to question their collective efficacy.

Concerns about time, frustration with imperfect implementation, and impatience for results can all have a negative effect on the collective efficacy of a teacher team. Without the right support, even a strong team can progress well through steps 1–3 of the CLEAR process and then hit a bump in the road. Sometimes, those bumps are challenging enough to completely derail a team's belief in itself and subsequently stop their collective growth.

Coaches and leaders who want to build the collective efficacy of their teacher teams must help teams activate and apply what they have learned through expert coaching. A critical element of this coaching is "social persuasion," which Bandura (1997) identifies as one of the primary sources of individual and collective efficacy beliefs. After step 3 of the CLEAR process, coaches and leaders must support the team's growth by activating new learning through coaching, practice, and implementation (step 4)—that is, through social persuasion. Let's take a closer look at the research.

What the Research Says

Step 4 of the CLEAR process is based on the research about social persuasion (Bandura, 1997) and its influence on self-efficacy and collective efficacy. After mastery experiences and vicarious experiences, social persuasion is the next-most-powerful influence on efficacy beliefs. Social persuasion is encouragement, coaching, and support from a trusted colleague or mentor that helps to boost efficacy beliefs. The research shows that the self-efficacy of a person or the collective efficacy of a group can be positively influenced by the encouragement and support of a trusted mentor or coach (Chin et al., 2021; Dortch, 2016; Lazarides & Warner, 2020; Loo & Choy, 2013). While this source of efficacy is not as impactful as mastery experiences and vicarious experiences, it still can enhance the collective efficacy of a person or group. Especially in a school setting, social persuasion provided by a trusted coach or leader can be an important support to collaborative teams that are trying to do the right work for students. This is particularly true of novice teachers or teachers being asked to implement new content or different strategies. Olli-Pekka Malinen and colleagues (2013) found that social persuasion experiences were more powerful for novice teachers implementing inclusive practices because they did not have years of mastery experiences to draw upon. Leaders and coaches who are working to build the collective efficacy of their teacher teams can capitalize on this research through carrying out step 4 of the CLEAR process.

Teams that have had powerful vicarious experiences through observing effective teams, consulting with fellow educators, and reviewing high-quality products will be ready to implement the practices themselves. Implementation will involve digesting all the models they have seen and the practices they have observed and determining how to apply what they have learned in their own practice, in their own school, with their own students. This is a complicated process that can overwhelm some teams. In addition, this is work that takes time. Results will not come overnight. And, as previously mentioned, it will be imperfect, even messy, in the beginning. For teams to build their collective efficacy during this part of the work, it is critical to provide them with coaching that is supportive, skilled, and ongoing. This kind of coaching includes social persuasion, characterized by high levels of expertise, productive relationships, differentiated support, and meaningful feedback.

Social persuasion, or input from others that informs our efficacy beliefs, "serves as a further means of strengthening people's beliefs that they possess the capabilities to achieve what they seek" (Bandura, 1997, p. 101). In other words, when we approach a task, if there is another person who tells us that they believe we are capable of performing the task, it just might help us to feel more confident. Think of the parent teaching their child to ride a bike awkwardly running next to their child who is trying to balance—"You can do this! You got this!" Hearing another person express faith in your capabilities can increase your self-efficacy.

One of the most consequential aspects of social persuasion is how it affects our willingness to persevere with a challenging task. Bandura (1997) explains, "People who are persuaded verbally that they possess the capabilities to master given tasks are likely to mobilize greater effort and sustain it than if they harbor self-doubts and dwell on personal deficiencies when difficulties arise" (p. 101). If you are the child learning to ride a bike or the team learning to collaborate on assessments, having a person you trust tell you that you can do it helps you to keep trying, increasing your chances of success. Social persuasion is not as powerful as mastery experiences or vicarious experiences, but it can have a positive effect on efficacy, especially if the person providing the encouragement is viewed as trustworthy, capable, and knowledgeable. In addition, the coaching itself needs to be supportive, differentiated, and based on best practice.

Bandura's (1997) explanation of how social persuasion works makes it clear that there are two critical elements: (1) the characteristics of the coach, and (2) the dynamics of the coaching process itself. Let's examine the research about the characteristics of an effective coach.

In the 2000s, coaching has been hailed and used as a strategy to help individuals and teams improve their performance across many disciplines. The desire for effective business coaching has given rise to a multibillion-dollar industry that employs tens of thousands of individuals (Blackman, Moscardo, & Gray, 2016). Significant resources have been allocated to increase team performance and results in many fields. Numerous researchers have conducted studies to try to define the characteristics of an effective coach. Many of these studies show that effective coaches demonstrate integrity by proving they are trustworthy, by maintaining confidentiality, being honest, following through on their commitments, and providing long-term support of their coaches (Blackman et al., 2016; Darling-Hammond, Hyler, & Gardner, 2017; Frazier, 2020; Killion, Bryan, & Clifton, 2020; MacCrindle & Duginske, 2018; National Center for Systemic Improvement [NCSI], 2015). Coaches who demonstrate a high level of integrity are better able to use social persuasion to build collective efficacy because their teams have a high level of confidence in what their coach says and does.

Effective coaches have a high level of expertise. They share their knowledge, are current on best practices, provide accurate feedback, provide expert support, and have earned the respect of their colleagues (Frazier, 2020; Killion et al., 2020; NCSI, 2015). As a result of their expertise, effective coaches have a high level of credibility with their clients (Blackman et al., 2016, Darling-Hammond et al., 2017; NCSI, 2015). Coaches with a high level of expertise inspire confidence and trust in their teams; therefore, they are able to provide social persuasion that helps teams to grow.

Effective coaches demonstrate excellent interpersonal skills. They communicate clearly, are good listeners, help clients to recognize their strengths and needs, provide meaningful feedback, and build trust with clients (Darling-Hammond et al., 2017; Killion et al., 2020; Martens & Vealey, 2024. In addition, effective coaches demonstrate empathy, warmth, patience, and high levels of collaboration (Blackman et al., 2016; Darling-Hammond et al., 2017; Hall & Simeral, 2008). Coaches with a high level of people skills build a strong bond with their teams. As a result, they are powerful providers of social persuasion—coaching and encouragement—as they work to build the collective efficacy of their teams.

A common link across different studies shows that there are important themes and characteristics of effective coaches that are consistent in the literature. Effective coaches for teachers and teacher teams must be experts in the field, who can build trust and credibility with their clients through demonstrating their expertise. Furthermore, effective teacher coaches use effective communication and coaching strategies and follow through on what they promise. They build relationships with teams so that they are positioned to provide guidance and feedback that teams will accept and act on.

The themes in this research align with Bandura's findings about the role of social persuasion in building the efficacy beliefs of individuals and teams. Bandura (1997) was the first to explain that the impact of social persuasion, or input from another person, would always be influenced by perceptions about who was providing the feedback: "Persuasory efficacy appraisals have to be weighted in terms of who the persuaders are, their credibility, and how knowledgeable they are about the nature of the activities" (p. 106). For encouragement to provide a real boost to our self or collective efficacy, we have to believe that the person providing the encouragement is someone we can trust and someone who knows what they are talking about. Credibility and relationships are key to effective coaching.

This is particularly true when coaches are working to build the collective efficacy of collaborative teams in a PLC. Leaders and coaches who are working to build the collective efficacy of the collaborative teams in their PLCs must be experts in the PLC process and the critical tasks of teams. They must have a deep understanding of foundational concepts like what a PLC is and is not, the three big ideas that drive a PLC, and the four critical questions that propel the work of teams. For coaches to have credibility, they must be able to respond to teams' questions about their critical work, from establishing team norms to identifying essential standards, to using CFA, to providing targeted interventions for students. Coaches who build the collective efficacy of teams in a PLC are recognized experts in the top ten tasks of teams in a PLC, as outlined in chapter 2 (page 33). Teams must have confidence that their coach understands the key work of teams and can accurately assess where teams are and how to help them. As Bandura (1997) explains, "Self-appraisals are partly based on the opinions of others who presumably possess diagnostic competence gained through years of experience" (p. 104). Effective coaches are presumed to be skilled diagnosticians and trainers who can help move teams forward. Coaches must continuously build their own knowledge so that they are up to date on the most recent research and best practice. If a coach promotes a message or strategy that then is found to be out of alignment with current research, it can undermine the team's confidence in their coaching. (This is not to say that a coach will always have the perfect answer off the top of their head.) Effective coaches can also model the professional learning process by capturing the question and demonstrating how to research and find answers.

In addition to having and demonstrating expertise, effective coaches must have the communication and relationship skills that will allow them to connect with a team and help them grow. Bandura (1997) points out how this is especially important when providing feedback to teachers and teams:

> It is more difficult to instill enduringly high beliefs of personal efficacy by persuasory means alone than it is to undermine such beliefs. . . . People who have been persuaded that they lack capabilities tend to avoid challenging activities that cultivate competencies and give up quickly in the face of difficulties. (p. 104)

In other words, it is much easier to kill a team's confidence than it is to build it up. When a coach has established that she is an expert in the field and built a level of trust with the team, the team will tend to hang on every word the coach has to say. In this scenario, if the coach unleashes a careless dose of harsh criticism or negative judgment, it can undo a lot of positive work. However, I am not recommending that coaches should provide only "happy talk" about what a team is doing. Effective coaches must provide honest feedback that helps a team to take the next steps toward mastery. "Given the same level of performance, disparaging criticism lowers perceived efficacy and aspirations, whereas constructive criticism sustains aspirations and upholds or even bolsters a sense of personal efficacy" (Bandura, 1997, p. 104). Providing constructive criticism is key. Skilled coaches find the balance between pushing a team to go further while still building their collective belief in themselves. They should aspire to be what Bandura (1997) referred to as "skilled efficacy builders" (p. 106). Skilled efficacy builders personify the expertise and relationship skills that help teams to continuously improve as they work to ensure high levels of learning for all students.

Researchers have identified the personal and professional characteristics of effective coaches—individuals who can use social persuasion to help teachers and teams grow in their practice. Leaders and coaches should consider this research when hiring coaches, when identifying individuals for coaching assignments, when providing professional development experiences to the coaches themselves, and when considering their own leadership and coaching of teams. If leaders are serious about building the collective efficacy of their teams, they will invest time, effort, and resources to providing their teams with coaches of the highest quality. In addition, leaders will want to make sure that their coaches are implementing coaching practices that have been shown to have a positive effect on individuals and teams (Killion, Bryan, & Clifton, 2020; NCSI, 2015).

Now that we have studied the personal characteristics of effective coaches, let's review the current research about the critical elements of effective coaching—what does it look like when a competent coach provides clients with the supports they need to succeed? The research on the specific actions and practices of effective coaches reveals several common themes, including the importance of assessment, goal-setting, feedback, and job-embedded coaching. The most effective coaches help clients to engage in an honest assessment of where they are based on data and evidence. What is our starting point? This question leads to identifying specific strengths and needs (Aguilar, 2016; Blackman et al., 2016; Desimone & Pak, 2017; Knight, 2021; Kraft, Blazar, & Hogan, 2018).

Next, effective coaches help their clients to establish short-term and long-term goals (Blackman et al., 2016; Desimone & Pak, 2017). Coaches who are skilled efficacy builders will inspire teachers and teams to think beyond their current state. What do we want to become? What could we achieve if we work together? What would that look like in terms of short-term goals? What do we think we could accomplish over an extended period? Effective coaches develop clear action plans to help their clients achieve success (Aguilar, 2016; Knight, 2021). When effective coaches work with their clients, they carefully map out a plan of action. There is a rationale to their coaching actions and moves. Everything is designed to help clients grow and move forward.

While implementing their coaching plans, effective coaches provide ongoing communication, modeling, and feedback as they use job-embedded coaching to help clients improve their skills (Aguilar, 2016; Blackman et al., 2016; Darling-Hammond et al., 2017; Knight, 2021; NCSI, 2015). The heart of effective coaching is providing ongoing feedback that is constructive, helpful, based on data, and matched to the client's needs. Effective coaches work shoulder-to-shoulder with their clients and provide the guidance needed to improve practice.

Effective coaches work with their clients for a sustained period and help them to evaluate progress over time (Blackman et al., 2016; Desimone, & Pak, 2017; Darling-Hammond et al., 2017). This iterative, long-term process is effective because it allows opportunities for the coach and the client to evaluate and implement new practices in a considered rather than impulsive way as they move forward. See figure 6.1 for a summary of effective coaching characteristics and actions.

Characteristics of Effective Coaches	Specific Actions of Effective Coaches
Integrity • Trustworthy • Maintains confidentiality • Honest Expertise • Knowledgeable • Up to date on best practices Respected by colleagues High level of credibility Interpersonal skills • Excellent communicator • Active listener • Empathetic • Warm • Skilled at providing feedback	Assessment • Helping clients identify strengths and weaknesses Goal setting • Setting effective short-term and long-term goals Action planning • Customized plan for clients Job-embedded coaching • Modeling • Feedback • Communication • Endurance (Coaching over sustained period) • Evaluation

Source: Adapted from Aguilar, 2016; Blackman et al., 2016; Desimone & Pak, 2017; Knight, 2021; Kraft et al., 2018; NCSI, 2015.

Figure 6.1: SUMMARY OF EFFECTIVE COACHES AND COACHING.

The research discussed in the preceding pages aligns with Bandura's findings about how effective coaches can use social persuasion to build the collective efficacy of their teams. According to Bandura's (1997) research, skilled coaches build the collective efficacy of individuals and teams through careful planning of activities that move them to new learning without overwhelming them. He confirms the importance of planning this way:

> Skilled efficacy builders, therefore, do more than simply convey positive appraisals or inspirational homilies. In addition to cultivating people's beliefs in their capabilities, they structure activities for them in ways that bring success and avoid placing them prematurely in situations where they are likely to experience repeated failure. (Bandura, 1997, p. 106)

To accomplish this, effective coaches must be highly skilled in assessing where a team is in terms of their knowledge and performance. Skilled coaches use their assessment of teams to identify the next step, the next piece of incremental growth that will help teams to achieve their goals. This helps to build collective efficacy and encourage perseverance.

Building team efficacy to persevere and master new knowledge and skills is not a one-time effort. Effective coaching requires an investment of effort over time, ongoing design of team activities, and skillful coaching. As Bandura (1997) explains, "Social persuasion involves more than fleeting pep talks" (p. 106). Finally, effective coaches, through sustained support and guidance, help teams to set and achieve goals for personal and collective growth. The goal is for continuous improvement in process and student learning, not in terms of competition with peers (Bandura, 1997).

To summarize, the research confirms that social persuasion—supportive and effective coaching from trusted and respected mentors—can have a powerful effect on the collective efficacy of groups. This is especially true of teacher teams in a PLC who are working to implement effective practices to ensure high levels of learning for all their students. The coaching priorities that Bandura highlights align exceptionally well with how coaching of collaborative teams works within a vibrant PLC. Collaborative teams that are implementing the top ten tasks of teams in a PLC are dealing with complex content and major changes in their practice. Teachers who have been working in isolation need a lot of support to make the transition to working as a collaborative unit. Teachers who have only used their own assessments and have never compared results with another teacher need guidance and support to become collaborative teachers who use common assessment and enjoy learning from their teammates. Each of the top ten tasks requires learning new things, working through implementation, and bouncing back from mistakes. Without a supportive and skilled coach, it is very difficult for teams to be successful with these tasks. But when teams have a skilled and knowledgeable coach who also understands the value of effective coaching and social persuasion, the team has a much better chance of succeeding with their collaborative tasks and building collective efficacy.

A few important notes about effective coaching and its impact for principals, administrators, superintendents, and board members: As I mentioned at the beginning of this chapter, school and district leaders can serve as the on-the-ground coaches who provide social persuasion to build the collective efficacy of their teacher teams. In addition, educators in these roles have an extra responsibility in terms of system leadership and support of coaching. Studies have found that individuals who have responsibility at the school and district level must prioritize coaching and create the structures and systems to support this work (Blackman et al., 2016; Darling-Hammond et al., 2017; Desimone & Pak, 2017; Knight, 2021; NCSI, 2015). You can have the best coaches on the planet, but if the school or district does not create the conditions for high-quality coaching to occur, the possible benefits for staff and students will never be realized. This view is echoed by other researchers who advocate for schools, districts, and larger entities to devote resources to high-quality coaching for teachers and teacher teams (Blackman et al., 2016; Darling-Hammond et al., 2017; Desimone & Pak, 2017; Knight, 2021).

Social persuasion in the form of skilled coaching for teachers and teams can have a positive effect on the collective efficacy of collaborative teams as they work to implement new learning. In the next section of this chapter, we explore strategies and tools that coaches and leaders can use to build the collective efficacy of their teacher teams by providing social persuasion.

Making It CLEAR

To implement step 4 of the CLEAR process, skilled efficacy builders activate new learning through coaching, practice, and implementation by aligning with the research around effective coaching and social persuasion. As we saw in the What the Research Says section of this chapter (page 173), building collective efficacy through social persuasion involves: (1) paying attention to the qualifications of the coach (how the coach's team views his or her knowledge and skills), (2) the relationship that the coach has with the team (the level of trust the coach has built), and (3) the coach's coaching skills and methods (strategies to bring out the best in teams—time, activities, methods, measurement, and so on). Coaches and leaders who are working to build the collective efficacy of their teacher teams will need to invest time and effort into each of these areas to maximize the impact of their social persuasion coaching.

As we have seen with previous steps of the CLEAR process, effective implementation of step 4 requires preparation, engagement, and follow-through.

- **Preparation:** The preparation work that is required for step 4 of the CLEAR process happens on two levels: (1) personal preparation to develop and maintain overall coaching skills and knowledge, and (2) specific preparation for each coaching assignment and each coaching session. To fully prepare for step 4 of the CLEAR process, coaches must: (1) invest time and effort into their overall coaching knowledge and skills so that they are prepared to carry out the evolving demands of effective coaching, and (2) invest time and care into preparing for each and every coaching interaction with their teams in order to provide them with the support they need and deserve. Both types of preparation are essential in efforts to build the collective efficacy of teacher teams. We will explore both types of preparation in this chapter.

- **Engagement:** Effective engagement with teams is the essence of coaching. Leaders and coaches must see every interaction with teams as a precious opportunity to help the team to grow, learn, and be successful. For leaders and coaches working to build the collective efficacy of their teachers, engagement with teams is where skilled efficacy builders use social persuasion to help teams self-assess, set goals, work on their practice, and monitor growth. The foundation of this work is positive relationships with teacher teams, so we will explore how coaches can enhance their engagement with teams by demonstrating critical skills like active listening, empathy, and clear communication. Finally, efficacy builders skillfully engage with teams to provide expert guidance, constructive feedback, and ongoing encouragement to help their teams grow. In this chapter, we will delve deeply into the research-based coaching practices that help increase collective efficacy.

- **Follow-through:** Effective coaches do an excellent job of follow-through with their teams after coaching sessions. Follow-up notes, recommendations, resources, tools, and guidance help to ensure that the content and skills learned during coaching is reinforced and confirmed. Effective follow-through also plays a key role in building trust and credibility with teams. Coaches working to build the collective efficacy of their teacher teams understand the power of social persuasion and how effective follow-through can help to build a team's collective belief in itself. In addition, effective coaches will complete follow-through on a personal level, reflecting on their coaching and their interaction with their teams. We will examine both aspects of effective follow-through for step 4 of the CLEAR process.

By exercising effective preparation, engagement, and follow-through, coaches can use the power of social persuasion to build the collective efficacy of their teacher teams. This is true of coaches and leaders who fill a variety of roles in schools and school systems. Depending on the situation in the school or district, this social persuasion coaching might be provided by another teacher or by an administrator. Here are a few possible scenarios.

- A principal in a small school is working to build the collective efficacy of the teacher teams in her school. She is trying to create a strong PLC to serve students and staff. She does not have an assistant principal, and there are no teacher coaching positions on her staff. There is a district-level coach, but that person serves many schools, so he is unable to provide long-term intensive coaching for teams. The principal needs to serve as the primary guide, coach, and provider of social persuasion for her teams. Accordingly, she devotes time to preparation, engagement with teams, and effective follow-through to help her teams develop collective efficacy.

- Another school has a principal, assistant principal, and two instructional facilitators (IFs)—one for literacy and one for mathematics—on the staff. The IFs do the lion's share of working with collaborative teams. The principal and the assistant principal attend team meetings when they can, they encourage and support teams, and they work at the administrative level to promote PLC implementation. The two IFs, who are peers and colleagues of the teachers they support, are nonevaluative. Their role is to support teams and promote effective practices. They are the primary providers of social persuasion for the teams in their school. They work together to plan and prepare for work with teams, they engage with their teachers on a regular basis, and they follow through with teams to build their collective efficacy.

- In another school, the PLC journey hasn't really started, but there is a department chair who is committed to her students and her team, and she is looking for ways to guide her team to high levels of performance. She can be a powerful source of social persuasion for her teammates. She may be limited in terms of the scope of her influence, since the work is not happening across the school, but she can make a difference for her team and for her students. She can help build the collective efficacy of her department through providing social persuasion. The department chair also invests time in preparing for work with her department, uses engagement with her teammates to build collective efficacy, and follows through consistently to help her team grow.

Educators with different titles and positions can serve as providers of social persuasion for the teacher teams in their schools or districts. And though their positions may have different levels of power, the work of using social persuasion to build the collective efficacy of teams boils down to effective coaching.

Effective coaching for step 4 of the CLEAR process involves elements of preparation (building knowledge and credibility), engagement (building positive relationships and providing expert coaching characterized by guidance, feedback, and encouragement) and effective follow-through (ongoing support of teams and their growth, as well as personal reflection). Figure 6.2 provides an overview of this work. Let's take a closer look at each of these components.

	Overall Personal Work to Be an Effective Coach	**Specific Work With Teams in Coaching Sessions**
Preparation	Build personal knowledge and expertise on an ongoing basis through review of research, professional development, and reflection.	Develop a detailed preparation for every session and a personalized plan for teams. Provide clear advance communication before each session.
Engagement	Monitor interactions with clients to assure positive relationship skills like active listening, empathy, and clear communication. Monitor interactions with clients to ensure provision of expert guidance, constructive feedback, and ongoing encouragement.	Build positive relationships and strategies that increase trust. Provide teams with expert guidance, constructive feedback, and ongoing encouragement.
Follow-Through	Conduct frequent reflection and self-assessment to refine skills.	Provide follow-up communication (prompt, positive, personalized). Provide ongoing, sustained support.

Figure 6.2: OVERVIEW OF PREPARATION, ENGAGEMENT, AND FOLLOW-THROUGH FOR STEP 4.

In the reproducible "Coach's Planner for Step 4 of the CLEAR Process: Activate New Learning Through Coaching, Practice, and Implementation" in the appendix (page 226), I provide a detailed planner for leaders and coaches to use in implementing this part of the CLEAR process.

Preparation for Activating New Learning Through Coaching, Practice, and Implementation

To implement step 4 of the CLEAR process, coaches must deliver effective coaching and the type of social persuasion that helps teams to build their collective efficacy. Effective efficacy-building coaches prepare to deliver this type of coaching on two levels. First, they work on a personal level to develop their knowledge and expertise as a coach, continually looking for ways to upgrade their skills. Second, coaches must prepare for each coaching assignment and each specific session with their teams, doing the detailed work that is necessary to meet the needs of their clients.

Building Knowledge, Expertise, and Credibility

Skilled coaches who are working to build the collective efficacy of teams must be knowledgeable and credible. The social persuasion that they provide to teams is much more powerful if the teams regard the coach as an expert who knows what she is talking about. Therefore, the most effective coaches build their credibility by staying informed, providing teams with accurate information, and building on prior successes.

Effective coaches are well-versed in the latest research in their area of coaching (Blackman et al., 2016; Darling-Hammond et al., 2017; Killion et al., 2020; NCSI, 2015). In a coaching relationship, the coach helps those being coached to grow through sharing their knowledge and skills. Coaches must be constant consumers of educational research. They read professional journals, review online research, attend professional conferences, and read professional books to make sure that they are staying up to date and providing their teams with the latest research. Many effective coaches have a weekly routine of reviewing the latest educational research and journal articles. Leaders can subscribe to journals that provide a weekly summary of research via email, such as ASCD K–12 Leadership SmartBrief. Then, as effective coaches work with teams, they look for opportunities to share these recent studies and findings with their teams, thereby making sure that their clients are benefiting from the latest thinking in the profession.

In the context of a PLC, coaches also must be expert in all things related to PLCs and their implementation, including recent research. While the foundational concepts of PLCs have not changed in thirty years, practitioners are continually conducting action research and finding new ways to focus on learning, working collaboratively, and achieving results for students. Excellent studies, books, and articles are generated every year, providing today's practitioners with updated research on how to implement the PLC process in today's schools. Individuals who aspire to serve as effective coaches and builders of collective efficacy in schools must be diligent in staying up to date with the latest research and practice through professional reading, collaboration with peers, attending professional development sessions, and seeking feedback from colleagues. Coaches who remain current with best practice will be able to demonstrate the expertise that inspires trust and confidence in the teams they coach.

Coaches build their credibility by providing teams with accurate information and effective processes. Equipped with the knowledge they have gained through participation in regular study and professional development of their own skills, effective coaches supply their teams with current, relevant information about how to do the work and with proven processes for working as a team. When coaches provide their teams with solid content and process, they help establish their value as a coach.

Coaches can increase credibility with a team by sharing how they have done this work with previous teams and how those teams were able to achieve significant results. If a team hears and sees clear evidence that their coach has helped other teams to grow and reach their goals, especially in terms of increasing student achievement, the team may feel a greater sense of confidence in the coach's expertise. But there is a caveat with this aspect of building credibility. When I have worked as a consultant with teams around the nation, part of my story is how my teams at Viers Mill helped the school go from nearly being taken over by the state (due to low performance) to being a National Blue Ribbon School in five years. When new teams see what we were able to accomplish at Viers Mill and the student achievement that resulted from our teams' hard work, it gives me some credibility—maybe I know what I am talking about. But here's the caveat: Credibility based on past successes can be helpful in the beginning, but it has a short shelf life. Coaches who do not back up their past successes with demonstrated expertise in the current situation will lose the confidence of their teams rapidly. Teams can also tire quickly about hearing about school successes from years ago. Coaches can use examples from previous successes in the beginning stages of the coaching relationship, but they must shift quickly to proving expertise for their current team and their circumstances.

As we see in the preceding paragraphs, effective coaches can prepare for activating knowledge with their teams before ever actually sitting down with their clients. While this work to continually expand their expertise and stay current on the latest research is important, the detailed preparation for each session with a team is even more consequential.

Preparing for Coaching Sessions

A key aspect of demonstrating knowledge and expertise involves how the leader or coach prepares for each session with a team. Effective coaches must do their homework and prepare the necessary strategies and materials for working with each individual team. There are few things that ruin a coach's credibility with a team faster than showing up unprepared for a session. Coaches must remember that teacher time is precious, and every coaching session is an opportunity to build the collective efficacy of each team. Coaches should communicate with their teams in advance to clarify the focus of the upcoming coaching session. This can involve asking for updates and samples from the team to check on their progress and to identify any questions or current obstacles. Then, the coach should carefully prepare materials and strategies in advance to address the team's needs. When a team sees evidence that the coach has heard their questions and has prepared resources and materials to address their needs, it builds the team's confidence in the coach.

Critical questions for an efficacy-building coach when preparing to meet with a team include the following.

- What are this team's goals?
  - What are their student achievement goals?
  - What are their team process goals?
- What is the evidence we have regarding the team's progress on their goals?
- What is the highest priority coaching that this team needs to have now to help them achieve their goals?
- Does this team have a clear understanding of the why, what, and how?
- How can I help this team overcome any stress and anxiety they are feeling?
- Are there effective models or examples that I can share with them?
- What kinds of guidance, feedback, and encouragement does this team need to reach their goals?
- What happened in my last session with this team? Are there any important follow-up tasks or work we need to continue? Do I need to do anything differently than I did in our last session?
- What do I need to prepare in advance of the next session with this team?
- What do I need to communicate to this team in advance of our next session?
- What are my goals for this team in their next session?
- What is my plan for helping this team to reach their goals through the interaction and engagement we have in our next session?

An effective coach will also have the expertise to respond when a team brings up a question or issue that the coach had not anticipated. Skillful coaches draw on their expertise to respond to the team's questions in the midst of coaching sessions. This is a skill that grows through repetition and experience. Coaches who have had the opportunity to work with many teams in varied situations strengthen their expertise and ability to respond in the moment, especially if they regularly reflect on those sessions and think about what they could have done differently. In addition, coaches who have invested time in staying current on research and practice, as we discussed in the earlier part of this chapter, are better equipped to respond to questions on the fly. When an informed coach responds expertly to an unanticipated question from a team, this is a great opportunity to build credibility.

Of course, even the most knowledgeable coaches cannot anticipate every issue or question a team will raise. In these cases, it is critical for the coach to listen to the team's question, ensure that they have clarity about the question, and then promise to research and get back to the team. Effective coaches then follow up quickly with the information and guidance they were able to find. This becomes a great opportunity for coaches to demonstrate their reliability and trustworthiness—they promised the team that they would research and find an answer to their question, and they have followed through in a timely fashion so that the team can continue moving forward. Getting back to the team with research and guidance also gives the coach an opportunity to model an important practice for teams—how to respond when we encounter a question or area of confusion: we research, we learn, and we work together to figure it out.

Once coaches and leaders have completed their preparation work, both in terms of their personal skills and their planning for specific coaching session, they are ready to engage with their teams and apply all their expertise and credibility. Let's look at the critical engagement work for step 4 of the CLEAR process.

Engagement for Activating New Learning Through Coaching, Practice, and Implementation

To implement step 4 of the CLEAR process, coaches must engage effectively with their teams. Indeed, effective engagement is the heart of coaching. Skilled coaches who are working to build the collective efficacy of their teams will provide high-quality social persuasion that helps teams to make progress.

In the engagement phase of step 4, skilled efficacy builders do the following.

- Draw on the credibility they have established with their teams (through building their own knowledge and skills).

- Establish positive relationships with teachers and teams that make it possible to deliver effective social persuasion.

- Implement research-driven coaching strategies and practices that help teams to make progress and develop collective efficacy.

Let's look at each of these components and how they play out in the engagement phase of step 4.

Credibility

When coaches are working to build the collective efficacy of their teacher teams, it is critical that they have credibility with their clients because this validates their social persuasion. In the engagement phase of step 4, coaches demonstrate their knowledge, skills, and credibility, and this helps to build the collective efficacy of their teams.

Figure 6.3 (page 156) captures what it looks like, sounds like, and feels like when effective coaches demonstrate knowledge and credibility.

Looks Like	Sounds Like	Feels Like
The coach comes to the session prepared with knowledge, resources, and tools that are aligned with the team's need.	I know you all are working hard on how to unpack state standards in a way that makes sense for you and your students. I brought a few examples to share.	Our coach knows what she is talking about.
The coach demonstrates strategies for teams and explains the rationale behind the tools she provides.	I know this work can be confusing at the start. It just takes some practice working through these steps…	I think we can trust what our coach says and follow her advice.
Using her background knowledge and familiarity with resources, the coach is able to respond to questions from the team.	That's a really interesting question. It shows how deeply you are digging into this work. Here's what the research says, and here's how I have seen other teams respond to this issue.	All the information we have been getting is finally making sense. I really appreciate her expertise and her ability to explain things so I understand them.

Figure 6.3: USING SOCIAL PERSUASION TO BUILD COLLECTIVE EFFICACY—KNOWLEDGE AND CREDIBILITY.

As we can see, establishing credibility is an important component for effective engagement to build collective efficacy with teams. But it is important to remember that even coaches with a tremendous amount of knowledge who have kept up to date on the latest research will have limited impact on the teams if they do not develop positive relationships with those they are coaching. Effective coaches build trusting relationships with their teams through demonstrating skills and characteristics like active listening, empathy, reliability, honesty, and effective communication. These skills and characteristics also help put coaches in the position where they can use social persuasion to build the collective efficacy of their teams.

The best coaches demonstrate trustworthiness by showing that they are truly hearing their team's questions, understanding their struggles, and supporting their goals. When listening actively, for example, they may restate the issue, ask clarifying questions, and make note of the team's concerns. As we discussed in chapter 2 (page 33), when coaches and leaders demonstrate active listening, it helps to create an atmosphere of psychological safety. This safety helps teams to thrive. When a team thinks that the coach is not listening to them, it can shut off the gateway for building collective efficacy. This can happen when coaches get too attached to their own agendas. The teams try to raise questions or concerns, but the coach or leader cuts them off, so the team is left feeling that their concerns are not important to the coach. A coach who does not establish trust with a team will not be able to build that team's collective efficacy through social persuasion.

Coaches who are skilled efficacy builders demonstrate empathy with their teams by acknowledging the challenges of their work, while continuing to encourage teams to implement new skills to benefit students. In each session, effective coaches listen and look for indications about how the team is doing and how they are handling the demands and expectations that have been placed on them. They are sensitive to the load that teachers are carrying, but they use their coaching skills to lift teams out of any malaise they might be caught in. These coaches allow teams a little bit of space to vent, when necessary, but then get the team back on track through encouragement, focus, and engagement. Coaches who ignore their teams' concerns and struggles miss an opportunity to be responsive and supportive. They may think that teams should "tough it out," so they choose not to acknowledge the difficult circumstances that a team is facing. Coaches who take this approach—choosing not to empathize with their teams—miss an opportunity to provide support and subsequently build trust with their teams. In addition, through minimizing or ignoring a team's struggles, they may end up neglecting a critical issue that affects the long-term productivity of the team. Empathy is a key characteristic for coaches who are building the collective efficacy of their teacher teams in all types of schools.

Effective coaches are reliable individuals who follow through on what they say they will do. Especially in the early stages of a coach–team relationship, it is essential for coaches to be reliable and dependable. When a coach consistently demonstrates that they will do what they say they will do and follows through on all the commitments that they makes to teams, it helps the team to believe that the coach is trustworthy. When a team realizes that they can depend on a coach, they are more likely to value the coach's advice and follow through on their guidance. If, however, a coach fails to provide a team with a resource that was promised or doesn't respond when a team reaches out with a question, the team may doubt whether the coach is worthy of trust. This lack of trust will make it less likely that the team will value any input from the coach.

Effective coaches admit when they have made a mistake and take responsibility for their errors. We are all human. We make mistakes. We drop the ball. If a coach fails to follow through on a commitment to a team, it is critical that the coach acknowledge the failure and take responsibility. Sometimes, when a leader or coach admits a mistake and promises to do better, it ends up deepening a team's trust in their coach. Coaches who fail to own their mistakes or missteps lose credibility with their teams.

Effective coaches build positive relationships with their teams by consistently supporting them, being honest with them, and providing high-quality support. As the coach-team relationship grows, the coach demonstrates commitment to the team first by continuing to show up. Each time a coach works with a team is an opportunity to demonstrate competence, build credibility, and move the team forward. Coaches deepen trust by telling teams the truth and giving them honest constructive feedback. As teams see that following the coach's guidance is helping them to do the work better and getting some results, their trust in the coach increases. On the other hand, coaches who are inconsistent in their support will have limited impact on their teams.

Coaches who truly want to build the collective efficacy of their teams must use each engagement with their teams to build positive relationships. Effective coaches will keep this top of mind as they have sessions with teams and will be intentional in demonstrating behaviors that build trust and foster collective efficacy. Figure 6.4 (page 158) captures what it looks like, sounds like, and feels like when effective coaches build positive and productive relationships with their teams.

Looks Like	Sounds Like	Feels Like
When members of the team are sharing their questions and struggles, the coach actively listens and gives the speaker their undivided attention.	(Silent listening) Thank you for sharing that with me. Let me ask about that . . . Tell me more about what you are trying to do . . .	Finally, someone is really listening to us!
The coach listens to teams' concerns and empathizes with their challenges but expresses belief in the team and helps them to persevere.	I know this piece of the work is really challenging. It has challenged lots of teams. But we can figure it out together.	I think he understands that we have a lot on our plate, and this is challenging. I appreciate being able to vent a little.
The coach demonstrates reliability and follows through on what they promise.	Here is the tool I said that I would bring this time. Let's look at it together.	Some coaches promise stuff and then forget. I appreciate that he comes through with what he promises.

Figure 6.4 USING SOCIAL PERSUASION TO BUILD COLLECTIVE EFFICACY—RELATIONSHIP SKILLS.

In addition to credibility and positive relationships, efficacy-building coaches must implement high-quality, research-based coaching strategies that help teams to achieve their goals. The key elements of this high-level coaching are guidance, feedback, and encouragement. Let's look at critical coaching skills and methods involved in the engagement phase of step 4.

Guidance

Effective coaches provide expert guidance to their teams as they apply their new knowledge. Effective guidance involves helping teams assess where they and establishing a clear plan to address needs. Coaches must be skilled diagnosticians who can assess where teams are in their journey. Having a clear picture of where they are in terms of student learning and team processes helps coaches to start creating their plan for helping the team to be more successful and subsequently build their collective efficacy. Diagnosis of a team's effectiveness prompts two primary questions.

1. Is the team's work positively influencing student learning? What is the evidence?

2. Is the team's collective work demonstrating growth and effectiveness? Is the work that they are doing as a team improving in its quality, detail, and application? What is the evidence?

The primary evidence of a team's effectiveness is that their efforts are producing higher levels of student learning. This is the heart of collective teacher efficacy. Collective teacher efficacy only happens when teachers believe that they can collectively make an impact on student learning, above and beyond all other factors, and then *they see evidence that they are* (Hattie, 2018). There is no true collective teacher efficacy without clear evidence of increased student learning over time.

To analyze student learning results and the role the team plays in those results, coaches can use a tool like the student learning discussion tool (figure 6.5) to organize their questions and analyze the information. This is similar to the process that is done at the school level to establish the why, what, and how. Coaches must make sure that all teachers have a clear understanding of how to read the data and how to interpret what they mean. If teachers do not understand the data or if they doubt the data's validity, it will have limited value for the team. If, however, the team has a deep understanding of the data and trusts the information it provides, it can be a powerful tool to drive the team forward.

What student achievement goals did we set at the beginning of the school year?
What updated data do we have to help us assess our progress?
What do we see in the data? What can we celebrate? What are the areas that need attention?
What are our next steps? How can we build on strategies that are producing student learning? How can we adjust or replace strategies that are not producing student learning?

Figure 6.5: STUDENT LEARNING DISCUSSION TOOL.

In addition to reviewing student learning and setting appropriate goals, coaches should help teams to self-assess their team practices, processes, and products. Reviewing this evidence and setting appropriate goals for improvement gives the team another way to measure their growth and thereby helps to build collective efficacy. Teams can use the Top Ten Tasks of Teams in a PLC Reflection Tool shared in chapter 5 (figure 5.2, page 124) to conduct a self-assessment and coaches can guide them in this process. PLC teams that are looking to assess where they are in terms of collaborative team practices can also use the PLC at Work continuums in the fourth edition of *Learning by Doing* (DuFour et al., 2024). This book contains over a dozen detailed continuums that provide descriptions of teams at the preinitiating, initiating, implementing, developing, and sustaining levels of practice for the critical work of collaborative teams in a PLC.

As teams assess where they are and start to review their progress, effective coaches use social persuasion—specific feedback and encouragement from a trusted and credible source—to help teams recognize how they are growing and to encourage teams when their progress is slower than expected. Skilled efficacy builders will develop a clear plan, based on the assessment of where the team is, and lead them step by step to the next level of implementation. Effective coaches always point teams toward the next step and provide the support they need to get there. For example, a team might review the PLC at Work continuum on using frequent common formative assessments (DuFour et al., 2024, p. 188) and determine that they are currently working at the preinitiating level. An effective coach will point the team to the description of the initiating level and help them to identify the steps to achieve that level of implementation.

Feedback

Effective coaches provide feedback that is based on data. In addition, the most powerful feedback is honest, accurate, constructive, and helps a team move forward. The best coaches have established their expertise and credibility with teams and have also proven that they care about the team, their mission, and their work. When coaches have achieved this level of respect and trust with the team, the team will want to hear the coach's feedback and advice. Coaches who are working with teams must take this responsibility very seriously. When a coach has done the work to establish this relationship with a team, their feedback will carry a lot of weight. Coaches who use this influence carefully and effectively can make an enormous difference in the effectiveness of the team. In the same way that effective coaches are careful and strategic in their preparation, coaches must demonstrate the same mindsets when providing feedback. Coaches must be skillful, deft, and balanced in how they deliver feedback messages. It cannot be rosy fluff. Effective teams that are growing will know when their coach is just offering "happy talk" with no substance. Constructive feedback is based in facts and evidence and helps teams to see the next steps. And while we want to avoid the trap of superficial feedback, coaches should not use a scorched-earth approach with brutal comments that cause teachers to question their vocation. A coach's work requires balance and skill.

Constructive and supportive feedback is especially important for teams that have a low sense of collective efficacy. As we discussed in chapter 4 (page 89), coaches will find that some teams have a very low expectation of what they can accomplish as a team. They may have received harsh negative feedback in the past. They may have tried some strategies, only to see their results decline. A team in this state needs a coach who can see the positive skills that a team has and then point out the things that they are doing correctly. Over time, positive feedback based on evidence that comes from a trusted coach will help a team to believe that they can be successful. This is the essence of using social persuasion to build collective efficacy. It is also challenging coaching work that takes time. Even a team that has an extremely low sense of collective efficacy can build their collective belief in themselves through the guidance and support of a supportive coach functioning as a skilled efficacy builder.

Encouragement

As teams carry out their action plans and work to improve student learning and their team practices, there will be hard days and disappointing weeks. There will be times that an assessment doesn't work, a unit lesson plan bombs, or student learning results are disappointing. In these moments, skilled efficacy builders make the biggest difference to their teams. Coaches who use social persuasion effectively will help teams to get through the rough spots by offering evidence and encouragement about the good work that the team is doing. Skilled coaches will use social persuasion to convince teams to keep going and work through the challenging spots. One of the biggest dividends of collective efficacy is its impact on perseverance. Teams that are building their collective efficacy are more likely to stick with it and work through to the end than a team that has a low sense of collective efficacy. Skilled coaches will look for opportunities to build teams up and encourage them to carry on.

Make no mistake—implementing new collaborative team practices can be messy and imperfect, especially when first applying new knowledge. Teams and individuals will make errors, implement practices incorrectly, omit critical steps, and stumble a bit in their application. This happens, and it is not the end of the world. Teams can learn from their mistakes and improve their practice through reflection and collaboration. This is where the support of a knowledgeable and trusted coach can make such a difference. This is where effective social persuasion can help to build the collective efficacy of a teacher team—even when they are struggling.

For schools and district working to implement the PLC process, one of the most popular resources is *Learning by Doing* (DuFour et al., 2024). I have often thought that this is such an appropriate name for this critical book because implementing its research and guidance requires us to actually do the work. We will learn more by doing—actually implementing practices and applying new knowledge with real teachers, teams, and students—than we ever learn through reading or study.

"Learning by doing" can also be pretty stressful. Leaders and coaches who are skilled efficacy builders will remember how affective states, or the emotional state of their teams, can influence the collective efficacy the team has about their ability to impact student learning. Coaches who are working strategically to build the collective efficacy of the teacher teams will be deliberate about their teams' emotional states, especially when providing feedback during coaching.

As coaches use these social persuasion and coaching strategies to build their teams' collective efficacy, it is important for them to check on the stress level of their teams. As we learned in step 2 of the CLEAR process, addressing the affective states or emotional status of teachers and teams is a critical aspect of building collective efficacy. If teachers and teams have stress or anxiety that is not addressed, it can have a negative effect on their collective confidence. Therefore, effective coaches will monitor their teams and do a temperature check from time to time to make sure that their teams are not being stymied by emotional turmoil. This is particularly true as coaches implement step 4 of the CLEAR process— Activating new learning through coaching, practice, and implementation.

Effective leaders and coaches can check on the emotional state and stress level of their teams through several simple strategies.

- In advance of a coaching session, email members of the team to ask them what questions they have about what they are working on. Include an open-ended question like "What is producing the most stress right now?" This can give the coach advance notice about what might be happening with the affective states of the team in advance of their session.

- Start the coaching session with an activator that gives team members an opportunity to communicate that they are feeling stress about some aspect of the work. Begin the meeting by having teachers share one celebration they have about the work they are doing, one question they have, and one obstacle they are facing. Use the responses to have an honest conversation about the sources of stress and discuss strategies for working past them.

Some leaders and coaches will view this idea of checking on teams' stress level in step 4 as unnecessary or overkill. Others will worry that if they draw attention to the idea of stress levels for teams, it could actually dredge up feelings and concerns that don't need to be reawakened. Some will worry (ironically) that devoting time to checking on a team's anxiety could derail the progress they have made. The research begs to differ (Baker et al., 2019; Bandura, 1977; Edmondson, 2018; Merritt, 2021). When leaders and coaches intentionally check on the mental health of their teams, they are demonstrating care and concern for their teachers. This helps to create a culture of psychological safety where all staff members know that they can ask for help (Edmondson, 2018). This, in turn, helps to build the collective efficacy of teams.

As mentioned earlier, step 4 of the CLEAR process is critical in the effort to build the collective efficacy of teacher teams. Effective coach-team engagement based on credibility, positive relationships, and skillful coaching can have a major impact on teams. Figure 6.6 shows what it looks like, sounds like, and feels like when coaches engage teams with effective practices.

Looks Like	Sounds Like	Feels Like
The coach starts work with a team by asking questions about the work they have done.	I am excited to have the chance to work with you. I want to start by learning as much as I can about you, your team, the work you have done, and your goals for this year.	I get the feeling that she is invested in helping us grow as a team.
The coach helps the team to establish short- and long-term goals for student learning and for their team processes and products.	So, let's take a close look at what the student achievement data are currently telling us about where your students are working. That will help us to set some goals to drive the work. We can also look at your team products and brainstorm ideas about how to make them work for you and your students.	Having clear goals that we are working on together makes me feel like we are focused on the right things and that we are more likely to get some results for our hard work.
The coach has an organized plan each time she meets with the team. The plan is aligned to the team's goals.	Since you let me know you would be working on unit plans today, I brought a bunch of samples and tools that could be helpful. Let's figure out which ones work best for you.	I really appreciate how she helps us take the next step in each meeting. After each session, I feel like we are getting closer to our goals.
The coach provides expert feedback and helps the team to work through problems and challenges.	I know you are frustrated because your students' writing isn't improving the way you had hoped—yet. I think it would help if all of you agreed on a common rubric to use in evaluating student work. Let me show you how that would work.	Our coach knows how demoralizing it can be when you work hard and don't get a good result. She always encourages us, helps us to examine the problem, and teaches us a new way to get it done.

Figure 6.6: USING SOCIAL PERSUASION TO BUILD COLLECTIVE EFFICACY—COACHING PRACTICES.

Next, coaches must provide effective follow-through that reinforces the growth that was achieved through engagement.

Follow-Through for Activating New Learning Through Coaching, Practice, and Implementation

For coaches and leaders working to build the collective efficacy of their teacher teams, effective follow-through is essential. Skilled efficacy builders will reinforce their coaching in the short-term through follow-up communication to teams and, in the long-term, by providing reliable, sustained coaching over time. In addition, effective coaches will conduct follow-through on a personal level by intentionally reflecting on their coaching and its impact. Let's examine both types of follow-through for step 4 of the CLEAR process.

Follow-Up Communication

One of the best ways for coaches to reinforce the learning that happens in coaching sessions is by sending follow-up communication that is *prompt, positive,* and *personalized.*

- Prompt follow-through communication is sent within 24 hours of the coaching session. This communication thanks the team for their efforts and looks ahead to the next session.

- Positive follow-through communication highlights growth and breakthroughs that occurred during the session, reinforcing the message that the team is making progress.

- Personalized follow-up communication makes specific reference to the team and the session (no cookie cutters here!) that reflects that the coach is thinking about the specific team and their work. This is also where coaches might respond to specific questions that the team posed during the session.

For example, after a session with a high school science department, the coach might send an email the following morning:

Hi Jill, Jack, Jamie, and Justin!

Good morning! I really enjoyed our session yesterday. It is so clear that you are truly collaborating as a department and looking for ways to enhance learning for your students. The work you have done to create common expectations for student lab reports, as well as strategies for providing feedback, is really exciting. As we discussed, an important piece will be making sure that you have a system for recording the student data so that you can look for trends. I have attached a sample monitoring tool that might work for you. Please look it over and let me know if you have any questions. As always, please feel free to contact me at any time if I can help. I am looking forward to our next meeting. Have a great day!

—Jason

These types of follow-up communications support the work, remind teams of next steps, and reinforce the feeling that the coach is there to support the team's efforts. When combined with follow-up actions to support the teams and their goals, coaches nurture a team's growing sense of collective efficacy.

In addition to the short-term strategy of prompt, positive, and personalized follow-up messages, coaches commit, when possible, to ongoing sustained coaching support of teams.

Sustained Support

In order for coaching to have a significant effect, it cannot be a one-shot effort. The research shows that teacher teams gain very little from isolated, single-experience coaching sessions, but long-term, job-embedded coaching support is one of the most powerful influences on teacher practice (Darling-Hammond et al., 2017; Desimone & Pak, 2017; Knight, 2021).

Building the collective efficacy of teacher teams through social persuasion requires shoulder-to-shoulder job-embedded work with the team. The opportunities for genuine social persuasion occur as coaches are working in the trenches with a team on the tasks that are critical for the team and their students. Coaches demonstrate expertise, build credibility, establish relationships, develop a plan, implement high-level coaching, provide meaningful feedback and guidance, and celebrate team growth all while in the room with the team they are coaching. Teams will get the greatest social persuasion benefit from their coach if the team perceives that the coach is a partner in the work they are doing to serve their students (Knight, 2021).

Most coaches who are working with teams in schools will have some control over their schedule and how often they can visit with their teams, but many have limited say in how they use their time to support teams. School schedules, district guidelines, coaches who are shared among multiple schools, and other factors can make it difficult for coaches to provide their teams with the long-term, consistent support that the research says they need. Leaders at the school and district level have the responsibility for making sure that their teams are getting the support they need. If a school or district is serious about building the collective efficacy of their teacher teams, they will work to allocate resources to support research-based, job-embedded professional development.

Effective coaching is supported by systems and structures that allow the coaching to occur as planned and maximize the impact of the coaching program. Leaders and administrators at the school, district, and state level have the responsibility of establishing and supporting the structures that provide effective coaching to teacher teams. The research shows that if teams are provided with high-quality coaching over an extended period, teams can make significant growth in their practice. Effective practice by teams leads to enhanced results for students.

At the school and team level, coaches must have a plan to maximize the impact of their time with teams. Even in the best scenarios where the district or state has provided the staffing and opportunities necessary for coaching to occur, most coaches will still have limited time with each team. It is essential to have a plan for how to use the time efficiently so that each session helps to move the team forward. Figure 6.7 captures what it looks like, sounds like, and feels like when a coach provides effective follow-up communication and sustained support.

Looks Like	Sounds Like	Feels Like
The coach follows up every session with an email message that is prompt, positive, and personalized.	Thank you so much for the work you have been doing as a team. The evidence we reviewed in our session yesterday shows that it is positively impacting student learning. Well done!	It's really nice when someone outside of the team recognizes the hard work we are doing. And when our coach helps us to see the evidence of growth, it makes me start to believe we really can do this!
The coach provides steady support over an extended period.	It is hard to believe we are already halfway through the second semester. I hope you all are seeing the growth that you have had in your instructional practice and how that is starting to really make a difference in student learning.	Thank goodness we have been able to work with our coach throughout the school year. We accomplished so much more than we would have with a one-shot professional development session.

Figure 6.7: USING SOCIAL PERSUASION TO BUILD COLLECTIVE EFFICACY—FOLLOW UP AND SUPPORT.

As mentioned in the Making It CLEAR section of this chapter (page 149), effective coaches also practice follow-through on a personal level. For high-performing coaches, this involves reflection on coaching sessions, review of results and feedback, and plans for continuous improvement. For coaches who are working to build the collective efficacy of teacher teams, this reflection is focused on social persuasion and strategies that are aligned with the research on efficacy beliefs. Figure 6.8 (page 166) and figure 6.9 (page 167) provide reflection tools that coaches can use to assess their social persuasion and coaching skills. The first focuses on credibility, expertise, and relationships—key elements for effective social persuasion. The second focuses on specific coaching practices within work with a team. Both figures are completed to show how a coach might reflect on her practice.

N – Never R – Rarely S – Sometimes U – Usually A – Always						
Effective Social Persuasion Practice	**N**	**R**	**S**	**U**	**A**	**Evidence**
Expertise and credibility						
I stay up to date on research and best practice through professional reading, ongoing training, and consultation with colleagues.					X	I devote time every week to professional reading. I've attended two conferences this year and applied what I learned to my coaching.
I demonstrate expertise through providing feedback and guidance that is aligned with the latest research and best practice.				X		When I review my notes and reflect on sessions, I can see the connection between my advice and best practice.
Relationships						
I demonstrate active listening in my work with teams.			X			I have received positive evaluations and comments from teams, but I think I can do better with this.
I demonstrate empathy in my work with teams.				X		I do understand everything that teams are dealing with, and I work to communicate that in every session.
When I make a commitment to a team, I follow through and do what I said I would do.			X			I am fairly consistent with this, but I need a better system to make sure I get to 100% on this.
I am reliable, dependable, and trustworthy in my work with teams.				X		I show up for sessions. I am on time. I bring what I am supposed to bring.
I provide my teams with effective, honest feedback and guidance.					X	I highly value honest feedback and am diligent about providing that to teams during our sessions. Evaluations from teams reflects this.
In my work with teams, I admit when I have made a mistake.				X		I usually admit a mistake, but sometimes I gloss over.
I communicate effectively with the teams I coach in advance of coaching sessions.					X	I am very consistent in sending advance emails before sessions so that we can have productive sessions.
I communicate effectively with the teams I coach during coaching sessions.				X		I have received positive feedback from teams about my communication with them during our sessions.
I communicate effectively with the teams I coach by following up after coaching sessions.		X				As I review my emails, I sometimes forget to follow up with teams in a timely manner. I need to improve in this area.

Which areas need attention?

I need to do a better job of sending prompt follow-up communication after every coaching session. I am missing golden opportunities to reinforce sessions and demonstrate reliability with my teams.

What are some concrete action steps you could take to improve your coaching/social persuasion?

Establish a routine of (1) jotting down notes immediately after each coaching session to capture the key items to include in follow-up communications, and (2) sending follow-up emails in the evening.

Figure 6.8: COACH'S SOCIAL PERSUASION SELF-ASSESSMENT—EXPERTISE, CREDIBILITY, AND RELATIONSHIPS.

Visit **go.SolutionTree.com/PLCbooks** *for a free reproducible version of this figure.*

N – Never R – Rarely S – Sometimes U – Usually A – Always						
Effective Social Persuasion Practice	**N**	**R**	**S**	**U**	**A**	**Evidence**
I conduct a thorough diagnosis of each team's current state through review of data, examination of products, and work with the team.				X		I am getting better at this. Sometimes, I have not given this piece the time it deserves, and I rush into the current work. I am finding that I am a better coach when I have a clear sense of where the team is.
I help each team to establish short- and long-term goals for increasing student achievement.			X			I have been doing really well with long-term goals, but I am still figuring out how to help some teams set short-term goals.
I help each team to establish short- and long-term goals for team process and products.			X			I could do a more consistent job of helping teams set goals for improving their processes and products.
I develop a customized plan for coaching each team to help them achieve their team goals.				X		I work hard on customizing the plans, and I have received positive feedback.
I provide each team with feedback that is honest, constructive, and accurate.					X	I am very diligent about my role in providing honest, accurate, supportive feedback. I have received formal and informal feedback from teams that they value this aspect of my coaching.
I help teams to notice, acknowledge, and celebrate their growth in terms of student learning and team practice.				X		I am fairly consistent with this, but I could improve my advance planning for celebration.
I help teams to persevere through difficulty by providing evidence of growth and encouragement.					X	I see this as a key aspect to my work as a coach, so I devote a lot of effort into helping teams persevere. I have had many teachers tell me they appreciate my encouragement.
I provide ongoing support for teams to help them achieve their short- and long-term goals.				X		I am thankful that most of my coaching assignments are long-term, but some of that is beyond my control and there are teams I only see sporadically.

Which areas are your strongest?

Providing feedback and encouraging teams through rough spots

How can you build on those strengths to support your teams?

I could be more mindful of how I am modeling these practices (feedback and encouragement) in order to make sure that I am teaching teams how to do these things for themselves.

Which areas need attention?

Setting meaningful short-term goals and monitoring team processes and products

What are some concrete action steps you could take to improve your coaching/social persuasion?

Add clear steps for setting short-term goals into the differentiated plan for teams and then plan and follow through with setting short-term goals in one of the first two sessions with each team.

Figure 6.9: EFFECTIVE SOCIAL PERSUASION PRACTICE SELF-ASSESSMENT TOOL—COACHING PRACTICES.

Visit **go.SolutionTree.com/PLCbooks** *for a free reproducible version of this figure.*

While social persuasion is not the most powerful influence on the efficacy beliefs of individuals and groups when compared to mastery experience and vicarious experience, it can still have a significant impact on teacher teams when it is wielded by an effective leader or coach. School leaders and coaches who are serious about building the collective efficacy of their teacher teams must be strategic and deliberate in how they plan and deliver social persuasion through effective coaching. When combined with the vicarious experiences described in step 3 of the CLEAR process and the attention to the affective states we discussed in step 2, the social persuasion that coaches provide through step 4 helps teams to achieve the most powerful influence on efficacy beliefs—mastery experience. We will explore the power of mastery experience in chapter 7 (page 171).

Team Update

On a Wednesday in March, the grade 6 mathematics team at John Wooden Middle School is excited. It is the week before spring break, and they are having their weekly collaborative team meeting. The team is reviewing the latest CFA data. They are thrilled with the results! Over 85 percent of their students across the grade level achieved the proficiency target on the latest assessment. And while the team is very pleased with the overall performance level of their students, they are especially excited about the students who were previously working below grade level who have now grown to meet the grade-level standard. As the team reviews the results, they smile and point out the performance of individual students. Students who previously would struggle with common formative and summative assessments are now hitting the targets. They know that a big factor in this growth is their effective use of WIN (what-I-need) time, their Tier 2 intervention block. Earlier in the year, they felt like they were doing everything right, but they were not seeing any results. They were frustrated and felt like failures. Then, Pat Summit, the school's mathematics facilitator, started to meet with them on a regular basis. The team really appreciated their time with Ms. Summit. She was so knowledgeable about mathematics instruction and intervention strategies. She had been part of a team at another school that had implemented mathematics interventions, and their students' scores were now some of the highest in the state! Ms. Summit also had a calm approach, she was an excellent listener, and she knew how to talk to teachers to help them be motivated to try new strategies. When the team voiced their struggles earlier in the year, the principal, Mr. Lombardi, and Ms. Summit worked things out so that she could join them every other week during their collaborative team time. They looked at student data, identified the skills and concepts that individual students were having difficulty with, and researched effective interventions for those needs. Ms. Summit was there as they tried new strategies, refined their intervention plans, and improved their systems for keeping track of student data. She helped them to develop a plan for recognizing and celebrating students who made progress as a result of their work during WIN time. And when the road got rough, like when they had a dip in their results after posting some gains, Ms. Summit was there with calm, focused feedback that helped the team to identify high priority action steps. She also helped them review the progress they made in their team products and processes, like their intervention plans and team agendas. As the team reviews the newest results, Ms. Summit comes into the meeting and joins the celebration.

CLEAR Thoughts and Next Steps

Social persuasion—advice and encouragement from a trusted person—is a powerful influence on the efficacy beliefs of individuals and teams. Skilled efficacy builders use step 4 of the CLEAR process to build the collective efficacy of their teacher teams through developing their coaching expertise, establishing positive relationships, and delivering high-quality guidance, feedback, and encouragement. As we conclude our look at step 4, let's review some critical takeaways, reflect on the implications for our work, and plan next steps.

Let's review critical takeaways.

- Providing teachers and teams with differentiated coaching helps to build collective teacher efficacy through the social persuasion that Bandura identified as an important influence on self-efficacy and collective efficacy beliefs.

- Social persuasion is encouragement and support from a trusted and respected coach. Social persuasion can be a powerful influence on collective efficacy, especially in an educational setting.

- Effective coaches demonstrate credibility, expertise, and the ability to form positive and productive relationships. Establishing and reinforcing trust is a critical aspect of this part of the CLEAR process.

- Effective coaches also demonstrate research-based coaching methods that help to build the collective efficacy of teacher teams.

- Because this step of the CLEAR process puts significant pressure on teams as they work to apply what they have learned to their own situation, this is also an important point to check on the emotional well-being of the team (affective states).

Let's reflect on the content from this chapter.

1. In this chapter, we explored how social persuasion can help build the collective efficacy of teacher teams. This happens when coaches who have expertise and credibility build positive relationships with teams and use a sequence of research-based steps to help teams achieve their goals. Have you ever had a coach who demonstrated these qualities? When and where was that? How did the coach's characteristics and actions help you or your team to be successful?

2. Being an effective coach requires making an investment in staying up to date with the latest research and thinking in the field. What are your current methods for "sharpening your saw"? Do you have a practice or routine for professional reading and research? What could that look like?

3. Being an effective coach also requires interpersonal skills. How often do you reflect on the interpersonal aspects of your leadership and coaching? How could you improve and enhance your relationships with your teachers and teams?

Let's plan an action step.

Before going into your next session with a team, consider what you need to do to be fully prepared to provide them with trusted guidance (social persuasion) that will help them to grow as a team. How does that affect your mindset and preparation?

_____

_____

_____

_____

_____

_____

_____

_____

_____

_____

CHAPTER SEVEN

Step 5 of the CLEAR Process:

Review Results, Celebrate Growth, and Set New Targets

FOR LEADERS AND coaches working to build the collective efficacy of their teacher teams, the fifth and final step of the CLEAR process involves helping teams to recognize their efforts have had an effect, to celebrate their gains, and to set new aspirational goals. After clarifying the why, what, and how (step 1), listening to teachers' fears, anxieties, questions, and concerns (step 2), exploring examples, models, best practices, and proven processes (step 3), and activating new learning through coaching, practice, and implementation (step 4), the fifth and final step in the CLEAR process to build the collective efficacy of teacher teams is to *review progress, celebrate growth, and set new targets* (step 5). Step 5 of the CLEAR process is built on the research that shows mastery experiences (clear successes supported by data) are the most powerful influence on individual and collective efficacy beliefs. When teams see clear evidence that their hard work has paid off in measurable results, it provides an incredible boost to their collective efficacy—"Look what we achieved! We can do anything!"

In this chapter, we examine the research about mastery experiences and their impact on individual and collective efficacy beliefs. We also explore practical strategies for helping teams get the most out of their mastery experiences through regular review of evidence, purposeful celebration, and strategies to sustain success through setting new goals, and a real-world-inspired scenario showing teams doing this work. At the end of the chapter, we review key points, reflect, and plan an action step in the CLEAR Thoughts and Next Steps section.

Now, let's imagine a scenario where an entire school district devoted itself to improving practice and, through hard work and with the support of skilled efficacy builders, they have come to the point where they are reviewing results and celebrating their growth.

Meet the Team

It is the last week of school, and all across the Mountaintop School District (MSD), teacher teams are feeling proud, accomplished, and powerful. Though they are a small district with just three schools—elementary, middle, and high, Mountaintop is making big things happen.

At the elementary school, teams are celebrating their student learning data that show that they achieved their school goals in reading. At the beginning of the school year, all teams established goals that were aligned with the district targets. They carefully monitored student progress through regular, common formative and summative assessments, and they have seen great growth among their K–5 students. Though they will not get the state test results for their 3–5 students for several weeks, the teachers are confident that the students did well. After all, they have been gathering evidence of student learning all year and posting it on their team data walls. They have a crystal-clear picture of where each student started and where they are performing now. They are delighted not only in the students who performed at or above grade-level targets all year, but especially those who started the year far below grade-level proficiency and demonstrated excellent growth throughout the year. They know that their work as a team has made a difference for students, and they can see the evidence of growth.

At the middle school, teacher teams are also celebrating increases in student achievement over the course of the year and reflecting on how their collaborative efforts as teachers had made an impact. They remember how they were stressed at the beginning of the year about a new approach to providing interventions to students who were not being successful with grade-level content. They recount stories about when they started to see that the intervention plan was making a difference. They remind each other of how excited they were when the progress monitoring data showed that students were learning and beginning to master grade-level concepts and skills. They express pride in their students and how hard they worked. The middle school teachers, like their elementary counterparts, will not see the state test results for several weeks, but they are confident that their students will do well and exceed last year's performance.

At the high school, teachers take pride in the work they have done to help all students master content and skills. They celebrate the progress they have made as teams, which is evident not only in increased student learning but in the products they have created as departments: clear essential standards that are aligned across grade levels and courses, common scoring tools for student writing and presentations, systematic plans for using the school's intervention period to provide students with support, and so on. They recall how excited they were when their review of student writing using a common tool started to show improvement.

In all three schools, these celebrations come at the end of a journey that has been very challenging at different points. But through it all, their principals, coaches, and teacher leaders helped them work through tough spots and to grow as teams. Coaches were clear about why they were asking teacher teams to change practice, what the changes would involve, and how they would measure growth and success. They helped teams to develop and use strategies and tools to monitor student achievement more regularly, so that they were not just waiting to see how students would do on the state test. School leaders also created a space for teachers to share questions and concerns, and yes, even fears and anxieties about new practices. Teacher input was welcomed, and their concerns were respected. This built trust and helped all teacher teams feel more empowered for the work ahead. School and team leaders followed up expectations about practice with training, resources, examples, supports, and many opportunities to grow. Each team received differentiated coaching to help implement the new practices with confidence and effectiveness.

In their conversations with each other, teachers shared how they felt very committed to the work that was being done in Mountaintop. Some admitted that they were almost to the point of leaving teaching before the district started this new work to support teams and their collective efficacy. Now they feel empowered and want to keep being a part of making great things happen for students. They knew that there would certainly be challenging days ahead and circumstances beyond their control—the crisis of the moment—but now they feel confident that their teams, their schools, and their district will be able to meet the challenges, keep the focus on students and their learning, and work together to make sure that all students succeed.

The teacher teams in the Mountaintop school district are experiencing the excitement and fulfillment of collective teacher efficacy—a powerful belief that they, as teacher teams, can take the necessary actions to ensure student learning. Further, they have come to believe that their collaborative efforts can overcome any obstacle that students may face and that their collective agency is more powerful than students' socioeconomic status or any other disadvantage. This collective efficacy was born out of repeated and consistent implementation of effective practices and monitoring progress. As they saw that their efforts were connected to increases in student learning, it inspired them to focus even more on strategies that were working and fueled their perseverance when circumstances got difficult.

Seeing evidence that their efforts have led to increased student learning has been a powerful mastery experience for the teams in Mountaintop. The teams have reviewed concrete data that clearly demonstrate that their work has made a significant difference in the achievement levels of their students.

What the Research Says

Bandura's research on how people form efficacy beliefs confirmed that mastery experiences are the most powerful influence on self-efficacy and collective efficacy. As he explains, "mastery experiences are the most influential source of efficacy information because they provide the most authentic evidence of whether one can muster whatever it takes to succeed. Successes build a robust belief in one's personal efficacy" (Bandura, 1997, p. 80). Studies in numerous fields have concluded that mastery experiences build self-efficacy and collective efficacy and, consequently, improve individual and group performance in academics, project management, athletics, and health care (Bruton et al., 2016; Capa-Aydin et al., 2018; Elaldı, 2016; George & Feltz, 1995; O'Neil, 2023; Sheu, Lent, Miller, Penn, Cusick, & Truong, 2018; Warner et al., 2018). For example, in their meta-analysis of 104 studies conducted over thirty-seven years, Hung-Bin Sheu and colleagues (2018) find that mastery experiences were a strong influence on individuals and their efficacy beliefs in science, technology, engineering, and mathematics (STEM). Olakunle Taofeek Lemboye (2019) finds a relationship between mastery experiences and the likelihood that project managers would be successful in leading complex work. Researchers have found that mastery experiences are critical in helping individuals adopt healthier lifestyles (Buckworth, 2017) and eliminate unhealthy habits like smoking (Warner et al., 2018). Other studies have determined that mastery experiences are very influential in the progress of medical students (Elaldı, 2016), young people studying the sciences in high school (Capa-Aydin et al., 2018), and secondary music students (Zelenak, 2015). In the field of nursing, Signe Egenberg and colleagues (2015) find that facilitating mastery experiences through a simulation training dramatically increased the effectiveness of treatment and patient results. Raj and Kumar (2009) found that coaching parents of children with autism and facilitating mastery experiences was an effective model for building the self-efficacy of the parents involved, and Mary Sara Wells, Mark A. Widmer, and J. Kelly McCoy (2004) determined that mastery experiences were critical when working with parents of at-risk youth. In the field of athletics, numerous researchers have confirmed the importance of mastery experiences for self-efficacy, collective efficacy, and team performance (Bruton et al., 2016; George & Feltz, 1995; O'Neil, 2023).

Mastery experiences have also been shown to have a powerful effect on educators in different settings. In their meta-analysis of forty-three studies with over 9,000 participants, Robert M. Klassen and Virginia M. C. Tze (2014) found a strong relationship between the self-efficacy teachers gain through mastery experience and the quality of their evaluated teaching performance. Doris Holzberger and Elisabeth Prestele (2021) pointed out the relationship between teacher mastery experiences and classroom management. Researchers have also determined that mastery experiences are critical to teacher success in different subjects, including science (Knaggs & Sondergeld, 2015), English as a foreign language (Phan & Locke, 2015), and music (de Vries, 2013). Several researchers find that mastery experiences are a critical component for beginning teachers. Franziska Pfitzner-Eden (2016) and Maria Martins, João Costa, and Marcos Onofre (2015) identified a link between mastery experiences during student teaching and preservice and later success of novice teachers. Jennifer VanSlander, Sarah W. Sharpe, and Victoria Cardullo's (2022) study of novice teachers confirmed that coaches can build the self-efficacy and effectiveness of novice teachers by deliberately constructing mastery experiences for them during their training. Other studies have found that mastery experiences are a key component of teacher training and success in inclusive education and instruction. In their systematic review of the literature of the factors influencing teacher self-efficacy for inclusive education, Emma Wray, Umesh Sharma, and Pearl Subban (2022) found that the key factors that affected teacher's level of confidence for implementing inclusive practices were the mastery experiences they had gained through teaching experience, preservice education, professional learning, and experiential contact. Claire Wilson, Lisa Marks Woolfson, and Kevin Durkin (2020) confirmed that teacher mastery experiences were a strong predictor of teacher self-efficacy when it came to implementing inclusive practices in their classrooms. Olli-Pekka Malinen and colleagues (2013), in their study of teacher self-efficacy and inclusion practices in China, Holland, and Finland, found that mastery experiences and prior practice in teaching special education were prime predictors of teacher success with inclusive education.

The research shows that when a person or team of people takes on a task and then sees clear evidence that they have achieved a positive result, it can increase their belief that they have the necessary skills and attributes to be successful with that task in the future. As Bandura (1997) explains, "People act on their efficacy beliefs and assess the adequacy of their self-appraisal from the performances they manage to achieve" (p. 81). Bandura (1997) also, however, warns against over-simplifying how mastery experiences build self-efficacy and collective efficacy, pointing out that there is a complex learning process taking place:

> The simplistic view that efficacy beliefs are solely reflections of past performance does not survive empirical scrutiny. Knowing how various factors affect the cognitive processing of performance information clarifies the conditions under which people get the most out of their mastery experiences. (p. 81)

For individuals or groups to get the most out of their mastery experiences, cognitive processing of the experience is essential. In other words, individuals and groups gain the greatest boost in efficacy beliefs when they think about, reflect on, and gain understanding of themselves through the mastery experiences they have. It is not as simple as "I was successful with this before, so I will be successful again." Building self-efficacy and collective efficacy through mastery experiences involves learning to how to think, behave, and persist when confronted with tasks. As Bandura (1997) explains, "Building a sense of personal efficacy through mastery experiences is not a matter of programming ready-made behavior. It involves acquiring the cognitive, behavioral, and self-regulatory tools for creating and executing effective courses of action to manage ever-changing life circumstances" (p. 80). This reminder is important for leaders and coaches who are working to build the collective efficacy of their teacher teams. It is not enough to high-five a team when they achieve a goal. Skilled efficacy builders will engage the team in careful review of what they did to achieve their goals. This squeezes the greatest benefit out of the mastery experience and helps a team to feel very solid in their collective efficacy. When leaders and coaches strategically engage their teams in reviewing results, celebrating growth, and setting new targets in step 5 of the CLEAR process, they are completing some of the most important actions involved in building the collective efficacy of teams.

Bandura (1997) further explains:

> Changes in perceived efficacy result from cognitive processing of the diagnostic information that performances convey about capability

rather than from the performances per se. Therefore, the impact of performance attainments on efficacy beliefs depends on what is made of those performances. The same level of performance success may raise, leave unaffected, or lower perceived self-efficacy depending on how various personal and situational contributors are interpreted and weighted. (p. 81)

In Bandura's work, the "various personal and situational contributors" include a person's or group's perceptions about their own capabilities and the difficulty of the task. People also consider the amount of effort they give, the level of external help they receive, any circumstances that might impact their performance, and the successes and failures they have in the process of completing the task. Bandura's research shows that we consider all these factors as we make judgments about our own efficacy. We do this by taking all the input and interpreting it for ourselves. The impact of our mastery experiences is determined by how "these enactive experiences are cognitively organized and reconstructed in memory" (Bandura, 1997, p. 81). Skilled efficacy builders help their teams to *cognitively organize* their experiences and *reconstruct them in memory* so they get and sustain a significant boost in their collective efficacy (Bandura, 1997).

Studies have also found that when individuals or teams are successful in the face of difficult circumstances, they can develop an even deeper sense of collective efficacy because they know they achieved something that was challenging. Bandura (1997) explains, "If people experience only easy successes, they come to expect quick results and are easily discouraged by failure. A resilient sense of efficacy requires experience in overcoming obstacles through perseverant effort" (p. 80). Sometimes, when an individual or team is facing an enormous challenge, it is the greatest opportunity to build individual and collective efficacy. This was evident during the COVID-19 pandemic when teachers and teams around the globe were presented with the most challenging conditions in decades. Schools were closed, teachers had to shift to virtual instruction with little to no preparation, and the process of collaborating was tested by distance and isolation. Yet many teams and schools persevered through these challenges, went the extra mile to support one another, and came out on the other side as stronger teams and more unified schools. The daunting challenge of the pandemic gave them the opportunity to prove to themselves that they could overcome overwhelming obstacles by working as teams and focusing on student learning. The experience of living through that challenge together promoted an attitude of "If we can handle that, we can handle anything!" and enhanced their collective belief in themselves and what they could accomplish (Long, 2021; Varela & Fedynich, 2021). In the postpandemic era, teachers and teams are still dealing with difficult circumstances, so there is a continuing opportunity to build the collective efficacy of teams by helping them to react, adapt, and thrive in the current atmosphere.

Genuine mastery experiences change the way our mind views and interprets challenges. When we are successful with a task, it creates a mental and emotional marker that will influence our view of that task in the future, providing critical information that we will draw on the next time we encounter the task. The more powerful the mastery experience is, the greater its effect on our perceptions of our own efficacy. This is especially true when we take the time to reflect on the mastery experience and process all the information we have gained through our successful completion of the task. And when our mastery experience involves overcoming substantial obstacles, the impact on our individual and collective efficacy is even stronger.

When we consider how to build the collective efficacy of teacher teams through mastery experiences, it is critical that we understand the crucial role of clear goals in this process. Step 5 of the CLEAR process is to review progress, celebrate growth, and set new targets. Each of the three processes is critical to mastery experiences, and we can accomplish none of them if we have not established clear goals. A team cannot review their progress toward a goal if they have not first identified a clear target. A team cannot celebrate growth unless they have data that show they are getting closer to their primary goal. A team cannot set new targets without evidence that they have reached the goals they had already set. Step 5 of the CLEAR process is tied very closely to clear team goals—although team goals have, of course, been a key ingredient throughout the CLEAR process. For example, in step 1, clarifying the how is centered on "How will we know if this is working?" and clear goals are an essential ingredient. Through steps 2, 3, and 4, coaches remind teams of their goals to help them focus their efforts on improving processes and student learning. In step 5, those goals are critical in helping teams to recognize their growth and celebrate their success.

As I previously discussed, when teams set goals that are specific, measurable, attainable, results oriented, and timebound (SMART), it provides them with a clear purpose and a common objective (Conzemius & O'Neill, 2014). In a PLC, high-performing collaborative teams work interdependently to achieve goals for which they are mutually accountable (DuFour et al., 2024). When the members of a team have reviewed data and set a common SMART goal, it galvanizes the team's efforts and provides a key data point that they can monitor to mark their progress.

As we have worked through the CLEAR process, we have reviewed a significant amount of data that confirms the link between clear goals and collective teacher efficacy (Conzemius & O'Neill, 2013; Donohoo, 2018; Hoogsteen, 2020; Muhammad & Cruz, 2019). As we get to step 5 of the process, it is worth reminding all leaders and coaches that your efforts to build the collective efficacy of your teacher teams will be more efficient and more productive if you take the time to engage teacher teams in setting clear goals and teaching them how to monitor progress.

Making It CLEAR

In step 5 of the CLEAR process, leaders and coaches work to build the collective efficacy of their teacher teams through reviewing pertinent data, facilitating reflection and analysis, celebrating evidence of progress, and reinforcing mastery experiences. Let's explore these components and examine how coaches and leaders can implement this work effectively with their teacher teams.

As we have seen in each of the previous steps of the CLEAR process, effective implementation of step 5 involves careful preparation, effective engagement with staff, and meaningful follow-through. In step 5 of the CLEAR process, coaches must prepare, engage, and follow through as they review progress with teams, celebrate growth, and set new targets.

- **Preparation:** Coaches who are implementing step 5 of the CLEAR process must be thorough in collecting and preparing data and evidence of the team's growth. This data will primarily consist of evidence of student learning, which could include assessment results, work samples, and any other documentation that shows that students are making academic gains. Coaches will also gather artifacts from the teams' work on different tasks as evidence of the team's growth. In addition, coaches must prepare a plan for how they will review this information with teams. Through careful organization of the available data and development of a plan to review the information, coaches can put their teams in the best position to benefit from their mastery experience. We will cover these items in detail later in this chapter.

- **Engagement:** The heart of step 5 of the CLEAR process is engaging with teams so that they can see their growth and the impact of their work to build their collective efficacy. Skilled efficacy builders will develop a plan for helping teams to review and reflect on their results and their work so that they see the connection between their hard work and positive results. Coaches facilitate celebration and guide teams to acknowledge their productive work as a team. Effective coaches also help teams when their results are flat or declining. This is where the coach's skills for encouragement and building confidence are most crucial. We will explore these different scenarios later in this chapter.

- **Follow-through:** In step 5 of the CLEAR process, after coaches have reviewed results and celebrated growth with their teams, they lead them to set new targets. Coaches encourage and motivate teams to continue the journey to achieve great results and higher levels of collective efficacy.

Figure 7.1 provides an overview of the critical preparation, engagement, and follow-through work that coaches do to implement step 5 of the CLEAR process.

	Reviewing Progress With Teacher Teams	Celebrating With Teacher Teams	Setting New Targets With Teacher Teams
Preparation	• Coaches gather and analyze data regarding student achievement. • Coaches review team goals to determine how teams are progressing. • If the coach has data in advance, they plan how to help the team respond to the data. • Coaches gather and analyze evidence regarding team practice, products, and so on.	• Coaches organize the data and evidence that shows the team's growth. • Coaches prepare the data to help teams recognize and celebrate their efforts. • Coaches prepare processes for helping the team to celebrate.	Coaches gather and analyze information regarding team data and targets at the school, district, and state level.
Engagement	• Coaches use protocols and other tools to lead teams through examination of all pertinent data. • Coaches lead teams to assess where they are in terms of progress toward their team goals. • Coaches provide honest, supportive feedback. • Coaches help teams deal with disappointing data by pointing out data that do show growth and encouraging them to persevere. • Coaches help teams to celebrate and reflect on positive data—see Celebrations.	• Coaches help teams to see the progress they are making in student learning and team practice and back it up with evidence. • Coaches encourage teams to take a moment to celebrate their hard work. • Coaches engage teams in reflection on their success and the actions that produced it.	Coaches use strategies and protocols to engage with teams and set new SMART goals to pursue and monitor.
Follow-Through	• Coaches help teams to address their needs and build on their successes through continued coaching. • Coaches follow through on any action steps that are created as a result of reviewing data and progress on team goals. • If the data has been difficult, coaches check in on teams to assess their mood, stress level, and perseverance. • Coaches set a regular schedule and process for teams to review data and products.	• Coaches help teams to reflect on their mastery experiences, examining how their actions led to the improved data. • Coaches help teams to process the mastery experience so that they remember their success and use it when approaching new challenges.	Coaches follow up with teams to continue monitoring of student achievement data and evidence of team process and products.

Figure 7.1: OVERVIEW OF PREPARATION, ENGAGEMENT, AND FOLLOW-THROUGH IN STEP 5 OF THE CLEAR PROCESS.

In the reproducible "Coach's Planner for Step 5 of the CLEAR Process: Review Results, Celebrate Growth, and Set New Targets" in the appendix (page 228), I provide a detailed planner for leaders and coaches to use in implementing this part of the CLEAR process.

In the following sections, I will go into more depth about the preparation, engagement, and follow-through work that effective coaches do to ensure that their teams experience the power of mastery experiences and, thus, build their collective teacher efficacy.

Preparation for Reviewing Results, Celebrating Growth, and Setting New Targets

The preparation work for step 5 of the CLEAR process focuses on gathering and organizing evidence that the team's work is making a difference in student learning. Coaches also gather artifacts that demonstrate the team's growth as a collaborative team. Whether the coach is reviewing results, celebrating growth, or setting new targets, the critical building block is evidence that shows what the team has done and its effect on students and learning.

To prepare for step 5 of the CLEAR process, coaches will gather all the pertinent data that they can to review with their teams. This will include student learning data as well as evidence of team growth in PLC process and products. Having the widest array of data possible on hand will provide for the most complete review of information. Collecting and organizing data and evidence also provides the information necessary to assess progress on team goals.

We notice here a parallel between step 1 of the CLEAR process and step 5. In step 1, we clarify the why. How do we do that? We examine information about student learning and determine where we are not fulfilling our fundamental purpose of ensuring high levels of learning for every student. Our review of data exposes our critical student learning need and establishes our why. We also establish our what by determining the best strategies for addressing our student learning needs. In step 1, we also establish our how. How do we do that? We agree on school and team goals and commit to monitoring our progress on those goals. We don't just identify issues with student learning and promise to give them attention. We establish clear goals and monitor progress on a regular basis. This is our commitment and responsibility.

In step 5, we are continuing to fulfill our commitment and meet this responsibility. In the preparation phase of step 5, we collect as much information as we can. If we have access to district or state databases for student data, we gather that information and organize it for analysis with teams. We may also ask the school or teams to share data with us so we can have a clear picture of student learning. We ask teams to share data from CFAs, benchmarks, and unit tests, so we can help them dig in and make sense of all the information. Note: this is another spot where building trust with a team has a benefit. A team that trusts their coach will be more forthcoming with team data and information.

Once the data are collected and organized, coaches should conduct an initial analysis to determine strengths, needs, and trends. In particular, efficacy coaches are looking for evidence of growth and progress because these data points can support mastery experiences and boosts in collective efficacy. Reviewing all necessary information ahead of time also allows the coach to be prepared for what the data say and how the team will react to it.

Next, coaches develop a plan for engaging their teams in analysis of the data. They might use a tool like the student learning discussion protocol that was shared in chapter 3 (page 57). It is critical to have a plan for the discussion. Data reviews with teams can be somewhat unpredictable. It is not always easy or possible to anticipate how teams will react to the data or the discussion. Coaches must be aware, flexible, and ready to respond to team needs. But it should start with a clear plan for engaging teams in review of the data.

Again, whether coaches are reviewing results, celebrating growth, or setting new targets, the first steps are to gather the pertinent data, conduct an initial analysis, and create a plan for reviewing the data with teams.

Engagement for Reviewing Results, Celebrating Growth, and Setting New Targets

After collecting data, analyzing it, and making a plan for engagement, effective coaches engage teams in collaborative review of the information. As skilled efficacy builders, coaches work to help teams to notice and acknowledge areas of growth and use social persuasion to reinforce the mastery experience for the team. This is true whether coaches are working with teams to review results, celebrate growth, or set new targets.

Reviewing Results

As skilled coaches implement step 5 of the CLEAR process with their teams, the first critical action is to review progress. This involves looking at different types of data and information together to determine how much progress the team has made in pursuing their team SMART goals. The work of reviewing progress, of course, also falls under step 4 of the CLEAR process as coaches work through the social persuasion coaching plan and help teams to review their team goals and any progress they have made. In this chapter, I will focus more on how to coach teams through the review of data, how to encourage celebration, and how to set new aspirational goals.

When reviewing student learning data, the results generally fall into one of three scenarios.

1. The data show clear evidence of student growth—they are making progress!

2. The data do not show evidence of student growth—scores are flat or declining.

3. The data are mixed—students are scoring higher in some areas, but it is not consistent.

Teachers on the team will obviously have different reactions to each of these scenarios. They will be encouraged or even elated if the data show clear evidence of student growth, especially if they are nearing or have achieved their SMART goal. They may be discouraged, or even depressed, when the data show students have not made progress and may even be taking a step back. When a team that is hoping to make steady progress toward their SMART goal instead sees data that indicate they have taken a step backward, it can be very disconcerting. If the data are mixed, the teams will likely have a mixed reaction, although most teachers will dwell on the negative results and feel bad that student learning is not increasing across the board.

In each of these scenarios, an effective coach needs to be prepared for how to work with the team. For a coach who is working to strategically build the collective efficacy of their teacher teams, this preparation is even more critical. Skilled efficacy builders will be prepared for any review of data with strategies that will help to build the collective efficacy of their teams.

If the data show clear evidence of student growth, the coach's main responsibilities are these.

- Help the team to fully understand and embrace that their efforts have created a positive result.

- Facilitate reflection so that they process this success and collaboratively discuss the question, How did we achieve this result? This helps teams to process and internalize the mastery experience and also makes it more likely that they will be able to (1) repeat the success (because they are clear about a strategy that works), and (2) explain to another team how they used the strategy to effect the result.

- Encourage (strongly) the team to take a moment to actually celebrate the fruits of their hard work. I will share more about celebrations later in this chapter (page 184).

An important aspect of reviewing progress, celebrating growth, and setting new targets is using social persuasion with teams to help them see and acknowledge their growth and success. When we help teams to see and embrace the evidence that their efforts are making a difference, we are ushering them into a mastery experience.

Social persuasion is also critical when a team's review of data reveals that they are not achieving their goals. When student results are flat or decline, teams can be devastated, especially if they are putting an extraordinary amount of effort into the process. Skilled efficacy builders will acknowledge the disappointment and the need to get better results, while also providing constructive feedback that will help the team to adjust and move forward. When teams are just starting to implement research-based collaborative practices, they have a steep learning curve and a lot of heavy lifting in the beginning. It often takes weeks or months of this effort to produce tangible student or team results. There is often a period when teams are exerting great effort and not yet seeing results. Many teams are tempted to quit at this point. They say, "All this work and it is not changing our results! Why are we working so hard if it doesn't make a difference?" Teachers and teams at this point in the journey also consider how hard they are working, and it is difficult for them to imagine how they will be able to sustain this level of effort. "We can't keep working at this level! We are burning out!" This is when a team needs an effective coach the most. A skilled efficacy builder will empathize with the team's frustration and stress, help them to see the ways that their practice is changing and making a difference, provide honest and encouraging feedback to help them plan next steps, and bolster the team's perseverance by being the voice of hope in the process.

When working with an overwhelmed team that is not yet getting the results they hope for, an effective efficacy coach will draw on the research about building the collective efficacy of teams. One effective strategy is to walk teams through the steps they have completed in the CLEAR process. For example, a coach working with a team that has just reviewed some disappointing data might say:

> OK, folks. I know you are disappointed with the results of the latest benchmark assessment. I know you were hoping for greater gains this time. You have been working so hard, and it is natural to want to see scores go up right away.

> Let's remember why we are doing this. I know you care deeply about your students, and you want them to be successful in this grade and in future grades. The data at the beginning of the year showed us that we had some work to do. So, we committed ourselves to working as a collaborative team and using the strategies that have been shown to increase student learning. And we set goals to measure our progress. We talked through what stressed us about this new challenge and anticipated that there would be rough spots along the way.

> We looked at how other teams have done this work before and watched the video of the team in Illinois as they worked together, and we tried to emulate their best practices.

> And, as your coach, I can tell you that there absolutely is evidence that your efforts are making a difference. We might not see the results on this benchmark, but there is evidence all around us. Think about where you are now with CFA compared to the beginning of the year. In September, you didn't know the first thing about using CFA. In last week's team meeting, when you reviewed that CFA on main idea and supporting details, you compared results, talked about effective strategies, and left the meeting with a plan for interventions and extensions. That's tremendous growth! And, while I know it is disappointing that your efforts did not show up as big increases on the benchmark, I know that your efforts will, in time, raise your scores.

> This doesn't happen overnight. That team that you watched on video—it took a full year of doing that work before they really saw results. You just need to hang in there and keep doing the work and you will get the gains you are hoping for. I believe in you.

> Now, let's talk about what we need to do next to get the results that you want for your students.

When a coach provides this type of skilled and caring support, teams are more likely to persevere through the rough spots and continue their work toward mastery experiences.

When I am working with a team or a school that is going through some difficulty, and the staff is feeling overwhelmed by the work, I try to encourage them by sharing stories of other schools and teams that have come through the same rough waters and emerged on the other side as a stronger, more unified teaching staff. I explain that I have had the privilege to work with teacher teams throughout the United States. In a number of schools and districts, I have had the opportunity to coach teams over a two-year or three-year period. Invariably, schools and teams that implement research-based collaborative practices see increases in their student learning data and teacher empowerment. But, as noted above, it doesn't happen overnight. It takes sustained effort over time. But it does happen. And seeing how teams grow and then create amazing results for their students is the greatest joy of coaching.

When I work with a team, school, or district over an extended period, I take time at the end of our work together to provide feedback. I ask them how they felt about the work at the beginning of the process, what they found most helpful, what their "aha" moments were, and what advice they would give to a team that is just starting the process. The question about advice for other teams provides some excellent insights. Several consistent messages emerge. Here are a few actual teacher responses that reflect the typical answers I hear.

- Trust the process, even when it gets hard and confusing!

- Sometimes it gets hard, you want to quit, it's overwhelming and time-consuming, but it's worth it to see the students grow in knowledge.

- You can do hard things! Work together as a team. Cry, laugh, scream, and then get back to work.

- Take it one task at a time—you will make it. Reach out to others and ask questions.

- Eat the elephant one bite at a time.

A higher sense of efficacy gives individuals and groups the ability to persevere and work through challenging circumstances and difficult tasks. Coaches play an incredibly important role when teachers are overwhelmed. Skilled efficacy builders are messengers of hope that convince teacher teams to stick with it and keep working for their students and for each other.

Reviewing results with a team provides excellent opportunities for coaches to boost the collective efficacy of teams. Next, we look at engagement strategies for celebrating when the results are positive.

Celebrating Growth

Most leaders and coaches understand the importance of celebrating progress and team members who have done great work and accomplished important tasks. In all fields, workers perform better in an organizational culture that is positive and motivating: celebration and acknowledgment are important components of a supportive organizational culture (Jalilianhasanpour, Asadollahi, & Yousem, 2021; Taheri, Motealleh, & Younesi, 2022; Williamson & Blackburn, 2023). This kind of intentional celebration is especially important when one considers the research about mastery experiences and their impact on individual and collective efficacy. Recognition and acknowledgment of achievement are key elements in mastery experiences. As I discussed, when a worker or team sees evidence that their efforts have made a positive difference, this is a boost to their efficacy beliefs. When this success is also recognized by superiors and celebrated within the workplace, the mastery experience is galvanized. For workers and teams in the organization, the combination of evidence of success with recognition by supervisors and the organization as a whole produces a powerful mastery experience that builds individual and collective efficacy beliefs.

Leaders and coaches who are working to build the collective efficacy of their teacher teams must understand and embrace the importance of carefully monitoring progress and providing teams with meaningful positive feedback. Most teacher teams need help recognizing that their efforts are making a difference, and a trusted coach is the perfect person to provide this input. Skilled efficacy builders use social persuasion techniques to help teams to see that their work is paying off. Many teacher teams are so focused on the end-of-year goals or the end-of-year state test that they do not take the time to review their progress and acknowledge incremental gains. For teacher teams, recognition of their efforts can be a powerful boost to their collective efficacy. Leaders and coaches who are working to build the collective efficacy of their teacher teams should consider how celebration provides a mastery experience and look for ways to integrate regular celebration into their organizational culture.

While the merits of celebration can be easy to see in theory, recognition and celebration are not always easy to implement—even when the leader is carefully monitoring progress. As I have worked with principals, supervisors, and leaders around the country, I have encountered a significant number who, when the idea of celebration is raised, grimace a bit and admit that they are not very good at leading the celebration part of their school culture. They say things like, "I know I should do more of that, but it just hasn't happened." When I probe to understand why the supervisor (most often the principal), has not facilitated regular celebration with their staff, the underlying mindset usually falls into one of the following categories.

- I'm afraid that my staff will think that I am playing favorites.
- We don't have time for silly celebrations in our staff meetings.
- What do I do about the teams that are not doing anything worth celebrating?
- I don't know how to organize celebrations like that. It's just not my thing.

Let's look at a few strategies that can help address these concerns and mindsets.

In *Learning by Doing*, DuFour and colleagues (2024) offer four keys for incorporating celebration into the culture of your school or district.

1. **Explicitly state the purpose of celebration:** DuFour and colleagues remind leaders to explain that the reason they are celebrating certain acts, achievements, or staff members is to reinforce the shared purpose, vision, collective

commitments, and goals of the organization (school/district). By celebrating these efforts, we drive and sustain our efforts to fulfill our fundamental purpose and become the school/district we hope to be.

2. **Make celebration everyone's responsibility:** The authors argue that the principal or supervisor should not be the "sole arbiter of who will be recognized," because this leads to the rest of the staff critiquing the choices. Instead, leaders must create processes and traditions that allow all staff members to recognize and appreciate each other.

3. **Establish a clear link between the recognition and the behavior or commitment you are attempting to encourage and reinforce:** DuFour and colleagues (2024) stress that it should be abundantly clear to all staff why an individual or team is being recognized or celebrated. The most effective way to do this is to tell a story that links the team's actions or behaviors to the shared mission, vision, commitments, or goals of the school.

4. **Create opportunities for many winners:** The authors warn against creating restrictions about how many teachers or teams to recognize or imposing arbitrary qualifications to be eligible for celebration. When many staff members and teams are celebrated by everyone, it provides a powerful boost to the organizational culture.

When coaches intentionally facilitate the celebration process with their teams, it does more than just make them feel good. As we saw in the What the Research Says section of this chapter (page 173), mastery experiences are most powerful when they are mentally processed and configured in memory. If a team implements practices that produce student results, but they spend no time reflecting on or celebrating that result, they will not get the full benefit of the mastery experience. This happens often when teachers are busy and driven to do the next task, and they do not take time to reflect and celebrate. I have worked with teachers who feel guilty if they stop for a moment to celebrate the work they have done. This is where a skilled coach, a dedicated efficacy builder, can intervene and help the team to pause and embrace the great work they have done. This will give the teacher team the genuine congratulations that they deserve, but, more importantly, it will cement the mastery experience and provide a substantial boost to the collective efficacy of the team.

Coaches can use the team celebration and reflection protocol in figure 7.2 to lead this process. While this type of protocol works well when reviewing end-of-year state test or midyear district benchmark scores, it is also appropriate when teams are reviewing midyear reading levels, the results of a mathematics unit test, or the culmination of a grade-level student writing assignment. A protocol like this helps focus teams on thinking deeply about what they have done and how it affected student learning.

1. Review student achievement data that has improved.

2. Give team members time to reflect on the following questions. Invite them to jot down their thoughts on Post-it notes.
 	
  a. When you review these results, how does it make you feel? What are some words you would use to describe how you feel?
 	
  b. When you review these results, what do you attribute them to? How were you, as a team, able to achieve these results? Try to be specific as possible in your reflections. What were the specific actions that members of your team took to achieve the results we are reviewing?

3. Initiate a sharing of team members' answers to the questions, beginning with the emotions felt at reviewing the results and then moving on to sharing thoughts about the actions that produced the results. Have team members post their thoughts on charts as they share them.
4. After all team members have had a chance to share, facilitate a discussion that helps them to see the connections between the data/results you reviewed and their specific actions. The goal of this part of the process is to help the teachers understand that it was their actions as a team that led to the results. Many teachers will be quick to give credit to their students. While acknowledging that students deserve mention for their hard work, help the teacher team to embrace the fact that the learning and growth did not happen in a vacuum, but is the result of the collaborative team's work to focus on student learning.

5. Lead a team discussion of the following questions.
 	
  a. How would you help another team to accomplish the same results?
 	
  b. What would you tell them? What would you emphasize? Which tools or strategies would you share with them?

Figure 7.2: TEAM CELEBRATION AND REFLECTION PROTOCOL.

Celebration is a key element in helping teacher teams build collective efficacy. Taking the time to acknowledge and embrace success in achieving goals (mastery experience) has a profound effect on a team's belief in themselves. Skilled efficacy builders will be careful not to skip over this critical piece.

Setting New Targets With Teacher Teams

When teams have achieved their goals and coaches have facilitated the appropriate and necessary celebration, it is then time to set new targets. Effective coaches will use the momentum and excitement of meeting targets to launch teams into setting new goals. First, coaches engage teams in reflecting on the targets they had set previously and discuss what new goals might look like based on where they've arrived in their work.

Coaches will often need to support teams as they think through how high to set their new goal. Teams that have been successful will feel the pull to set ambitious goals, but they are often nervous about setting a goal too high. They have just experienced how good it feels to set and achieve a goal, and they may be fearful of setting a goal and failing to attain it. Skilled coaches will help teams to recognize the power they have as a collaborative team. Coaches guide teams to see that they can have a profound influence on student learning through their instruction, support, and collaboration. Coaches should assess where teams are and help them to set true stretch goals that are also attainable. Coaches can use a protocol like the one in figure 7.3 to lead teams to review previous goals and set new targets.

---

1. Review previous student achievement goals.

   a. What were the goals we set at the beginning of the year?

   b. What level of growth did we need to achieve to reach our goals?

   c. What did we do to achieve those goals? (This is a brief restatement of the discussion that the team had in the Celebration and Reflection protocol on page 187.)

2. Turn attention to setting new goals.

   a. What are our students' current levels of performance?

      i. What do we know about how are students are learning?

      ii. What are their strengths?

      iii. What are the areas of need?

   b. Are specific students or groups of students underperforming?

   c. What is our strategy for supporting students who are not demonstrating proficiency yet?

   d. When we think about setting new learning targets, what makes sense as our next stretch goal? How much growth do we think we can accomplish by continuing to apply and refine the strategies that are already working?

   e. What do we see when we look at data student by student—by name and by need? How many students can we move from below proficient to proficient by a given date? How many students can we move from proficient to advanced?

3. Lead team members to propose draft goals. Discuss proposals. Facilitate the team discussion.

4. Based on the team discussion, focus the team on a draft goal. Work toward consensus agreement on the new goal.

5. Once the new goal has been agreed to, begin the process to establish or refine the team's action plan for achieving the goal.

Figure 7.3: PROTOCOL FOR REVIEWING GOALS AND SETTING NEW TARGETS.

Through using a protocol like the one in figure 7.3, coaches help teams believe in themselves and their ability to set and achieve goals. This is a critical piece of the efficacy research and the power of mastery experiences: When a dedicated team of teachers sets ambitious student learning goals and then works hard and achieves them, it gives them their first taste of collective efficacy (we worked hard, and together we made a difference in our students' learning). When that same team sets new goals and meets their targets a second time, it exponentially increases their collective efficacy. When a team reaches the point that they have set student learning goals and achieved them by working together five, ten, or fifty times, they develop an incredibly high sense of collective teacher efficacy that produces exceptional student learning results while also dramatically improving teacher morale, empowerment, and commitment. This is the goal of the CLEAR process for building collective teacher efficacy.

Follow-Through for Reviewing Results, Celebrating Growth, and Setting New Targets

After engaging teacher teams in reviewing results, celebrating growth, and setting new targets, effective coaches will follow through with teams to reinforce the master experiences and set the stage for new ones. Whether coaches are working with teams to review ongoing student results, celebrating growth on the team's SMART goal in reading, or setting new targets for the end-of-year benchmark because the midyear results were so terrific, coaches follow through and provide ongoing support. Efficacy-building coaches will help teams to focus on goals and results in every session. They will help teams to review their data so that they notice areas that need attention, but also recognize where there is growth that they can celebrate. And coaches will help teams to continue to set stretch goals so that they, and their students, can reach their highest potential.

Step 5 of the CLEAR process is a key in building the collective efficacy of teacher teams. Mastery experiences are critical to building the collective efficacy of teacher teams. In our exploration of step 5 of the CLEAR process, I have shared research, practical advice, and tools to conduct this work with teacher teams. In my experience as a coach, I have found that there are some unique challenges to implementing this work with today's teachers. To wrap up our discussion of step 5, I offer the following insights about teachers, teacher teams, and a few teacher quirks that may arise as you work to reinforce mastery experiences. These insights are important to keep in mind when you are working to build the collective efficacy of teacher teams, especially when you are trying to reinforce and maximize the mastery experiences they have earned.

Teachers Sometimes Need Help Recognizing and Celebrating Their Own Efforts

When teacher teams get focused on student learning, they become skilled at a variety of tasks, including organizing for instruction, using team meeting time efficiently, accurately assessing student growth, planning for interventions, and analyzing student work together. As teacher teams learn these skills, they get very good at focusing their time on these tasks and using every minute intentionally to help them reach their goals. Ironically, they are not usually adept at celebrating the gains that their efforts create. Many high-performing teams must be reminded to stop for a moment, notice the growth they have achieved, and take a moment to celebrate their success for students. Leaders and coaches are often in a great position to encourage, if not require, teams to celebrate.

Effective coaches will look for opportunities to direct their teams' attention to positive data both as a planned activity and as an in-the-moment coaching move. Let me explain. Coaches should be vigilant and thorough in identifying the data sources that are tied to teams' goals. If a team establishes a goal to increase reading proficiency as measured by a district benchmark assessment, coaches should learn as much as they can about the assessment, including when the assessment is taken and when the results are available. Then, coaches should communicate with teams when data are available and recommend that they spend part of a session reviewing the data. If the coach is able to review some of the data in advance, perhaps by obtaining it from school administration, the coach can review the scores and look for results to celebrate. The coach can then highlight the positive data in the session with the team and nudge the team to acknowledge and celebrate the results. In this case, the coach has some advance notice and can prepare to lead this review in a session with the team.

There will be other times that the data present themselves without warning, and a skilled coach will be ready to point out the positive results. Imagine a team has established goals in student writing, and they have been monitoring student progress in this area. The coach attends a session with the team. They have planned to review student writing samples, but the coach has not seen any of the student writing in advance. As the coach and the team are reviewing student writing, if the coach sees a student paper that demonstrates growth, the coach should call it out and draw the team's attention to it, ideally helping them to make a direct connection between the student writing, their team goal, and the strategies that they have been implementing. A coaching move like this encourages a team to notice growth and to take a moment to celebrate it when it happens. Skilled efficacy builders will always be looking for opportunities to provide teams with a mastery experience based on their work and students' learning.

Teachers' Conscientiousness Sometimes Robs Them of Deserved Celebration

An interesting phenomenon I have noticed as I have worked with teacher teams usually goes like this: I am sitting with a team at the end of a school year or the end of a coaching cycle, and we have just reviewed exciting data that shows, indisputably, that their students are learning, making progress, and reaching targets better than ever before. And while this should be a clear time to focus solely on the great work that they have done, I will notice one teacher looking a little sad. This is a sign that teacher conscience and teacher perfectionism are about to join the conversation. Almost invariably, that teacher will say something like, "I am really happy about the great results we got this year, and I am excited for our students, but it tears me up to think about the students we had last year, and three years ago, and five years ago. I wish we had been working this way when we had them as students." Other teachers will start to nod and soon everyone is feeling sad! I have learned to respond to this phenomenon by telling teachers that I appreciate their teacher's hearts, their compassion, their conscientiousness, but I insist that they can't beat themselves up about previous years. I assure teachers that they were doing the best they could with the knowledge, tools, and skills they had at the time, and the best thing to do is to concentrate on keeping their current efforts going. Leaders and coaches who are taking teacher teams through the CLEAR process should watch for these reactions, especially at a point where the team is celebrating improvements in student learning.

Coaches can head off teacher regret and perfectionism by anticipating these responses, especially when teams are reviewing positive data, and preparing comments, in advance, so that they are ready to address regret and perfectionism when they arise. By taking these steps, coaches can protect a team's mastery experience and help ensure that they get a collective efficacy boost from their positive results.

Teachers Sometimes Forget to Reflect on What They Did Right to Achieve Student Gains

When hard-working teacher teams are in the midst of implementing new practices and seeing results from their efforts, they sometimes find it hard to stop and take a moment to reflect on *how* they are getting results. They are so focused on the ongoing work to ensure high levels of learning for their students that they do not devote time to consider how this is happening. Coaches who are working to build the collective efficacy of their teacher teams should intervene and encourage teams to take some time to reflect on their actions and results and in doing so accomplish three important goals. First, it helps the team to recognize their success and the fact that it was their efforts that produced the results. This helps teams to build their collective efficacy by providing them with a powerful mastery experience. When teams take the time to note the connection between their concrete efforts and positive results in student learning and team processes, it cements their collective belief in themselves. It makes them take a moment to say "We did this! This wouldn't have happened without us and what we did!" This is the essence of collective teacher efficacy. Second, when teacher teams take the time to reflect on their practice and make note of it, they are more likely to repeat that practice and the accompanying success in the future. Busy teams that do not take the time to reflect and document their successful practices will sometimes find themselves in the next school year trying to remember what they did to achieve a high level of student success. Third, when successful teams take a moment to reflect on their successful practices, it helps them prepare to share their effective strategies with other teams. This, then, becomes an opportunity for one team's mastery experience to inform and help another team.

Helping teams to stop and reflect on what they did, collectively, to achieve their results is key to maximizing the benefit of the mastery experience. The research shows (Bandura, 1997) that people get a bigger boost in their efficacy beliefs when they cognitively process and reflect on their success with a task. When a team of teachers is coached to stop and think about how they were able to achieve gains in learning, it galvanizes the mastery experience for them as educators.

Team Update

On the first day of preservice, the teachers at all three schools in the Mountaintop School District are feeling positive and excited about the school year. While they wouldn't have minded another week or two of summer break, they are looking forward to building on the successes they had last year. It has been four years since the principals and teacher leaders at each school implemented the CLEAR process in the hopes of building the collective efficacy of teacher teams. There is abundant evidence that this effort has paid off for teachers and for students.

Student achievement has steadily grown over the last four years. The data from state tests show that Mountaintop students have demonstrated remarkable growth and now score among the top districts in the state. At the school level, teachers and teams at the elementary, middle, and high school have seen their students' proficiency in all content areas, especially literacy and mathematics, blossom over the past four school years. With each year's increases, teachers and teams became more and more convinced that it was their efforts that were responsible for the students' growth. With that realization, their collective teacher efficacy increased.

In addition, teacher morale and empowerment have increased across the district. Teachers are excited about the growth in student learning, and they are eager to make it happen again. There have been some rough spots along the way, but the teams have persevered and gotten the work done. For example, the scores for students who receive special education services dipped unexpectedly from year 2 to year 3. Teachers and teams were disappointed and frustrated. But they knew that they could figure it out together. They had done this for so many other learning challenges and they had a deep belief that they could address any achievement issue if they worked together and were consistent in practice. They studied the problem, identified research-based strategies, set new goals, and got to work. They talked through the questions and concerns they had. They looked for examples and connected with other schools that had demonstrated success with students receiving special education. They encouraged each other as they tried new approaches and monitored data. Then, they celebrated as they saw that certain strategies were working and doubled down on successful techniques. The teachers and teams relied on each other, and through their collaborative work, they were able to achieve dramatic increases in student learning.

The school principals and teacher leaders have relied on the research-based steps of the CLEAR process as they have worked each year to build the collective efficacy of their teacher teams. They have started each year with an in-depth study of student data and then established a clear why, what, and how. They have established a routine where teachers and teams know that they will have opportunities to share and discuss their stress about the why, what, and how. Leaders and coaches have developed extensive resource banks full of proven tools and strategies and established processes for teams to visit other schools and learn from each other. They have refined their coaching techniques to guide teams, provide effective feedback, and encourage them through the rough spots. Finally, they have established traditions for celebrating excellent work and student progress, while also pushing teams to set new goals. Their consistent efforts to address affective states, provide vicarious experiences, coach through social persuasion, and celebrate mastery experiences, have increased the level of collective efficacy on the staff each year.

As the principals and teacher leaders planned for implementation of the CLEAR process in year 4, they realized that most of the teams were beginning to implement the process for themselves. The teams had reached a level of collective efficacy where they did not need as much administrator/coach direction or support to do the necessary work. The teams embraced the why, what, and how each year and personalized it for their themselves and their students. They set ambitious goals and used every team meeting to focus their pursuit of those goals. They were very intentional about how they used instructional time and collaborative sessions. When they felt stressed, they took a moment to talk through it and came up with strategies to help them keep from getting overwhelmed. When they got stuck, they looked for examples and models and reached out to other teams and schools. They encouraged each other through the rough spots, but also held each other accountable for the work they were doing together. They had difficult conversations when necessary to make sure that they were all implementing the plan and ensuring success for their students. Teams regularly reviewed data and student work. They celebrated growth and identified areas of need. Then, they worked as a cohesive unit to address the areas of need so that the results would be better the next time they looked at data. With each round of this process, they grew in their collective efficacy.

Now, as preservice is about to start, the principals, teacher leaders, coaches, and teacher teams of Mountaintop district know that there will be challenges in the school year ahead. But they are approaching the school year with a high sense of collective efficacy and the belief that they can address any challenge if they continue to work together. It is going to be a great year.

CLEAR Thoughts and Next Steps

The final step of the CLEAR process for building the collective efficacy of teams, review progress, celebrate growth, and set new targets, is linked to mastery experiences, the most powerful influence on efficacy beliefs. And though the daily work of teacher teams should provide multiple opportunities for coaches to connect teachers to mastery experiences (think of the number of times that individual students finally demonstrate understanding of a concept), practical experience shows that it can be challenging to engage teachers in careful review of progress, celebrating gains, and setting new goals. As we have seen, teachers are extremely busy; they are always running off to the next task, they do not always take the time to reflect, they can be resistant to celebrating their own success, and they often have a heavy streak of perfectionism. All these factors can reduce the possibility that teacher teams have the mastery experiences that they should. A skilled coach, equipped with the CLEAR process and an understanding of mastery experiences and collective efficacy, can serve as a driver and facilitator of these experiences. And when that happens, we have teachers who know their hard work is paying off for students, have evidence that it is happening, have reflected on their effective strategies, have shared their ideas with other teachers, and have the energy and joy that comes from mastery experiences so that they can go back to school and do it again the next day. And when teacher teams have these mastery experiences repeatedly, they will reach a level of collective teacher efficacy that is associated with high levels of student learning, increased teacher morale, higher teacher retention, and improvements in school climate.

Let's review critical takeaways.

- The most powerful source of self-efficacy and collective efficacy beliefs is mastery experience. When a person or a group is successful with a task, that experience provides a powerful boost to efficacy beliefs.

- The most powerful mastery experience for teacher teams is when they see indisputable evidence that their collective efforts have resulted in increased student learning. It is also a powerful mastery experience for a teacher team when they can see that their work as a team—team products, processes they have mastered, the efficiency of their team meetings, their focus on student learning—has grown and deepened.

- Leaders and coaches who are working to build the collective efficacy of their teacher teams must be very intentional about how they support, facilitate, celebrate, and reinforce mastery experiences for their teams.

- Mastery experiences are more powerful and effective when individuals and groups take the time to cognitively process, reflect, and remember the experience. Coaches can play a critical role in making sure that teacher teams take the time to reflect so that they get the full benefit of the mastery experiences they have earned.

Let's reflect on the content from this chapter.

1. When you think about your time as a leader or coach, are there mastery experiences that come to mind? What are your most powerful memories of being successful in your work as a leader or coach? What made that experience so powerful?

2. When coaches work with a teacher or team, it is natural to want them to be successful. How have you strategically planned for teams to experience growth and success? What could you do differently to be intentional about providing teams with mastery experiences?

3. How can you help your teams to get the most out of their mastery experiences? Think of a team that you have worked with that has achieved their goals. How could you have enhanced their mastery experience by helping them reflect on their efforts?

Let's plan an action step.

The next time that you work with a team, commit yourself to identifying some point of growth or improvement that the team has achieved. Focus the team's attention on it and point out that they should celebrate this growth. Ask them to take a moment to stop and think about what they did together to achieve that growth.

_____

_____

_____

_____

_____

_____

_____

_____

_____

_____

CHAPTER EIGHT

How to Put It All Together

I N CHAPTERS 3-7, I presented the five steps of the CLEAR process to build the collective efficacy of teacher teams. To recap, the research-based steps of the CLEAR process are the following.

1. **Clarify the why, the what, and the how:** We provide a solid foundation for building collective efficacy by clarifying why we are taking on a task, what the task involves, and how we will measure success. This step is supported by research that shows an important link between building collective efficacy and having clarity about purpose, strategy, and goals.

2. **Listen to teachers' fears, anxieties, questions, and concerns:** We build collective efficacy by giving teachers space to share their concerns, thereby building trust and creating a psychologically safe environment. This step is supported by the research on affective states and their influence on efficacy beliefs.

3. **Explore examples, models, best practices, and proven processes:** We build collective efficacy by providing teams with high-quality models and evidence that the work can be done. This step is supported by the research on vicarious experiences and their influence on collective efficacy.

4. **Activate new learning through coaching, practice, and implementation:** We build collective efficacy through high-quality coaching, feedback, and encouragement. This step is supported by the research on social persuasion.

5. **Review progress, celebrate growth, and set new targets:** We build collective efficacy through helping teams to acknowledge their growth, celebrate their success, and strive for additional gains. This step is supported by the research on mastery experiences and their powerful influence on efficacy beliefs.

Within each chapter, I have unfolded the research that supports each step of the process because I want leaders and coaches who read this book to understand that the CLEAR process I have presented has a strong research base. I provided scenarios that describe what this work looks like in today's schools because a process to build the collective efficacy of teacher teams is only useful if it can be implemented in the schools we have. I have described and explained the practical steps that principals, teacher leaders, and coaches can take to build up the collective efficacy beliefs of teacher teams because I know educators of all types have their hands full and a practical process is a valuable tool. I have also tried to illustrate what happens in schools when leaders and coaches do not work strategically to support the collective efficacy of teachers.

In this chapter, we put it all together.

What does it look like when the entire five-step CLEAR process is implemented in a variety of settings? I provide three detailed scenarios that follow coaches and leaders in different situations with a variety of factors in play as they lead a team through the CLEAR process. The key variables that are reflected in the scenarios are the role or position of the coach, the current status of the team, the task to be implemented, school and team characteristics, and where the school is on the PLC journey. Here is an overview of our three CLEAR process stories.

1. An experienced instructional coach in a midsize middle school is working with a literacy team to identify essential standards in reading and language arts and develop learning targets. The school as a whole is at the very beginning of their development as a PLC, and the coach is supporting the team as they try to complete this critical task.

2. A grade-level team leader in an elementary school is working with his team of fourth-grade teachers to develop and use CFAs in mathematics. The school has done some PLC work and using CFAs is the next step of implementation.

3. The principal of a large high school is working with multiple teams to develop and implement systematic interventions and extensions for students in reading and mathematics. The school is several years into the PLC journey, and there are a lot of critical PLC practices in place. The principal is trying to move the school to the next level by refining their systems for responding when students don't learn.

It is my hope that most readers will be able to see themselves in one or more of these scenarios. I also hope that these detailed narratives will help all readers to understand that the CLEAR process for building the collective efficacy of teacher teams in a PLC can be implemented by individuals in various roles who are working with many different variables.

CLEAR Scenario 1—Ms. Gonzalez, Middle School Mathematics Teams, and Essential Standards

Emilia Gonzalez is an instructional coach at Carter Middle School (CMS), a midsize school that serves 1,100 students in grades 6–8. She works with teachers and departments to implement strategies that improve student learning in reading and language arts. Ms. Gonzalez has read a lot about the PLC process, and she is interested in implementing strategies that could build teacher capacity and increase student learning. Her school is at the very beginning of the PLC journey. They have not implemented many PLC strategies, but they are starting to talk about how working as PLC might benefit the students at CMS. In particular, they have started to explore answering PLC critical question 1: What do students need to know and be able to do? The administrative team is encouraging all teams to look at their curriculum documents and discuss what is most important for students to learn in each grade level and course. The principal has not presented a very clear rationale, besides stating that it is "something that PLCs do." It is also not clear yet exactly what teams are expected to do or how this new effort will be evaluated. Still, Ms. Gonzalez sees value in the effort, and she wants to help all her teams be successful. In addition, she really wants to build the collective efficacy level of her teams. She decides to use the CLEAR process to implement the initiative.

Step 1

Ms. Gonzalez starts by preparing how she will clarify the why, the what, and the how.

She thinks about the why—why should the teams invest time in reviewing curriculum and identifying essential standards? The easy answer is "because the principal said to, and every other team is doing it" but this seems like an unsatisfactory and less-than-inspiring why. Thanks to her reading, Ms. Gonzalez knows that the research indicates that focusing on essential standards helps teachers to teach and students to learn the most critical skills. She plans to share that information with her teams. But Ms. Gonzalez knows that the most powerful why will also be a compelling student achievement need.

She refers to the CLEAR process guidelines for step 1 and begins by asking questions about student performance in reading and language arts and writes them down. How are our students doing compared to district and state targets? Are there areas that are strengths or weaknesses for our students? What do the trends look like from grade 6 to grade 7 and grade 7 to grade 8? Ms. Gonzalez accumulates data from the district website and slides that had been shared with the school leadership team. Ms. Gonzalez analyzes the data and notes the key points in the students' reading scores. She sees there are some areas of relative strength (vocabulary) but serious needs in identifying main idea and supporting details and citing evidence from the text.

Next, Ms. Gonzalez brainstorms ideas about how to engage teams in looking at the data. She doesn't just want to tell them what she found in her analysis. She wants them to explore the data themselves to see what they notice. She develops a plan to use in her next meetings with teams. When she meets with them, she leads an activity that engages them in looking at user-friendly reports and summaries that she has prepared. She asks them to share what they "notice" and "wonder" about the data they see. This leads to a great discussion about what the teams see in the student scores. Ms. Gonzalez and the teams build a shared understanding of how their students are doing on the state test in reading and language arts.

Next, Ms. Gonzalez helps the team to identify areas for attention. Which skills should we give some extra attention to in hopes of improving student performance? She reminds them that this is not just about the state test, but about preparing their students to be successful in high school and beyond. The teams confirm that students need extra work and instruction in identifying the main idea and supporting details and citing evidence from the text. Ms. Gonzalez states that clearly and confirms it with an email to the teams. She also promises to help them with this work in their sessions this school year. Ms. Gonzalez also helps the teams to see that the school focuses on identifying essential standards fits perfectly with their findings. If we identify critical skills, such as identifying main idea and supporting details and citing evidence, and focus on them as collaborative teams, it is likely to improve our students' performance.

In her next session with teams, Ms. Gonzalez helps her teams to understand the what. What do we have to do to identify essential standards? To prepare for this meeting, she asks herself some questions about this work. What are the best tools or processes for this work? She accumulates information, tools, and resources from institutes she has attended. She looks them over and decides on a tool to use in starting the work with her teams.

She brainstorms a plan for engaging her teams. She will introduce the REAL (Readiness, Endurance, Assessment, and Leverage) criteria for identifying essential standards. This engages teachers in reviewing curriculum standards and determining: (1) Does this standard promote *readiness* for another grade level? (2) Does this standard represent a skill that has *endurance*, meaning that it will be used far beyond the current grade level? (3) Is this skill *assessed*—meaning is it a skill that is important enough to be included on high-stakes assessments? and (4) Does this standard or skill provide *leverage* across other subjects? She leads the activity with her teams, building shared knowledge about all the standards and their relative importance. The sessions go well with most groups. They are able to develop a draft list of four to five essential standards per semester that they will focus on. The seventh-grade team struggles a bit. They are able to develop a draft list, but there seems to be an extra level of stress with the grade 7 group.

In the next session with her teams, Ms. Gonzalez plans to raise the question, "How will we know if this is working?" The school has not yet established clear schoolwide goals for student performance in reading, but Ms. Gonzalez really wants her teams to have a way to monitor progress, to see growth, and to celebrate success.

Ms. Gonzalez starts by considering some questions about the current data and possible goals. She reviews the data she accumulated and the teams' data findings. She analyzes the information and arrives at some possible draft goals for her teams. She brainstorms ideas about engaging her clients in the goal-setting process. She plans an activity to have them think through possible ranges for team goals: If our students are currently performing at this level (55 percent meeting the standard on the state test), and we are working together to implement strategies to make a difference in this result, what is a reasonable goal for our students this year? What makes sense as a midyear, one-semester goal? Ms. Gonzalez works with the teams during their team meeting time and builds shared knowledge about setting clear goals. She walks teams through the SMART goal acronym and helps teams to understand what a clear goal might look like. Ms. Gonzalez supports teams as they create a draft SMART goal for reading for the current school year. Now, all the teams know *why* they are trying something new (to make a difference in students' futures by helping them become better readers), *what* the change involves (being strategic about the most essential reading skills, giving them extra attention, and ensuring all students learn them), and *how* we will measure support (student performance in reading).

Step 2

In her next session with teams, Ms. Gonzalez decides to create a space for listening to teachers share their questions, concerns, and, yes, even fears and anxieties, about this new focus on essential standards. She asks teachers to participate in a four-square activity where teachers use Post-it notes to express:

- What is most exciting about this change (identifying and focusing on specific essential standards or team focus)?

- What are your biggest hopes for what this change could accomplish?

- What is most scary about this change?

- What questions do you still have about this effort?

She sees that teachers are enthusiastic, for the most part, about being able to focus on fewer standards. She also notes that they have some questions about how students will learn the skills that they do not identify as "essential."

As Ms. Gonzalez is meeting with the seventh-grade team, one teacher, Mrs. Simms, a twenty-five-year veteran who has been at CMS for over twenty years, begins to tremble. She raises her voice and shouts "What about these other skills? When will students learn them? Why do I have to change my units? They are great units and I do not want to change them!" With that, she storms out of the meeting. Ms. Gonzalez followed up with Mrs. Simms later in the day. The veteran teacher shared how the new work on essential standards was causing her a tremendous amount of stress. Ms. Gonzalez listened and gave Mrs. Simms the space to share her feelings. As she listened, Ms. Gonzalez understood that Mrs. Simms was frightened by the prospect of not teaching the same way she had for years. She was threatened by the idea that she would have to modify her units and focus on certain essential standards to match the rest of the team. Ms. Gonzalez said that she understood that this was a change, and that change could be scary. She offered to work with Mrs. Simms so that she would feel more comfortable with the new approach. Mrs. Simms said that she appreciated Ms. Gonzalez's understanding.

Step 3

Next, Ms. Gonzalez builds the collective efficacy of her teams by exploring examples, models, best practices, and proven processes. As the teams began to work on identifying essential standards and developing their lists, Ms. Gonzalez arrived at a team meeting with some examples to share. She had connected with another middle school coach at a school where they had done this work the previous year. When the teams saw examples of how other middle school teams had identified and organized their essential standards, it helped them to believe that they could be successful too. Even Mrs. Simms appreciated seeing the models, and she chimed in with some ideas about how to apply what they saw in the other teams' examples to work with their own students.

Step 4

Next, Ms. Gonzalez activated new learning through coaching, practice, and implementation. After the teams had identified their essential standards, they started to plan their long-term calendar and units of instruction to ensure that all students would learn the essentials. At this point, some of the teams struggled with how to fit everything in. Ms. Gonzalez worked shoulder-to-shoulder with them, providing feedback, asking questions, and encouraging their work. In time, they were able to develop a draft plan that they thought would work. Ms. Gonzalez continued to check in with teams to make sure things were going well. In particular, she touched base with Mrs. Simms to reiterate her willingness to help.

Step 5

Next, Ms. Gonzalez led her teams to review progress, celebrate growth, and set new targets. By the midpoint of the school year, the teams were starting to see evidence that their new approach was working. Students were demonstrating a higher level of proficiency on identifying the main idea and supporting details. They were even citing evidence from the text without being reminded. In her meetings with the teams, Ms. Gonzalez guided them to reflect on why they thought this was happening. The teams talked about how they had focused more on these skills. They were very intentional when they taught them, and they took time in team meetings to review student work and share ideas with each other. The teams started to realize that when they worked together, they were more effective in meeting the needs of their students. Ms. Gonzalez led them to think about this new success as they planned new goals to pursue.

CLEAR Scenario 2—Mr. Williams, the Fourth-Grade Team, and Common Assessments

Malcolm Williams is a fourth-grade teacher at Jefferson Elementary School, a rural elementary school that serves 450 students. Mr. Williams has been teaching for eight years. For the last two years, he has served as the fourth-grade team leader. He also serves on the school's guiding coalition (GC). Jefferson's principal initiated the guiding coalition two years ago as the school moved into a new phase of implementing the PLC process. Before the establishment of the GC, teams at Jefferson had explored PLC ideas like collaborating, but they had not yet organized and focused the effort. Over the last two years, the GC has led a staff-wide process to relaunch the school's mission statement, vision statement, collective commitments, and shared goals. In addition, the GC has established clear expectations about what collaborative teams do in a PLC and has provided ongoing professional development to support team implementation of team norms, SMART goals, essential standards, clear expectations for proficiency, and the use of common assessments. There has been steady, if slow, progress in these areas, and most teams are implementing practices and learning as they go.

The fourth-grade team has not come as far as some of the other teams. There are several possible reasons for this. For several years, the teachers in fourth and fifth grade were departmentalized—one teacher taught reading and social studies, and the other teacher had responsibility for teaching mathematics and science. This was somewhat more convenient for teachers—they could concentrate on preparing for fewer subjects—but it did not support teacher-to-teacher collaboration at the grade level. As the school embraced the importance of collaborative teams, they decided to stop departmentalizing and instead have all teachers at the grade level teach both reading and mathematics. Thus, all teachers would have collaborative partners for the subjects they taught, which lends itself to more meaningful collaboration, which is associated with higher levels of student learning.

Because of this change, several teachers were now teaching content that they either had not taught before or had last taught years ago. They had a steep learning curve, and it has caused some stress. On the fourth-grade team, this was exacerbated by the fact that the team had two novice teachers. In Mr. Williams' first year as the team leader, he tried to lead implementation of PLC processes, but he spent a lot of time dealing with teammates' stress and frustration about the change. As a result, they did not make as much progress as some other teams. As the new school year is starting, Mr. Williams is planning a "restart" by using the CLEAR process. He knows his teammates are good teachers and good people and they just need support and a new mindset to do this work together. Mr. Williams plans to focus his process on developing and using CFAs.

Step 1

Mr. Williams begins by working with his team to clarify the why, the what, and the how. He takes what has been discussed and established for the whole school and helps his team to apply it to their work with their fourth graders. In their initial planning session, Mr. Williams and his team address some common questions, including:

- *Why are we doing this?* We are doing this because our student data show that over 40 percent of our students are not meeting standard on the state test in mathematics. We must respond to this data and adjust our practice so that more students will be prepared to be successful in mathematics in grade 4, grade 5, middle school, high school, and beyond.

- *What does it mean to use CFAs? What are we expected to do?* We are expected to identify essential standards in mathematics, plan instructional units to support student learning of these essentials, and use common assessments to monitor student progress. We are expected to develop high-quality efficient and rigorous assessments that give us insight into how students are learning and what they are struggling with. We are expected to review common assessment data and analyze student learning, discussing which instructional strategies are working. This is our opportunity to learn from each other so that our students can learn at higher levels.

- *How will we know if this working? How will we monitor progress?* We will use common formative and summative assessments in our units, and we will monitor student proficiency in critical mathematics standards throughout the school year. Our goal is to increase the percentage of grade 4 students meeting the proficiency target on the state test in mathematics from 54 percent in 2024 to 75 percent in 2025. This team goals aligns with our school goal to have at least 75 percent of all students at Jefferson to score proficient on the state test.

Mr. Williams leads team discussions and makes sure that everyone on his team of four teachers has a clear understanding of the why, what, and how.

Step 2

Next, Mr. Williams listens to teachers' fears, anxieties, questions, and concerns. He knows that currently his team is in the Insecure Resisters quadrant of the step 2 matrix tool (figure 4.8, page 109). He listens patiently and lets his teammates vent their frustration with having to teach new content ("I liked it better when we departmentalized."), their concern about the amount of work involved ("Learning new content and develop assessments is too much, and it takes so much time!"), and their lack of confidence about the assessment piece ("I was never trained to develop assessments."). As team leader, he has limited power over resources, professional development, or assignment of staff, but he can support his team within their work together, and he promises to help each member of the team with what they need.

Step 3

Next, Mr. Williams engages his team in exploring examples, models, best practices, and proven processes. He does his own research online and finds some examples of how elementary teachers have developed common assessments. He shares those with his team. This proves to be very helpful, because several of the teammates had a preconceived notion that CFAs needed to be big, complex tests and that teams needed to do extensive research to develop each assessment item. When Mr. Williams showed his team examples of efficient assessments that provided a lot of useful information, but only required students to answer five questions, their stress about CFAs diminished. They saw how a well-designed CFA could be given as an exit ticket, and they feel more capable of completing this task. He reaches out to the fifth-grade team leader, who is also a GC member, and asks about their work on common assessments. Mr. Williams and the fifth-grade teacher organize a joint team session where the fourth- and fifth-grade teams work together to examine essential standards and compare ideas about how to assess student learning. Since the fifth-grade team is a little more advanced in this work, it is a powerful learning experience for the fourth-grade team.

Step 4

Next, Mr. Williams works to build the collective efficacy of his team by activating new learning through coaching, practice, and implementation. He continues to do his own research and brings in information and tools to help his team do their work. They appreciate his expertise and efforts to help them. The team members work through creating their own CFAs, and Mr. Williams encourages them to persevere through the tough parts of the process. He notices that the stress level is rising again with several team members. He hits the pause button to try to understand what is happening and determine how he can respond. He leads a team chat, and it becomes clear that two teammates are terrified that they would not be able to figure this out, and it would cost them their jobs. They are struggling with learning new content, and they don't feel confident planning and teaching those lessons—and adding the complexity of developing and analyzing assessments on top of that is too much. They are feeling overwhelmed and are ready to give up. Mr. Williams gives some space for his teammates to share their concerns. He then responds to each of the worries they express and tries to help them understand that the whole team will do this work together—they will all learn at the same time. They will make mistakes and use those experiences to learn more. He assures them that the principal and the GC know that this is new work for the team and understand that it will take some time for team members to learn what to do. They just need to keep trying, keep learning, and keep moving forward. The two team members recognize that they have to keep trying—the goal is to help their students. This resolution helps the team to move on, and they start to regularly use CFAs and common unit assessments with their mathematics units.

Step 5

Next, Mr. Williams builds the collective efficacy of his team by reviewing progress, celebrating growth, and setting new targets. It has taken some time, but now it is February, and Mr. Williams' team members are really hitting their stride in their use of CFAs. It is no longer a discussion about whether or not they will develop CFAs when they plan a unit. They jump right into discussing what needs to be assessed, what the proficiency target looks like, and how they can construct the assessment items to get the best information about how their students are learning. The grade 4 team has also gotten very skilled at reviewing the CFA data together. Now, without fail, they meet within two days of giving an assessment to review the results, analyze student work, and discuss instructional strategies.

During this February meeting, Mr. Williams leads his team to reflect on how far they have come. He shows them the first CFA they created in September, and they grimace and groan. "Wow, we tried, but that is not a very good assessment." Mr. Williams then has them review their most recent assessment and leads them to acknowledge how their work on assessments has dramatically improved, not only in terms of design of assessment items but also their use of assessment data. He continues this reflection by having the team look at the latest data, which show that more and more students are demonstrating mastery of essential standards like multiplication and problem solving. Just then, the principal joins the meeting. She acknowledges how hard the team has worked and thanks them for the work they have done and their commitment to students.

CLEAR Scenario 3—Dr. Harris, Adams High School, and Systematic Interventions

Dr. Alicia Harris is the principal of a large suburban high school, Adams High School (AHS). She has been working for several years to implement PLC processes, strategies, structures, and culture in her building, and this work has produced visible results. All the teachers at AHS work in collaborative teams. Even the singletons on the staff, teachers who are the only person to teach their particular courses, meet as a team and collaborate around common skills and outcomes. The master schedule provides time for all teams to meet twice a week to complete the critical tasks of collaborative teams in a PLC. All of the teams have established norms, and they use them to be effective and efficient in their team meeting times. All teams have established team SMART goals that are aligned with the school and district goals. All departments have worked collaboratively to identify the essential standards and learning targets for each subject area. Every team works to implement the teaching-assessing cycle. They plan units in advance, develop a common summative assessment (unit test), agree on proficiency targets for students, decide on the pacing of instruction, and agree on the timing for CFAs. When they implement a unit, they administer the CFAs and then meet as a team to review student learning. They use these collaborative reviews as an opportunity to discuss instructional strategies and learn from each other. They also use the data to identify students who are struggling as well as students who are ready for extension or enrichment on the essential skills. These efforts have resulted in gains in student achievement, and teams are beginning to see the evidence that their work is positively affecting student learning.

While Dr. Harris and the staff at AHS are clearly working at a high level in their implementation of PLC practices, they are not satisfied with their student learning results. Despite their efforts to date, they still have a significant percentage of students who are not meeting grade-level and course targets. Every year, the school has 10 to 15 percent of students who do not demonstrate proficiency in their coursework. This is reflected in the number of students who fail to earn course credit in critical classes. In addition, these same students do not perform well on district benchmark assessments, state tests, and key data points like advanced placement tests. For several years, Dr. Harris and the guiding coalition of AHS have worked to address this need. They have identified the students who are having difficulty and have worked to provide them with supports to help them be successful. The school counselor has recruited teachers to serve as mentors to check in with students on a weekly basis. The school has provided after-school study halls and tutoring to provide additional assistance.

Despite these efforts, the student learning results have not improved for this group of students. Dr. Harris and the guiding coalition have read the research on effective implementation of response to intervention (RTI) and multitiered systems of support (MTSS). They even sent members of the GC to a conference on best practices in RTI. They know that effective intervention needs to be timely, specific, mandatory, and provided during the student day, but their master schedule does not allow for interventions to be provided during the school day. To provide effective interventions during the student day would require a full reworking of the master schedule—a challenge that Dr. Harris and the guiding coalition have been avoiding. They kept hoping that their other intervention efforts would have an effect. Dr. Harris has come to realize that this change, though difficult, is necessary. She works with the GC to develop a new master schedule and strategies for providing students with systematic interventions during the student day. Now, Dr. Harris and the GC of AHS must work with staff to implement this new strategy. They decide to align their plan with the research on collective teacher efficacy. They decide to use the CLEAR process for building the collective efficacy of teacher teams in a PLC.

Step 1

Dr. Harris and her GC are clear on the why: the school's current way of doing things is not meeting the needs of all students. AHS is not accomplishing their fundamental purpose of ensuring that all students learn at high levels. As long as 10 to 15 percent of students are failing to work at grade-level targets, the work of Dr. Harris and her staff is not done. The leadership of AHS is also clear now on the what. They must implement Tier 2 interventions during the student day. They must follow the research that says that effective student interventions are timely, specific, mandatory, targeted, fluid, flexible, and delivered by trained staff. They develop two draft schedules that provide a thirty-five-minute block four days per week for students to receive Tier 2 supports. They create this block by reducing the other periods by four or five minutes. Dr. Harris and the GC are also clear on the how. They develop draft school goals for student performance in reading and mathematics and map out how they will monitor progress as students receive interventions.

Dr. Harris and the GC plan how to engage all staff in review of student data, research about interventions, and building shared knowledge about systematic Tier 2 supports. They carry out staff meetings that help all staff to understand the critical student need, learn about the intervention practices that have been proven to increase student learning, and the schoolwide goals and monitoring systems that will help them to measure success. They give all staff opportunities to ask questions about the draft schedules and conduct sessions with each department to explain the two drafts and how it would affect each team. They invite feedback on the two options and present the findings to a full staff meeting.

Step 2

Next, Dr. Harris and the GC listen to teachers' fears, anxieties, questions, and concerns. They started their process by developing a Google Doc survey to distribute to all staff. They made it clear that the responses would not be connected back to staff members and assured the staff that the results would be shared, discussed, and acted upon. When Dr. Harris and the GC reviewed the results, they found that the biggest stressors for staff were (1) concern that they would be losing time from their class periods in order to create the intervention block in the master schedule; (2) concern about the extra preparation they would have to do to provide effective interventions; (3) belief that they had not received enough training to be able to provide effective interventions; and (4) concern among some teachers that their students might not get the help they needed because some staff members were perceived as being unqualified to provide interventions. Dr. Harris and the GC shared the results at a staff meeting and addressed each concern. They explained professional development and resources that all teachers would receive to help them maximize the instructional time they had, to support planning for interventions, and to provide Tier 2 supports that would help students to make progress. Dr. Harris addressed the concern about staff members' qualifications—which was a trust issue—by encouraging all staff to work together. She described how leadership would be committed to regular monitoring, effective communication, and support for all staff. The great majority of staff responded well to these assurances. However, one of Dr. Harris's assistant principals told her that the mathematics department was still upset about the plan for interventions. Dr. Harris met with the team to discuss their concerns. It was clear that the team was in the Confident Resisters quadrant of the step 2 matrix tool (figure 4.8, page 109). The team felt that the changes were unnecessary because their students were doing fine. They felt it was an unnecessary imposition on them as mathematics teachers, because it was obvious that the intervention block was being implemented to address student performance in reading. Dr. Harris listened patiently to the team's concerns. Then, she responded by getting the mathematics team to agree that any high school that called itself a PLC should do whatever it could to make sure that students who graduate are at least functional readers—and that even if that effort caused some discomfort or change, it was worth it in the end. Dr. Harris also shared data that showed that while the reading results were definitely a bigger concern, student performance in mathematics had dipped in the last two years. She stated that the school also had a responsibility to make sure that students were performing at a high level in mathematics. She asked them to try to see the possibilities of how their classroom instruction, when combined with systematic intervention supports could help struggling students to be successful. By the end of the meeting, the mathematics department felt that their concerns had been heard, and they understood that they needed to support this effort to increase student learning.

Step 3

Next, Dr. Harris and the AHS GC built the collective efficacy of their teacher teams by exploring examples, models, best practices, and proven processes. Dr. Harris explored the PLC model schools on the www.allthingsplc.info website, looking for high schools similar to AHS. She found a school in a neighboring state, less than a two-hour drive away, that was similar in size with comparable demographics. Most importantly, their PLC story on AllThingsPLC detailed how they had designed and implemented a system for student interventions. Once they had put this system into place, they saw dramatic gains in student achievement and went on to become a model PLC school. Dr. Harris contacted the principal of the model school and asked for guidance. The two principals decided they would arrange a time for a team from AHS to visit the model school and see their interventions in action. Dr. Harris worked with the GC to identify a team of eight people to visit the school, making sure to include a representative from the mathematics department. The AHS team gathered early at school one day and made the drive to the model school. They got to see the intervention block in practice, and they were amazed by how engaged students were and how enthusiastic teachers were about their system. The team from AHS stayed for lunch and had an opportunity to talk to a team of representatives at the model school about the system they had put in place and the steps they took along the way. The whole drive home, the AHS teachers talked about ideas to refine their system. The following week, the teachers who had visited the model school presented their findings and observations to the full staff. Their ideas were incorporated into the system at AHS, and everyone saw that the adjustments were positive and productive.

Step 4

As the new Tier 2 block is implemented at the beginning of the school year, Dr. Harris and members of the GC work to provide ongoing coaching and support to all staff who are implementing the new system. They develop plans to help each department with executing their piece of the process and encourage teams and teachers when there is a problem or miscommunication. They help teams to recognize the incremental growth they are achieving and provide honest and constructive feedback to help with the overall implementation.

Step 5

Finally, Dr. Harris and the GC build collective efficacy by reviewing progress, celebrating growth, and setting new targets. At the last staff meeting before spring break, Dr. Harris and members of the GC lead a presentation recognizing and celebrating the work that all teams and teachers have done to implement the Tier 2 block and systematic interventions for students at AHS. They share data that show the progress that students have made. They share celebrations about individual students and groups of students who have made excellent progress as a result of the support they have received. Dr. Harris and the GC also point out specific actions that teams have taken to make sure that students are receiving the necessary interventions. They help all staff to understand what they have achieved and how it will change students' lives.

These scenarios illustrate how the CLEAR process can be used to build the collective efficacy of teacher teams by people in different roles (principal, instructional coach, team leader), in different types of schools (large suburban high school, midsize middle school, small elementary school), to support implementation of different tasks (identifying essential standards, using CFA, implementing systematic interventions), and at different points in the PLC journey (initiating, implementing, developing, and sustaining). Regardless of the circumstances, the process remains the same, because it is based on the research about how we, as humans, develop our individual and collective efficacy beliefs and then act on them.

CLEAR Thoughts and Next Steps

The CLEAR process for building the collective efficacy of teacher teams works because it is based on the research about how people develop efficacy beliefs. For most of this book, we have discussed the research and the process in sequence from step 1 to step 5. It is also instructive to think of the process in reverse. For all of us, the most powerful influence on our individual or collective efficacy is a mastery experience (step 5). When we work hard at something important and we have success, it significantly increases our belief in ourselves (self-efficacy) and our belief in our team (collective efficacy). This is especially true if we take the time to reflect on our success, dissect how it happened, and share our knowledge with others. We are often led to these mastery experiences by trusted mentors and coaches who provide social persuasion and all kinds of support and encouragement (step 4). They believe in us, and that helps believe in ourselves. They guide us to try, to persevere, and to overcome. We also learn by watching others and seeing a peer excel at a task helps us to feel that we can be successful too (step 3). Whether we actually get to see them do the work, have a chance to talk to them about the strategies, or review the excellent products of their labor, these models provide vicarious experiences that boost our efficacy beliefs. All these influences help us to overcome the low efficacy beliefs, individually and collectively, that we may have developed in response to failures, criticism, or negative feedback (step 2). Our lack of success leads to fear, which leads to avoidance, which leads to resistance, apathy, and even anger when presented with a task that conjures up traumatic memories. It takes a lot to overcome deep-set beliefs about what we can and cannot do. It takes even more to get us to move from what is familiar and safe to what could be amazing and life-changing for us and others. And all this work starts with a clear understanding of why we are doing something, what it involves, and how we know if it is working (step 1). Efforts to improve ourselves or to learn something new are more successful when they start with a clear grasp of purpose, strategy, and goals. When these ideas are put into action in a school with teachers who work with students, the potential for changing lives in wonderful ways is multiplied.

Let's review critical takeaways.

- Leaders and coaches of all kinds can use the CLEAR process to deliberately and strategically build the collective efficacy of their teams. When leaders and coaches understand the four sources of self-efficacy and collective efficacy and how people develop their efficacy beliefs, they can design their support of teams to intentionally build their teams' belief in themselves and their ability to succeed.

- In a school setting, the CLEAR process can help to develop the collective efficacy of teacher teams regardless of the specific position of the leader or coach, the level of school, the school's demographics, or the school's point on the PLC journey.

- When leaders and coaches working with teacher teams organize their efforts around clarifying the why, what, and how, listening to teachers' fears and anxieties, providing examples and models to explore, guiding teams through skilled coaching, and facilitating mastery experiences, they greatly increase the likelihood that their teams will develop a powerful sense of collective efficacy.

- Implementing the CLEAR process in all settings requires leaders and coaches to plan and prepare for interactions with teams, engage effectively with teachers to guide them through the process, and follow through in order to reinforce coaching and maximize growth.

Let's reflect on the content from this chapter.

1. When you read the descriptions of different types of leaders and coaches working diligently to build the collective efficacy of their teacher teams, do you see yourself? Do you believe you can do this work? Why or why not?

2. What would you, as a leader or coach, have to do differently to harness the power of collective teacher efficacy in your school? What is stopping you from strategically developing collective teacher efficacy in your teams, a force that we know has a powerful and positive influence on student achievement and teacher morale?

Let's plan an action step.

Now, imagine that you fully implement the CLEAR process as it is explained in this book. Imagine that, over time, the strategies work and you see a significant rise in student achievement, teacher empowerment, and collective teacher efficacy. What would that look like in your school? What would you have to do? What affect would it have on teams? What changes would occur? What results could you achieve? Try to get specific about details. Then write it down. Capture a few bullets or a write a narrative like the three stories shared in this chapter. How does imagining it and writing it down help you to identify the actions you need to take?

_____

_____

_____

_____

_____

_____

_____

_____

_____

_____

_____

EPILOGUE

CLEAR Thoughts and Next Steps

*P*UBLIC SCHOOL EDUCATORS around the world are facing some of the greatest challenges ever. Rebounding from a worldwide pandemic that disrupted instruction across the globe, we are working hard to help students learn and make up the ground they lost. At the same time, teachers are reporting higher levels of stress and burnout than ever before. Teacher morale is low, more people are leaving the teaching profession, and fewer are choosing education as their career. Educational leaders, principals, administrators, coaches, and lead teachers everywhere are working to respond to these crises and looking for answers about how to support their students and their teachers more effectively.

At the same time, we are living in an age where there is more educational research and solid information about what works in schools than any time in history. Educational studies since the turn of the millennium have produced some of the most important findings ever about how to help students learn, how to organize schools for success, and how to empower teachers to get great results, while also helping them to stay healthy in the profession so that they can do great work over time.

Some of the most powerful research concerns the promise of collective teacher efficacy—a group of teachers' collective belief that they have the power to influence student learning and that this power is greater than any of the obstacles and issues that students face. Study after study shows a strong link between the levels of collective teacher efficacy and higher student achievement. In addition, the research shows repeatedly how collective efficacy in a school is associated with higher levels of teacher morale, greater feelings of teacher empowerment, increased rates of teacher retention, and overall teacher wellness. With its dual positive influence on student learning and teacher morale, collective teacher efficacy is clearly the win-win strategy we need as we move deeper into the 21st century.

And while there seems to be universal agreement that collective teacher efficacy in schools is a good thing, there has been relatively little practical guidance about how to build collective efficacy on a team or in a school. What should leaders and coaches do to build the collective efficacy of their teacher teams?

In this book, I have presented and explained the CLEAR process, a practical, five-step process that leaders at any level and in many different circumstances can use to build the collective efficacy of their teacher teams. I felt compelled to write this book after seeing the power of collective efficacy in many districts and schools around the United States. I have been fortunate to see, in all kinds of schools, the amazing things that can happen when teams of teachers really believe in themselves and their ability to help students learn.

I developed the CLEAR process for building the collective efficacy of teacher teams in a PLC in hopes of providing guidance and tools for more educational leaders to make these great things happen in their own districts, schools, and teams. My deepest hope is that the CLEAR process will help more leaders to strategically and deliberately develop collective efficacy in their teacher teams and thereby address the many challenges that public educators are facing today.

I hope the information contained in this book helps you to coach your teams and build their collective efficacy, so that more teachers feel energized, supported, and inspired in the profession, and more students learn at the higher levels that help them to pursue and achieve their dreams.

APPENDIX

*I*N THIS APPENDIX, leaders and coaches will find a variety of tools that help in planning and executing the CLEAR process with teacher teams. Specifically, there is a coach's planner tool for each step of the CLEAR process. These tools will help coaches and leaders to carry out the critical preparation, engagement, and follow-through strategies that build collective teacher efficacy. In addition, there is a specific tools and resources guide for step 1 of the process. Leaders and coaches are encouraged to use these tools as they work to harness the power of collective teacher efficacy in their schools.

REPRODUCIBLE

The Five Steps of the CLEAR Process

Step 2:

LISTEN

to Teachers' Fears, Anxieties, Questions, and Concerns:

Affective States

Create the space to hear teacher concerns and honor questions. Continue throughout Steps 3–5.

Step 3:

EXPLORE

Examples, Models, Best Practices, and Proven Processes:

Vicarious Experiences

Show evidence that it can be done.

Step 4:

ACTIVATE

New Learning Through Coaching, Practice, and Implementation:

Social Persuasion

Coach teams to apply what they have learned through feedback and guidance.

Step 5:

REVIEW

Results, Celebrate Growth, and Set New Targets:

Mastery Experiences

Dig into the data on SMART goals, celebrate success, and chase higher targets.

Step 1: CLARIFY the Why, the What, and the How

Build a solid foundation for collective teacher efficacy to grow by clarifying Why we need to change practice, What the change will involve, and How we will measure the impact of the change.

Tools and Resources for Step 1 of the CLEAR Process

Clarifying the Why

Resources for collecting, analyzing, and presenting data:

Boudett, K. P., City, E. A., & Murnane, R. J. (Eds.). (2020). *Data wise: A step-by-step guide to using assessment results to improve teaching and learning* (revised and expanded edition). Cambridge, MA: Harvard Education Press.

Schildkamp, K., Handelzalts, A., Poortman, C. L., Leusink, H., Meerdink, M., Smit, M., et al. (2018). *The data team procedure: A systematic approach to school improvement.* New York: Springer International Publishing.

Datnow, A., & Park, V. (2014). *Data-driven leadership.* New York: John Wiley & Sons.

Fisk, S. (2021). *Leading data-informed change in schools.* Bloomington, IN: Solution Tree Press.

Clarifying the What

Resources for identifying and understanding research-based practices:

Websites

ERIC – The Education Resources Information Center (https://eric.ed.gov/)

Education Source – EBSCO (https://www.ebsco.com/products/research-databases/education-source)

Harvard Graduate School of Education: Gutman Library's "Online Resources for Educators" (https://www.gse.harvard.edu/community/library/online-resources-educators)

JSTOR (https://www.jstor.org/)

The Library of Congress (https://www.loc.gov/)

Books

Robert Marzano and associates have conducted high-level research into effective instructional strategies for several decades. *The New Art and Science of Teaching* is a comprehensive guide to instructional strategies that work (Marzano, 2017).

Another excellent resource is *Visible Learning* by John Hattie, which I cited in chapter 1 while sharing the effect size data about collective teacher efficacy. In Hattie's book, he not only shares the effect sizes and impact of hundreds of school strategies, including instructional methods, but he also provides an overview of each strategy and offers suggestions on where to find additional information (Hattie, 2023).

Harnessing the Power of Collective Teacher Efficacy © 2025 Solution Tree Press • SolutionTree.com
Visit **go.SolutionTree.com/PLCbooks** to download this free reproducible.

REPRODUCIBLE

Clarifying the What (continued)

Education Journals

Teachers and Teaching: Theory and Practice	*The New Educator*
The Teacher Educator	*Professional Development in Education*
Action in Teacher Education	*Teacher Development*
Cognition and Instruction	

Clarifying the How

Resources for setting goals and reviewing progress:

Conzemius, A. E., & O'Neill, J. (2013). *The handbook for SMART school teams: Revitalizing best practices for collaboration.* Bloomington, IN: Solution Tree Press.

DuFour, R., DuFour, R., Eaker, R., Many T., & Mattos, M. (2024). *Learning by doing:* A handbook for professional learning communities at work (4th ed.). Bloomington, IN: Solution Tree Press.

Ferriter, W. M. (2020). *The big book of tools for collaborative teams in a PLC at Work.* Bloomington, IN: Solution Tree Press.

Working With Adult Learners

Key points from the research:

Leaders and coaches should always bear in mind that they are working with adult learners, and they should plan sessions that will meet the needs of their clients. Most researchers in the adult learning field agree that there are several critical components to effective adult learning sessions (Aguilar, 2016; Bouchrika, 2024).

Adults learn better when they know why they have to learn something—so it is important to have clear objectives and a rationale for why the content is necessary. Coaches and leaders implementing the CLEAR process can also connect the training session back to the why. For example, it is helpful to begin training sessions with a clear statement of why the content is important, how it will help teachers and teams, and how it will help students.

Adults learn better when they get to collaborate and solve problems—so it is important to engage adults in active discussion and study of meaningful content, rather than lecturing/presenting. For example, rather than showing slide after slide and reading the content to teachers, coaches can pose a problem or scenario and ask teachers to work in small groups to come up with a solution.

Adults learn better when they have an opportunity to make decisions about how they learn something—so it is important to give options during training sessions. It is also very helpful to give adult learners options about how to continue their learning or practice what they learned. For example, leaders and coaches can prepare online materials and modules that teachers and teams can review at their own pace.

Harnessing the Power of Collective Teacher Efficacy © 2025 Solution Tree Press • SolutionTree.com
Visit **go.SolutionTree.com/PLCbooks** to download this free reproducible.

Coach's Planner for Step 1 of the CLEAR Process: Clarify the Why, the What, and the How

Preparation Work for Step 1

Before engaging teachers and teams to clarify the why a change is necessary, what the change is, and how the change will be measured, leaders and coaches must prepare, by completing the following actions.

Coach or Leader Task	Guiding Questions	Desired Product	Actions and Notes
Generate questions about their students and their learning (the why), strategies to address learning needs (the what), and possible goals (the how).	What do I want to know about my students and their learning, research-based strategies, and shared goals?	An exhaustive list of your questions about your students and their learning, high-leverage practices, and draft goals.	
Collect and organize all the data and information about their students and their learning. Collect and organize research about effective practices. Collect and organize information about previous school and team goals.	Where can I find the data and information needed to better understand our students' current level of achievement, strategies to improve learning, and goals to measure our progress?	A comprehensive list of sources and a compilation of all the data and research you need to answer your questions.	
Conduct an initial analysis of the achievement data to identify strengths, areas for growth, trends, patterns, and the most critical student learning needs. Conduct an initial review of the research on best practices. Conduct an initial review of school and team goals.	What does our analysis tell us about the state of student learning at our school? What does our research tell us about how we can address our student needs? What should our shared goals be and how will we monitor progress?	A clear and concise analysis that captures the main themes in your students' data, the most promising practices to address your need, and strategies for setting goals and monitoring progress.	

page 1 of 3

REPRODUCIBLE

Coach or Leader Task	Guiding Questions	Desired Product	Actions and Notes
Develop plans for engaging teachers and teams in collaborative learning with the data so that they understand the compelling student learning need (the why), research-based strategies to address the need (the what), and draft goals for measuring progress (the how).	How can we engage teachers and teams in meaningful activities that will build shared knowledge about student learning, effective strategies, and shared goals? How can we plan activities that will build shared knowledge and increase ownership?	A clear and cohesive training plan for engaging teachers and teams in reviewing student data, research-based practices, and draft goals.	

Engagement Work for Step 1

Skilled efficacy builders clarify the why, the what, and the how by engaging teacher teams in collaborative activities that build shared knowledge.

Coach or Leader Task	Guiding Questions	Desired Product	Actions and Notes
Implement the training plan to engage staff in collaborative learning about student achievement data (the why), high-leverage practices (the what), and draft school goals (the how).	How can we best engage our teachers and teams in building shared knowledge about our current levels of student learning, best practices to implement, and strategies for setting goals and monitoring progress?	A high-quality training plan that meets the needs of adult learners, gives adequate time for discussion and reflection, and engages all staff in collaborative learning.	
Build shared knowledge about student learning, best practices, and shared goals, so that all teachers and teams have a clear understanding of the why, the what, and the how.	How can we facilitate learning activities so that all participants gain knowledge and understanding and help to establish our why, what, and how?	Specific training activities and processes that build awareness and ownership.	
Before completing the engagement with staff, confirm what you have learned through building shared knowledge and establish the why, the what, and the how for all staff.	What processes can we use to engage staff, work through a great deal of information, and establish a clear why, what, and how for the school year?	A clear, one-page statement of the school's why, what, and how that captures the focus and commitments for all staff.	

Harnessing the Power of Collective Teacher Efficacy © 2025 Solution Tree Press • SolutionTree.com
Visit **go.SolutionTree.com/PLCbooks** to download this free reproducible.

Follow-Through Work for Step 1

Skilled efficacy builders reinforce the why, the what, and the how through ongoing communication and targeted professional development.

Coach or Leader Task	Guiding Questions	Desired Product	Actions and Notes
Reinforce the why (the identified student learning needs), the what (the identified high-leverage strategies to address the need), and the how (shared school goals and a plan for monitoring progress) in ongoing communications with staff.	How will I use formal and informal communications to regularly reinforce the importance of the school's why, what, and how? How will I keep these items "front of mind" for all staff?	Written plan for using formal communications (staff bulletin, staff meetings, notes to teams, etc.) and informal communications (chats with teachers and teams, classroom visits) to reinforce the why, what, and how.	
Provide all necessary supports to teams and teachers to enable them to focus on the why, the what, and the how. Provide any and all professional development and coaching support that teams need to be successful in implementing the why, the what, and the how.	What supports and professional development opportunities will teachers and teams need to be successful with the why, what, and how? How will I check in with teams to see what they need? How will I support teams that struggle to implement the why, what, and how?	Written plan and regular notes to provide teams with the support they need. Notes from conversations with teams. Training schedules that respond to team needs.	
Monitor team progress, assess team stress levels, and provide support as needed.	How will I continue to check on teams and monitor their stress level?	Written schedule and regular routine for touching base with teams. Note-taking system to capture input and responses.	

Harnessing the Power of Collective Teacher Efficacy © 2025 Solution Tree Press • SolutionTree.com
Visit **go.SolutionTree.com/PLCbooks** to download this free reproducible.

Coach's Planner for Step 2 of the CLEAR Process: Listen to Teachers' Fears, Anxieties, Questions, and Concerns

Preparation Work for Step 2

Skilled efficacy builders prepare for Step 2 by creating a plan for collecting meaningful feedback from teams through multiple methods and using that information to assess the stress level of teachers and teams.

Coach or Leader Task	Guiding Questions	Desired Product	Actions and Notes
Leaders and coaches plan how they will communicate with teachers and teams about collecting input on fears, anxieties, questions, and concerns.	How will I explain why I am asking teachers and teams to share their perspectives? How will I encourage them to accept and trust the process?	Written plan, comments for presenting this effort to staff. Messages that confirm the plan to collect the data	
Leaders and coaches develop the meeting plans, surveys, comment walls, and suggestion box strategies to gather input.	Which tools would be best to use to gather the most accurate picture of how teachers and teams are feeling about the why, what, and how?	Written plan detailing tools to be used, dates for deployment and collection, estimated dates for sharing data and action steps	

Engagement Work for Step 2

Skilled efficacy builders engage with staff through multiple methods to collect meaningful data and develop a clear understanding of staff needs. They also communicate how they will respond to the concerns and assure teams of ongoing support.

Coach or Leader Task	Guiding Questions	Desired Product	Actions and Notes
Leaders and coaches hold face-to-face meetings with teachers and teams.	What combination of whole staff, team level, and individual teacher meetings will help me to get the most accurate read on staff and their stress levels?	Detailed notes and products from whole staff meetings, team chats, and individual conferences	
Leaders and coaches distribute surveys with directions, guidance, and due dates.	How will I encourage full participation in completing the survey?	Collected survey results and analysis	
Leaders and coaches deploy suggestion box and comment wall strategies to gather staff input.	How will I make it easy for staff to provide input? How will I monitor and collect the information?	Collected comments and analysis	

Harnessing the Power of Collective Teacher Efficacy © 2025 Solution Tree Press • SolutionTree.com
Visit **go.SolutionTree.com/PLCbooks** to download this free reproducible.

Follow-Through Work for Step 2

Skilled efficacy builders provide follow-through that demonstrates that they have heard staff concerns and shows that they will provide necessary supports.

Coach or Leader Task	Guiding Questions	Desired Product	Actions and Notes
Leaders and coaches honor the input from staff by sharing their analysis of the data and their action steps within two weeks of collecting the data.	How do I demonstrate to staff that their input was valued?	Written analysis of combined data	
Leaders and coaches communicate clearly about the high-priority action steps they have, based on the data, to support teachers and teams in their work on the why, the what, and the how.	How do I clarify how I will follow up to address teacher and team concerns and questions?	Written list of high-priority action steps	
Leaders and coaches follow through and execute the action steps and provide the promised supports. They continue to monitor teams and check on team stress on a regular basis.	How do I follow up with concrete actions that build trust and help teams to move forward with the why, the what, and the how?	Ongoing communication and evidence of follow-through	

Harnessing the Power of Collective Teacher Efficacy © 2025 Solution Tree Press • SolutionTree.com
Visit **go.SolutionTree.com/PLCbooks** to download this free reproducible.

REPRODUCIBLE

Coach's Planner for Step 3 of the CLEAR Process: Explore Examples, Models, Best Practices, and Proven Processes

Preparation Work for Step 3

Skilled efficacy builders prepare for Step 3 by identifying team needs and identifying appropriate models to help teams grow.

Coach or Leader Task	Guiding Questions	Desired Product	Actions and Notes
Leaders and coaches help teams to identify their specific needs and desired learning topics.	What tasks or skills does the team need to learn about? How do they want to increase their proficiency?	Team self-assessment tool completed by the team	
Leaders and coaches identify a model that can help the team to grow, whether it is a work product, a team to consult with, or a team to observe.	Where can I find an appropriate model that will help the team to grow?	Clear identification of a model and how it matches with the team's needs	
Leaders and coaches organize a plan for engaging the learning team with the model. In the case of consultations or observations, this includes working out all logistical details.	What arrangements need to be made to facilitate the team learning from a model?	Written plan for engaging with products or detailed logistical plan for consultation or observation	

Harnessing the Power of Collective Teacher Efficacy © 2025 Solution Tree Press • SolutionTree.com
Visit **go.SolutionTree.com/PLCbooks** to download this free reproducible.

Engagement Work for Step 3

Skilled efficacy builders facilitate the engagement of their teams with quality examples and model teams.

Coach or Leader Task	Guiding Questions	Desired Product	Actions and Notes
Leaders and coaches facilitate the interaction between the learning team and the model, whether they are reviewing team products, consulting with a team, or observing a model team in action.	How will I maximize the effectiveness of the interaction between the learning team and the model team? How can the learning be focused?	Detailed agenda and notes from the review of team products, the consultation, or the observation	
Leaders and coaches plan and execute facilitation strategies that serve to maximize collective learning.	What facilitation strategies will I use to make the most of the experience?	Notes that show that the session was productive and informative	

Follow-Through Work for Step 3

Skilled efficacy builders follow through to make sure that their teams gain the most through their vicarious experiences.

Coach or Leader Task	Guiding Questions	Desired Product	Actions and Notes
As soon as possible after the interaction with the model, leaders and coaches engage the learning team in deep reflection about what they saw, what they learned, what they observed, and what they took away from the experience.	How can I encourage deep reflection on the experience so that the learning team gains the most knowledge and insight?	Team notes that show a deep level of reflection on the learning experience	
Leaders and coaches ask targeted questions to help teams to process what they have learned and to plan how to apply it to their own practice.	How can I help teams to apply what they earned to their own work with students?	List of team action steps to follow up the learning experience	

Harnessing the Power of Collective Teacher Efficacy © 2025 Solution Tree Press • SolutionTree.com
Visit **go.SolutionTree.com/PLCbooks** to download this free reproducible.

REPRODUCIBLE

Coach's Planner for Step 4 of the CLEAR Process: Activate New Learning Through Coaching, Practice, and Implementation

Preparation Work for Step 4

Skilled efficacy builders prepare for Step 4 by building their own skills and by preparing in advance for every coaching session with teams.

Coach or Leader Task	Guiding Questions	Desired Product	Actions and Notes
Leaders and coaches build their own expertise and credibility through staying up to date on educational research and best practice.	What can I do to ensure that I am staying up to date on best practice?	Solid expertise and credibility with teams	
Leaders and coaches plan each coaching session in advance, working to maximize the value of each session for every team.	What does this team need in the next session? How can I build their collective efficacy through this session?	Written plan for the coaching session	
Leaders and coaches communicate in advance with teams about their needs, their current practice, and any new data or evidence they have.	What do I need to know in advance to make sure we have a valuable session? What do I need to communicate in advance?	Advance communications— emails, texts, etc.	

Harnessing the Power of Collective Teacher Efficacy © 2025 Solution Tree Press • SolutionTree.com
Visit **go.SolutionTree.com/PLCbooks** to download this free reproducible.

Engagement Work for Step 4

Skilled efficacy builders provide targeted coaching characterized by guidance, feedback, and encouragement.

Coach or Leader Task	Guiding Questions	Desired Product	Actions and Notes
Leaders and coaches provide individualized support to each team, based on their needs. Skilled coaches provide guidance for the team to improve, feedback to help teams understand their next steps, and encouragement to persist in the work, even when it is difficult.	What kind of coaching does the team need in this session? How can I provide them with what they need to grow in skill and collective efficacy?	Notes from session reflecting that the team is making progress.	

Follow-Through Work for Step 4

Skilled efficacy builders follow through to provide their teams with ongoing guidance and support as they apply what they have learned.

Coach or Leader Task	Guiding Questions	Desired Product	Actions and Notes
Leaders and coaches conduct their own self-assessment and reflect on how their coaching is impacting their teams.	How is my coaching impacting this team? Do I need to modify any practices?	Completed coach's self-assessment tool	
Leaders and coaches follow up with teams to provide ongoing support. They provide follow-up communication that is prompt, positive, and personalized. Leaders and coaches make sure to respond to any questions that team had or any resources/tools that the coach promised to provide.	What do I need to communicate to the team in the follow-up message that I send within 24 hours? How can I be prompt, positive, and personalize the message for the team?	Evidence of follow-up communication and follow-through on promised resources	

Harnessing the Power of Collective Teacher Efficacy © 2025 Solution Tree Press • SolutionTree.com
Visit **go.SolutionTree.com/PLCbooks** to download this free reproducible.

Coach's Planner for Step 5 of the CLEAR Process: Review Results, Celebrate Growth, and Set New Targets

Preparation Work for Step 5

Skilled efficacy builders prepare for Step 5 collecting evidence of the team's work and its impact on students.

Coach or Leader Task	Guiding Questions	Desired Product	Actions and Notes
Leaders and coaches gather and analyze evidence of the team's work, including team products and student achievement data.	Where can I find updated evidence of student learning?	Summary of updated data and the team's work products	
Leaders and coaches review team goals and progress that teams have made toward their targets.	How is the team doing in pursuit of its SMART goals?	Summary of updated data and progress toward goals	
Leaders and coaches develop a plan for how to engage their teams in examination of goals and data.	How can I use review of this information to build the collective efficacy of the team?	Written plan for reviewing the information with the team	

Harnessing the Power of Collective Teacher Efficacy © 2025 Solution Tree Press • SolutionTree.com
Visit **go.SolutionTree.com/PLCbooks** to download this free reproducible.

Engagement Work for Step 5

Skilled efficacy builders facilitate teams' review of their data, helping them to recognize their impact and reflecting on the mastery experience.

Coach or Leader Task	Guiding Questions	Desired Product	Actions and Notes
Coaches use protocols and other tools to help teams assess where they are in pursuit of their team goals.	Which protocols or strategies would work best for review of this data and information?	Team meeting notes that reflect thorough review of information	
Coaches provide feedback and guidance to help teams celebrate progress and plan for areas that need attention.	How can I provide feedback and guidance that will help to increase the team's collective efficacy?	Team meeting notes that reflect thorough review of information and reflection	
Leaders and coaches provide encouragement and coaching if the team's results are disappointing.	Will the team need encouragement due to some disappointing data? How can I provide that encouragement?	Team meeting notes that reflect thorough review of information and reflection	

Follow-Through Work for Step 5

Skilled efficacy builders follow through with teams through coaching that helps them to gain the greatest benefit from their mastery experiences as they set new goals to pursue.

Coach or Leader Task	Guiding Questions	Desired Product	Actions and Notes
Leaders and coaches provide ongoing support to help teams monitor their progress, celebrate growth, and set new goals.	What types of ongoing support does the team need to get results and build collective efficacy?	Written plan and evidence of providing communication and supports	
Coaches build credibility and trust by following through on requests from teams or any follow-up promised to a team.	What requests did the team have? What did I promise to follow up on?	Evidence of responding to team requests and following through on promises	

Harnessing the Power of Collective Teacher Efficacy © 2025 Solution Tree Press • SolutionTree.com
Visit **go.SolutionTree.com/PLCbooks** to download this free reproducible.

REFERENCES
AND RESOURCES

Adams, C. M., & Forsyth, P. B. (2006). Proximate sources of collective teacher efficacy. *Journal of Educational Administration, 44*(6), 625–642.

Aguilar, E. (2016, April 10). Asset-based coaching: Focusing on strengths. *Education Week.* Accessed at https://www.edweek.org/education/opinion-asset-based-coaching-focusing-on-strengths/2016/04 on July 13, 2024.

Alibakhshi, G., Nikdel, F., & Labbafi, A. (2020). Exploring the consequences of teachers' self-efficacy: A case of teachers of English as a foreign language. *Asian-Pacific Journal of Second and Foreign Language Education, 5,* Article 23.

Althauser, K. (2015). Job-embedded professional development: Its impact on teacher self-efficacy and student performance. *Teacher Development, 19*(2), 210–225.

Amitai, A., & Van Houtte, M. (2022). Being pushed out of the career: Former teachers' reasons for leaving the profession. *Teaching and Teacher Education, 110*(1), Article 103540.

Anderson, C. M., Summers, K. H., Kopatich, R. D., & Dwyer, W. B. (2023). Collective Teacher efficacy and its enabling conditions: A proposed framework for influencing collective efficacy in schools. *AERA Open, 9*(1), 1–16. https://doi.org/10.1177/23328584231175060

Atasoy, V., & Çakıroğlu, J. (2020). A study on examining relationship between pre-service teachers' collective efficacy and science teaching efficacy beliefs. *Hacettepe Universitesi Egitim Fakultesi Dergisi-Hacettepe University Journal of Education,* 466–479. https://hdl.handle.net/11511/38441

Bailey, K., & Jakicic, C. (2017). *Simplifying common assessment: A guide for Professional Learning Communities at Work.* Bloomington, IN: Solution Tree Press.

Bailey, K., & Jakicic, C. (2022). *Formative tools for leaders in a PLC at Work: Assessing, analyzing, and acting to support collaborative teams.* Bloomington, IN: Solution Tree Press.

Baker, E. L., Dunne-Moses, A., Calarco, A. J., & Gilkey, R. (2019). Listening to understand: A core leadership skill. *Journal of Public Health Management and Practice, 25*(5), 508–510.

Bandura, A. (1977). Self-efficacy: Toward a unifying theory of behavioral change. *Psychological Review, 84*(2), 191–215.

Bandura, A. (1982). Self-efficacy mechanism in human agency. *American Psychologist, 37*(2), 122–147.

Bandura, A. (1986). *Social foundations of thought and action: A social cognitive theory.* Englewood Cliffs, NJ: Prentice-Hall.

Bandura, A. (1993). Perceived self-efficacy in cognitive development and functioning. *Educational Psychologist, 28*(2), 117–148.

Bandura, A. (1994). Self-efficacy. In V. S. Ramachaudran (Ed.), *Encyclopedia of human behavior* (Vol. 4, pp. 71–81). New York: Academic Press.

Bandura, A. (Ed.). (1995). *Self-efficacy in changing societies.* New York: Cambridge University Press.

Bandura, A. (1997). *Self-efficacy: The exercise of control.* New York: Freeman.

Bandura, A. (2000). Cultivate self-efficacy for personal and organizational effectiveness. In E. A. Locke (Ed.), *The Blackwell handbook of principles of organizational behaviour* (pp. 120–136). Hoboken, NJ: Wiley.

Barnum, M. (2023, March 6). *Teacher turnover hits new highs across the U.S.* Accessed at www.chalkbeat.org/2023/3/6/23624340/teacher-turnover-leaving-the-profession-quitting-higher-rate on November 28, 2023.

Bartle, N. C., & Harvey, K. (2017). Explaining infant feeding: The role of previous personal and vicarious experience on attitudes, subjective norms, self-efficacy, and breastfeeding outcomes. *British Journal of Health Psychology, 22*(4), 763–785.

Berebitsky, D., & Salloum, S. J. (2017). The relationship between collective efficacy and teachers' social networks in urban middle schools. *AERA Open, 3*(4). https://doi.org/10.1177/2332858417743927

Blackman, A., Moscardo, G., & Gray, D. E. (2016). Challenges for the theory and practice of business coaching: A systematic review of empirical evidence. *Human Resource Development Review, 15*(4), 459–486.

Blazar, D., & Kraft, M. A. (2015). Exploring mechanisms of effective teacher coaching: A tale of two cohorts from a randomized experiment. *Educational Evaluation and Policy Analysis, 37*(4), 542–566.

Bong, M., & Skaalvik, E. M. (2003). Academic self-concept and self-efficacy: How different are they really? *Educational Psychology Review, 15*(1), 1–40.

Boogren, T. H. (2018). *Take time for you: Self-care action plans for educators.* Bloomington, IN: Solution Tree Press.

Boschi, H. (2020). *Why we do what we do: Understanding our brain to get the best out of ourselves and others.* Hoboken, NJ: Wiley.

Bouchrika, I. (2024). *Adult learning theory 2024: Methods and techniques of teaching adults.* Accessed at https://research.com/education/adult-learning-theory on March 26, 2024.

BrainyQuote. (n.d.). *Winston Churchill quotes.* Accessed at www.brainyquote.com/quotes/winston _churchill_103739 on November 29, 2023.

Broom, D. (2022, November 14). *Here's how COVID-19 affected education—and how we can get children's learning back on track.* Accessed at www.weforum.org/agenda/2022/11/covid19 -education-impact-legacy on November 27, 2023.

Brown, T. C. (2003). The effect of verbal self-guidance training on collective efficacy and team performance. *Personnel Psychology, 56*(4), 935–964.

Bruton, A. M., Mellalieu, S. D., & Shearer, D. A. (2016). Observation as a method to enhance collective efficacy: An integrative review. *Psychology of Sport and Exercise, 24,* 1–8.

Bryner, L. (2021). The teacher shortage in the United States. *Education and Society, 39*(1), 69–80.

Buckworth, J. (2017). Promoting self-efficacy for healthy behaviors. *ACSM's Health and Fitness Journal, 21*(5), 40–42.

Buffum, A., Mattos, M., & Malone, J. (2018). *Taking action: A handbook for RTI at Work.* Bloomington, IN: Solution Tree Press.

Buonomo, I., Fiorilli, C., & Benevene, P. (2020). Unravelling teacher job satisfaction: The Contribution of collective efficacy and emotions towards professional role. *International Journal of Environmental Research and Public Health, 17*(3), 736. https://doi.org/10.3390/ ijerph17030736

Butel, J., & Braun, K. L. (2019). The role of collective efficacy in reducing health disparities: A systematic review. *Family and Community Health, 42*(1), 8–19.

Cansoy, R., & Parlar, H. (2018). Examining the relationship between school principals' instructional leadership behaviors, teacher self-efficacy, and collective teacher efficacy. *International Journal of Educational Management, 32*(4), 550–567.

Capa-Aydin, Y., Uzuntiryaki-Kondakci, E., & Ceylandag, R. (2018). The relationship between vicarious experience, social persuasion, physiological state, and chemistry self-efficacy: The role of mastery experience as a mediator. *Psychology in the Schools, 55*(10), 1224–1238.

Carter, A. (2017). Mobilising the middle: The key to cultivating collective teacher efficacy. *Education Today, 4,* 22–24.

Carter, W. R., Nesbit, P. L., Badham, R. J., Parker, S. K., & Sung, L.-K. (2018). The effects of employee engagement and self-efficacy on job performance: A longitudinal field study. *The International Journal of Human Resource Management, 29*(17), 2483–2502.

Chambers Mack, J., Johnson, A., Jones-Rincon, A., Tsatenawa, V., & Howard, K. (2019). Why do teachers leave? A comprehensive occupational health study evaluating intent-to-quit in public school teachers. *Journal of Applied Biobehavioral Research, 24*(1), Article e12160.

Chin, C.-H., Tseng, L.-M., Chao, T.-C., Wang, T.-J., Wu, S.-F., & Liang, S.-Y. (2021). Self-care as a mediator between symptom-management self-efficacy and quality of life in women with breast cancer. *PLoS One, 16*(2), Article e0246430.

Choate, K., Goldhaber, D., & Theobald, R. (2021). The effects of COVID-19 on teacher preparation. *Phi Delta Kappan, 102*(7), 52–57.

Choi, A. (2023, May 31). *Teachers are calling it quits amid rising school violence, burnout, and stagnating salaries.* Accessed at www.cnn.com/2023/05/31/us/teachers-quitting-shortage-stress -burnout-dg/index.html on November 27, 2023.

Chong, W. H., & Kong, C. A. (2012). Teacher collaborative learning and teacher self-efficacy: The case of lesson study. *Journal of Experimental Education, 80*(3), 263–283.

Chow, G. M., & Feltz, D. L. (2014). Collective efficacy beliefs and sport. In M. R. Beauchamp & M. A. Eys (Eds.), *Group dynamics in exercise and sport psychology* (2nd ed., pp. 298–316). New York: Routledge.

Clark, S., & Newberry, M. (2019). Are we building preservice teacher self-efficacy? A large-scale study examining teacher education experiences. *Asia-Pacific Journal of Teacher Education, 47*(1), 32–47.

Clear, J. (2018). *Atomic habits: An easy and proven way to build good habits and break bad ones.* New York: Avery.

Çoğaltay, N., & Boz, A. (2023). Influence of school leadership on collective teacher efficacy: A cross-cultural meta-analysis. *Asia Pacific Education Review, 24*(3), 331–351.

Collins, J. (2001). *Good to great: Why some companies make the leap . . . and others don't.* New York: HarperBusiness.

Conzemius, A. E., & O'Neill, J. (2013). *The handbook for SMART school teams: Revitalizing best practices for collaboration* (2nd ed.). Bloomington, IN: Solution Tree Press.

Dampérat, M., Jeannot, F., Jongmans, E., & Jolibert, A. (2016). Team creativity: Creative self-efficacy, creative collective efficacy and their determinants. *Recherche et Applications en Marketing (English Edition), 31*(3), 6–25.

Darling-Hammond, L., Hyler, M. E., & Gardner, M. (2017). *Effective teacher professional development.* Palo Alto, CA: Learning Policy Institute.

de Carvalho, A. L., Durksen, T. L., & Beswick, K. (2023). Developing collective teacher efficacy in mathematics through professional learning. *Theory Into Practice, 62*(3), 279–292. https://doi.org/10.1080/00405841.2023.2226553

Dempsey, D., & Jennings, J. (2014). Gender and entrepreneurial self-efficacy: A learning perspective. *International Journal of Gender and Entrepreneurship, 6*(1), 28–49.

Desimone, L. M., & Pak, K. (2017). Instructional coaching as high-quality professional development. *Theory Into Practice, 56*(1), 3–12.

de Vries, P. (2013). Generalist teachers' self-efficacy in primary school music teaching. *Music Education Research, 15*(4), 375–391.

DeWitt, P. (2018). *School climate: Leading with collective efficacy.* Thousand Oaks, CA: Corwin.

DeWitt, P. (2019). How collective teacher efficacy develops. *Educational Leadership*, *76*(9), 31–35.

Dhingra, N., Samo, A., Schaninger, B., & Schrimper, M. (2021). Help your employees find purpose—or watch them leave. *McKinsey & Company*, 31.

Diliberti, M. K., Schwartz, H. L., & Grant, D. (2021). *Stress topped the reasons why public school teachers quit, even before COVID-19.* Santa Monica, CA: RAND.

Dimopoulou, E. (2012). Self efficacy and collective efficacy beliefs of teachers for children with autism. *Literacy Information and Computer Education Journal*, *3*(1), 609–620.

Di Pietro, G. (2023). The impact of Covid-19 on student achievement: Evidence from a recent meta-analysis. *Educational research review*, 100530.

Donohoo, J. (2016). *Collective efficacy: How educators' beliefs impact student learning.* Thousand Oaks, CA: Corwin.

Donohoo, J. (2017). Collective teacher efficacy research: Implications for professional learning. *Journal of Professional Capital and Community*, *2*(2), 101–116.

Donohoo, J. (2018). Collective teacher efficacy research: Productive patterns of behaviour and other positive consequences. *Journal of Educational Change*, *19*(3), 323–345.

Donohoo, J., Hattie, J. A. C., & Eells, R. (2018). The power of collective efficacy. *Educational Leadership*, *75*(6), 40–44.

Donohoo, J., & Hite, S. A. (2021). Addressing inequity with the power of collective efficacy. *Educational Leadership*, *78*(6). Accessed at www.ascd.org/el/articles/addressing-inequity-with -the-power-of-collective-efficacy on November 28, 2023.

Donohoo, J., & Katz, S. (2017). When teachers believe, students achieve: Collaborative inquiry builds teacher efficacy for better student outcomes. *The Learning Professional*, *38*(6), 20–27.

Dortch, D. (2016). The strength from within: A phenomenological study examining the academic self-efficacy of African American women in doctoral studies. *The Journal of Negro Education*, *85*(3), 350–364.

Dos Santos, L. M. (2020, October). Stress, burnout, and low self-efficacy of nursing professionals: A qualitative inquiry. In *Healthcare* (Vol. 8, No. 4, p. 424). MDPI.

Drury, J. (2018). The role of social identity processes in mass emergency behaviour: An integrative review. *European Review of Social Psychology*, *29*(1), 38–81.

DuFour, R. (2016). Loose vs. Tight. *All Things PLC Magazine*, Summer 2016, pg. 33.

DuFour, R., DuFour, R., Eaker, R., Many, T. W., Mattos, M., & Muhammad, A. (2024). *Learning by doing: A handbook for Professional Learning Communities at Work* (4th ed.). Bloomington, IN: Solution Tree Press.

DuFour, R., & Marzano, R. J. (2011). *Leaders of learning: How district, school, and classroom leaders improve student achievement.* Bloomington, IN: Solution Tree Press.

Eaker, R., Hagadone, M., Keating, J., & Rhoades, M. (2021). *Leading PLCs at Work districtwide: From boardroom to classroom.* Bloomington, IN: Solution Tree Press.

Earp, J. (2022, February 2). Teacher time pressures "impacting effective classroom practice." *Teacher Magazine.* Accessed at www.teachermagazine.com/au_en/articles/teacher-time -pressures-impacting-effective-classroom-practice on November 27, 2023.

Edmondson, A. C. (2018). *The fearless organization: Creating psychological safety in the workplace for learning, innovation, and growth.* Hoboken, NJ: John Wiley & Sons.

Edmondson, A. C. (2022, November 22). Leading in tough times: HBS faculty member Amy C. Edmonson on psychological safety. *Harvard Business School.*

Eells, R. J. (2011). *Meta-analysis of the relationship between collective teacher efficacy and student achievement* [Doctoral dissertation, Loyola University Chicago]. Loyola eCommons. https://ecommons.luc.edu/luc_diss/133

Egenberg, S., Øian, P., Bru, L. E., Sautter, M., Kristoffersen, G., & Eggebø, T. M. (2015). Can inter-professional simulation training influence the frequency of blood transfusions after birth? *Acta Obstetricia et Gynecologica Scandinavica, 94*(3), 316–323.

Elaldı, S. (2016). The effect of mastery learning model with reflective thinking activities on medical students' academic achievement: An experimental study. *Journal of Education and Training Studies, 4*(5), 30–40.

Elmore, R. F. (2002). *Bridging the gap between standards and achievement: The imperative for professional development in education.* Washington, DC: Albert Shanker Institute.

Errida, A., & Lotfi, B. (2021). The determinants of organizational change management success: Literature review and case study. *International Journal of Engineering Business Management, 13.*

Every Student Succeeds Act of 2015, Pub. L. No. 114-95, 20 U.S.C. § 1177 (2015).

Fackler, S., & Malmberg, L.-E. (2016). Teachers' self-efficacy in 14 OECD countries: Teacher, student group, school and leadership effects. *Teaching and Teacher Education, 56,* 185–195.

Fancera, S. (2016). Principal leadership to improve collective teacher efficacy. *Education Leadership Review, 17*(2), 74–85.

Farmer, D. (2020). Teacher attrition: The impacts of stress. *Delta Kappa Gamma Bulletin, 87*(1), 41–50.

Fathi, J., Derakhshan, A., & Saharkhiz Arabani, A. (2020). Investigating a structural model of self-efficacy, collective efficacy, and psychological well-being among Iranian EFL teachers. *Iranian Journal of Applied Language Studies, 12*(1), 123–150.

Ferriter, W. M. (2020). *The big book of tools for collaborative teams in a PLC at Work.* Bloomington, IN: Solution Tree Press.

Francisco, C. D. (2019). School Principals' Transformational Leadership Styles and Their Effects on Teachers' Self-Efficacy. *Online Submission, 7*(10), 622–635.

Fransen, K., Vanbeselaere, N., Exadaktylos, V., Vande Broek, G., De Cuyper, B., Berckmans, D., et al. (2012). "Yes, we can!": Perceptions of collective efficacy sources in volleyball. *Journal of Sports Sciences, 30*(7), 641–649.

Frazier, R. A. (2020). *The joy of coaching: Characteristics of effective instructional coaches.* Thousand Oaks, CA: Corwin.

García, E., & Weiss, E. (2020). *Examining the factors that play a role in the teacher shortage crisis: Key findings from EPI's "Perfect Storm in the Teacher Labor Market" series.* Washington, DC: Economic Policy Institute.

Gatti, R., Tettamanti, A., Gough, P. M., Riboldi, E., Marinoni, L., & Buccino, G. (2013). Action observation versus motor imagery in learning a complex motor task: a short review of literature and a kinematics study. Neuroscience Letters, 540, 37–42.

George, T. R., & Feltz, D. L. (1995). Motivation in sport from a collective efficacy perspective. *International Journal of Sport Psychology, 26*(1), 98–116.

Getachew, D. S., & Zhou, E. (2018). The influences of transformational leadership on collective efficacy: The moderating role of perceived organizational support. *International Journal of Organizational Innovation, 10*(4), 7–15.

Goddard, R. D., Bailes, L. P., & Kim, M. (2021). Principal efficacy beliefs for instructional leadership and their relation to teachers' sense of collective efficacy and student achievement. *Leadership and Policy in Schools, 20*(3), 472-493.

Goddard, R. D., Goddard, Y., Kim, E. S., & Miller, R. (2015). A theoretical and empirical analysis of the roles of instructional leadership, teacher collaboration, and collective efficacy beliefs in support of student learning. *American Journal of Education, 121*(4), 501–530.

Goddard, R. D., Hoy, W. K., & Woolfolk Hoy, A. (2000). Collective teacher efficacy: Its meaning, measure, and impact on student achievement. *American Educational Research Journal, 37*(2), 479–507.

Goddard, R. D., Hoy, W. K., & Woolfolk Hoy, A. (2004). Collective efficacy beliefs: Theoretical developments, empirical evidence, and future directions. *Educational Researcher, 33*(3), 3–13.

Goddard, R. D., Skrla, L., & Salloum, S. J. (2017). The role of collective efficacy in closing student achievement gaps: A mixed methods study of school leadership for excellence and equity. *Journal of Education for Students Placed at Risk, 22*(4), 220–236.

Goddard, Y., & Kim, M. (2018). Examining connections between teacher perceptions of collaboration, differentiated instruction, and teacher efficacy. *Teachers College Record, 120*(1), 1–24.

Goldhaber, D., & Holden, K. L. (2021). The early teacher pipeline: What data do—and don't—tell us. *Phi Delta Kappan, 103*(3), 13–16.

Gordon, D., Blundell, C., Mills, R., & Bourke, T. (2023). Teacher self-efficacy and reform: A systematic literature review. *Australian Educational Researcher, 50*(3), 801–821.

Grose, J. (2023, September 13). People don't want to be teachers anymore. Can you blame them? [Opinion]. *The New York Times*. Accessed at www.nytimes.com/2023/09/13/opinion/teachers-schools-students-parents.html on November 27, 2023.

Guo, Y., Connor, C. M., Yang, Y., Roehrig, A. D., & Morrison, F. J. (2012). The effects of teacher qualification, teacher self-efficacy, and classroom practices on fifth graders' literacy outcomes. *The Elementary School Journal, 113*(1), 3–24.

Haddad, S. I., & Taleb, R. A. (2016). The impact of self-efficacy on performance: An empirical study on business faculty members in Jordanian universities. *Computers in Human Behavior, 55*, 877–887.

Hall, B. (2022). *Powerful guiding coalitions: How to build and sustain the leadership team in your PLC at Work*. Bloomington, IN: Solution Tree Press.

Hall, P., & Simeral, A. (2008). *Building teachers' capacity for success: A collaborative approach for coaches and school leaders*. Alexandria, VA: ASCD.

Hammerstein, S., König, C., Dreisörner, T., & Frey, A. (2021). Effects of COVID-19-related school closures on student achievement: A systematic review. *Frontiers in Psychology, 12*, Article 746289.

Hattie, J. A. C. (2009). *Visible learning: A synthesis of over 800 meta-analyses relating to achievement*. New York: Routledge.

Hattie, J. A. C. (2017). *Visible Learning 250+ Influences on Student Learning*. Accessed at https://visible-learning.org/wp-content/uploads/2018/03/VLPLUS-252-Influences-Hattie-ranking-DEC-2017.pdf on August 5, 2024.

Hattie, J. A. C. (2018) [The Learning Pit]. *Hattie: Collective Efficacy* [Video]. Vimeo. https://vimeo.com/267382804

Hattie, J. A. C. (2023). *Visible learning: The sequel: A synthesis of over 2,100 meta-analyses relating to achievement*. New York: Routledge.

Hattie, J. A. C., Masters, D., & Birch, K. (2015). *Visible learning into action: International case studies of impact*. New York: Routledge.

Hersey, P. H., Blanchard, K. H., & Johnson, D. E. (2012). *Management of organizational behavior: Leading human resources* (10th ed.). Boston: Pearson.

Higgins, B. R., & Hunt, J. (2016). Collective efficacy: Taking action to improve neighborhoods. *National Institute of Justice Journal, 277*, 18–21.

Hipp, K. A., & Bredesqn, P. V. (1995). Exploring connections between teacher efficacy and principals' leadership behaviors. *Journal of School Leadership, 5*(2), 136–150.

Holzberger, D., & Prestele, E. (2021). Teacher self-efficacy and self-reported cognitive activation and classroom management: A multilevel perspective on the role of school characteristics. *Learning and Instruction, 76*(3), Article 101513.

Hoogsteen, T. J. (2020). Collective efficacy: Toward a new narrative of its development and role in achievement. *Palgrave Communications, 6*(1), 1–7.

Hussain, M. S., Khan, S. A., & Bidar, M. C. (2022). Self-efficacy of teachers: A review of the literature. *Multi-Disciplinary Research Journal*, 2320–2750.

Jackson, A. L. (2016). The combined effect of women's neighborhood resources and collective efficacy on IPV. *Journal of Marriage and Family, 78*(4), 890–907.

Jalilianhasanpour, R., Asadollahi, S., & Yousem, D. M. (2021). Creating joy in the workplace. *European Journal of Radiology, 145*, 110019.

Jugert, P., Greenaway, K. H., Barth, M., Büchner, R., Eisentraut, S., & Fritsche, I. (2016). Collective efficacy increases pro-environmental intentions through increasing self-efficacy. *Journal of Environmental Psychology, 48*, 12–23.

Kasalak, G., & Dagyar, M. (2020). The relationship between teacher self-efficacy and teacher job satisfaction: A meta-analysis of the Teaching and Learning International Survey (TALIS). *Educational Sciences: Theory and Practice, 20*(3), 16–33.

Keating, J., & Rhoades, M. (2023). A new era in district and school improvement: The critical role of the superintendent and school board. *AllThingsPLC Magazine, 7*(2), 8–14.

Killion, J., Bryan, C., & Clifton, H. (2020). *Coaching matters* (2nd ed.). Oxford, OH: Learning Forward.

Klassen, R. M., & Tze, V. M. C. (2014). Teachers' self-efficacy, personality, and teaching effectiveness: A meta-analysis. *Educational Research Review, 12*, 59–76.

Knaggs, C. M., & Sondergeld, T. A. (2015). Science as a learner and as a teacher: Measuring science self-efficacy of elementary preservice teachers. *School Science and Mathematics, 115*(3), 117–128.

Knight, J. (2021). *The definitive guide to instructional coaching: Seven factors for success.* Alexandria, VA: ASCD.

König, C., & Frey, A. (2022). The impact of COVID-19-related school closures on student achievement: A meta-analysis. *Educational Measurement: Issues and Practice, 41*(1), 16–22.

Kotter, J. P. (2007). Leading change: Why transformation efforts fail. In R. Sandell & R. R. Janes (Eds.), *Museum management and marketing* (pp. 20–29). New York: Routledge.

Kotter, J. P. (2012). *Leading change.* Boston: Harvard Business Review Press.

Kraft, M. A., Blazar, D., & Hogan, D. (2018). The effect of teacher coaching on instruction and achievement: A meta-analysis of the causal evidence. *Review of Educational Research, 88*(4), 547–588.

Kuhfeld, M., Soland, J., Lewis, K., & Morton, E. (2022, March 3). *The pandemic has had devastating impacts on learning. What will it take to help students catch up?* Accessed at www.brookings.edu/articles/the-pandemic-has-had-devastating-impacts-on-learning-what -will-it-take-to-help-students-catch-up on November 28, 2023.

Kuhfeld, M., & Tarasawa, B. (2020). *The COVID-19 slide: What summer learning loss can tell us about the potential impact of school closures on student academic achievement.* Portland, OR: NWEA.

Kumar Pradhan, R., Prasad Panigrahy, N., & Kesari Jena, L. (2021). Self-efficacy and workplace well-being: understanding the role of resilience in manufacturing organizations. *Business Perspectives and Research, 9*(1), 62–76.

Künsting, J., Neuber, V., & Lipowsky, F. (2016). Teacher self-efficacy as a long-term predictor of instructional quality in the classroom. *European Journal of Psychology of Education, 31*(3), 299–322.

Lambersky, J. (2016). Understanding the human side of school leadership: Principals' impact on teachers' morale, self-efficacy, stress, and commitment. *Leadership and Policy in Schools, 15*(4), 379–405.

Lazarides, R., & Warner, L. M. (2020). Teacher self-efficacy. In G. W. Noblit (Ed.), *Oxford research encyclopedia of education*. New York: Oxford University Press.

The Learning Pit. (2018). *Hattie: Collective efficacy* [Video file]. Accessed at https://vimeo.com/267382804 on November 27, 2023.

Lemboye, O. T. (2019). *Correlational analysis of the relationship among mastery experience, self-efficacy, and project success* [Doctoral dissertation, Walden University]. Walden Dissertations and Doctoral Studies. Accessed at https://scholarworks.waldenu.edu/dissertations/7028 on October 21, 2024.

Leo, F. M., Sánchez-Miguel, P. A., Sánchez-Oliva, D., Amado, D., & García-Calvo, T. (2013). Analysis of cohesion and collective efficacy profiles for the performance of soccer players. *Journal of Human Kinetics, 39*(1), 221–229.

Li, J., Jia, L., Cai, Y., Kwan, H. K., & You, S. (2020). Employee–organization relationships and team performance: Role of team collective efficacy. *Frontiers in Psychology, 11*, Article 206.

Long, C. (2021, May 14). NEA Today. Lean on me: how educators persevered through the pandemic. Accessed at https://www.nea.org/nea-today/all-news-articles/lean-me-how-educators-persevered-through-pandemic on July, 31 2024.

Loo, C. W., & Choy, J. (2013). Sources of self-efficacy influencing academic performance of engineering students. *American Journal of Educational Research, 1*(3), 86–92.

Loughland, T., & Nguyen, H. T. (2020). Using teacher collective efficacy as a conceptual framework for teacher professional learning: A case study. *Australian Journal of Education, 64*(2), 147–160.

Loughland, T., & Ryan, M. (2022). Beyond the measures: The antecedents of teacher collective efficacy in professional learning. *Professional Development in Education, 48*(2), 343–352.

Lyons, W. E., Thompson, S. A., & Timmons, V. (2016). "We are inclusive. We are a team. Let's just do it": Commitment, collective efficacy, and agency in four inclusive schools. *International Journal of Inclusive Education, 20*(8), 889–907.

MacCrindle, A., & Duginske, J. (2018, April 5). *Seven qualities of an instructional coach* [Blog post]. Accessed at www.ascd.org/blogs/seven-qualities-of-an-instructional-coach on November 27, 2023.

Maeker, P., & Heller, J. (2023). *Literacy in a PLC at Work: Guiding teams to get going and get better in grades K–6 reading*. Bloomington, IN: Solution Tree Press.

Malinen, O. P., Savolainen, H., Engelbrecht, P., Xu, J., Nel, M., Nel, N., et al. (2013). Exploring teacher self-efficacy for inclusive practices in three diverse countries. *Teaching and Teacher Education, 33*, 34–44.

Many, T. W., Maffoni, M. J., Sparks, S. K., & Thomas, T. F. (2018). *Amplify your impact: Coaching collaborative teams in PLCs at Work*. Bloomington, IN: Solution Tree Press.

Martens, R., & Vealey, R. S. (2024). *Successful coaching* (5th ed.). Champaign, IL: Human Kinetics.

Martins, M., Costa, J., & Onofre, M. (2015). Practicum experiences as sources of pre-service teachers' self-efficacy. *European Journal of Teacher Education, 38*(2), 263–279.

Mather, B. R., & Visone, J. D. (2024). Peer observation to improve teacher self-efficacy. *Journal of Educational Research and Practice, 14*(1). https://doi.org/10.5590/JERAP.2024.14.01

Merriam-Webster. (n.d.). Vicarious. In *Merriam-Webster's online dictionary*. Accessed at www.merriam-webster.com/dictionary/vicarious on November 27, 2023.

Merritt, M. R. (2021). Active listening in the diverse roles of international school leaders. *IMCC Journal of Science, 1*, 115–130.

Meyer, A., Richter, D., & Hartung-Beck, V. (2022). The relationship between principal leadership and teacher collaboration: Investigating the mediating effect of teachers' collective efficacy. *Educational Management Administration and Leadership, 50*(4), 593–612.

Moore, C. (2016, July 28). *Albert Bandura: Self-efficacy and agentic positive psychology*. Accessed at https://positivepsychology.com/bandura-self-efficacy on November 27, 2023.

Moosa, V. (2021). Review of collective teacher efficacy research: Implications for teacher development, school administrators and education researchers. *International Journal of Theory and Application in Elementary and Secondary School Education, 3*(1), 62–73.

Morris, D. B., Usher, E. L., & Chen, J. A. (2017). Reconceptualizing the sources of teaching self-efficacy: A critical review of emerging literature. *Educational Psychology Review, 29*(4), 795–833.

Muhammad, A. (2018). *Transforming school culture: How to overcome staff division* (2nd ed.). Bloomington, IN: Solution Tree Press.

Muhammad, A., & Cruz, L. F. (2019). *Time for change: Four essential skills for transformational school and district leaders*. Bloomington, IN: Solution Tree Press.

Muhammad, A., & Hollie, S. (2012). *The will to lead, the skill to teach: Transforming schools at every level*. Bloomington, IN: Solution Tree Press.

National Center for Systemic Improvement. (2015). *Implementation guide for effective coaching of teachers*. San Francisco: WestEd. Accessed at www.air.org/sites/default/files/NCSI_Teacher_Coaching_Implementation_Guide-508.pdf on November 27, 2023.

Navo, M., & Savage, J. J. (2021). *Collective efficacy in a PLC at Work: Lessons, paradoxes, and research from a turnaround district*. Bloomington, IN: Solution Tree Press.

Nikoçeviq-Kurti, E. (2021). Fostering student teachers' self-efficacy and professional identity through vicarious experiences. *International Journal of Education and Psychology in the Community, 11*(1 & 2), 140–163.

Nixon, P., Ebert, D. D., Boß, L., Angerer, P., Dragano, N., & Lehr, D. (2022). The efficacy of a web-based stress management intervention for employees experiencing adverse working conditions and occupational self-efficacy as a mediator: Randomized controlled trial. *Journal of Medical Internet Research, 24*(10), e40488.

No Child Left Behind (NCLB) Act of 2001, Pub. L. No. 107-110, § 115, Stat. 1425 (2002).

O'Neil, K. (2023). Using the sources of self-efficacy to improve motor performance. *Strategies, 36*(1), 49–52.

Perna, M. C. (2024). No more teachers: the epic crisis facing education in 2024. *Forbes*. Accessed at https://www.forbes.com/sites/markcperna/2024/01/03/no-more-teachers-the-epic-crisis -facing-education-in-2024/ on March 1, 2024.

Pfeffer, J., & Sutton, R. I. (2000). *The knowing-doing gap: How smart companies turn knowledge into action*. Boston: Harvard Business School Press.

Pfitzner-Eden, F. (2016). Why do I feel more confident? Bandura's sources predict preservice teachers' latent changes in teacher self-efficacy. *Frontiers in Psychology, 7*, Article 1486.

Phan, N. T. T., & Locke, T. (2015). Sources of self-efficacy of Vietnamese EFL teachers: A qualitative study. *Teaching and Teacher Education, 52*, 73–82.

Pierce, S. (2014). Examining the relationship between collective teacher efficacy and the emotional intelligence of elementary school principals. *Journal of School Leadership, 24*(2), 311–335.

Pizana, R. F. (2022). Collective efficacy and co-teaching relationships in inclusive classrooms. *International Journal of Multidisciplinary: Applied Business and Education Research, 3*(9), 1812–1825.

Prelli, G. E. (2016). How school leaders might promote higher levels of collective teacher efficacy at the level of school and team. *English Language Teaching, 9*(3), 174–180.

Pressley, T., Ha, C., & Learn, E. (2021). Teacher stress and anxiety during COVID-19: An empirical study. *School Psychology, 36*(5), 367–376.

Preston, B. (2022). *Mindfully organizing collective teacher efficacy: A case study of efficacious educator teams* [Doctoral dissertation, University of New England]. DUNE: DigitalUNE. https://dune .une.edu/theses/440

Qadach, M., Schechter, C., & Da'as, R. (2020). Instructional leadership and teachers' intent to leave: The mediating role of collective teacher efficacy and shared vision. *Educational Management Administration and Leadership, 48*(4), 617–634.

Raj, A., & Kumar, K. (2009). Optimizing parent coaches' ability to facilitate mastery experiences of parents of children with autism. *International Journal of Psychosocial Rehabilitation, 14*(2), 25–36.

Reeves, D. (2011). *Finding your leadership focus: What matters most for student results*. New York: Teachers College Press.

Reeves, D. (2021). *Deep change leadership: A model for renewing and strengthening schools and districts*. Bloomington, IN: Solution Tree Press.

Reeves, P. M., Pun, W. H., & Chung, K. S. (2017). Influence of teacher collaboration on job satisfaction and student achievement. *Teaching and Teacher Education, 67*, 227–236.

Ryan, M., & Hendry, G. D. (2023). Sources of teacher efficacy in teaching reading: Success, sharing, and support. *The Australian Journal of Language and Literacy, 46*, 1–14.

Rintaugu, E. G., Mwangi, F. M., & Toriola, A. L. (2018). Sources of sports confidence and contextual factors among university athletes. *Journal of Physical Education and Sport, 18*(2), 889–895.

Salanova, M., Llorens, S., & Schaufeli, W. B. (2011). "Yes, I can, I feel good, and I just do it!" On gain cycles and spirals of efficacy beliefs, affect, and engagement. *Applied Psychology, 60*(2), 255–285.

Salanova, M., Rodríguez-Sánchez, A. M., Schaufeli, W. B., & Cifre, E. (2014). Flowing together: A longitudinal study of collective efficacy and collective flow among workgroups. *The Journal of Psychology, 148*(4), 435–455.

Sánchez-Rosas, J., Dyzenchauz, M., Dominguez-Lara, S., & Hayes, A. (2022). Collective teacher self-efficacy scale for elementary school teachers. *International Journal of Instruction, 15*(1), 985–1002.

Santoro, D. A. (2021). *Demoralized: Why teachers leave the profession they love and how they can stay*. Cambridge, MA: Harvard Education Press.

Schwarzer, R., & Warner, L. M. (2013). Perceived self-efficacy and its relationship to resilience. In S. Prince-Embury & D. H. Saklofske (Eds.), *Resilience in children, adolescents, and adults: Translating research into practice* (pp. 139–150). New York: Springer.

Shahzad, K., & Naureen, S. (2017). Impact of teacher self-efficacy on secondary school students' academic achievement. *Journal of Education and Educational Development, 4*(1), 48–72.

Sheu, H.-B., Lent, R. W., Miller, M. J., Penn, L. T., Cusick, M. E., & Truong, N. N. (2018). Sources of self-efficacy and outcome expectations in science, technology, engineering, and mathematics domains: A meta-analysis. *Journal of Vocational Behavior, 109*, 118–136.

Sims, S., & Fletcher-Wood, H. (2021). Identifying the characteristics of effective teacher professional development: A critical review. *School Effectiveness and School Improvement, 32*(1), 47–63.

Skaalvik, E. M., & Skaalvik, S. (2019). Teacher self-efficacy and collective teacher efficacy: Relations with perceived job resources and job demands, feeling of belonging, and teacher engagement. *Creative Education, 10*(7), 1400–1424.

Skaalvik, E. M., & Skaalvik, S. (2023). Collective teacher culture and school goal structure: Associations with teacher self-efficacy and engagement. *Social Psychology of Education, 26*(4), 945–969.

Skinner, B. F. (1938). *The behavior of organisms: An experimental analysis.* New York: Appleton-Century.

Skinner, B. F. (2019). *The behavior of organisms: An experimental analysis.* Cambridge, MA: B. F. Skinner Foundation.

Smith, M. (2022). 'It killed my spirit': How three teachers are navigating the burnout crisis in education. CNBC. Accessed at https://www.cnbc.com/2022/11/22/teachers-are-in-the-midst -of-a-burnout-crisis-it-became-intolerable.html on October 21, 2024.

Sørlie, M.-A., & Torsheim, T. (2011). Multilevel analysis of the relationship between teacher collective efficacy and problem behaviour in school. *School Effectiveness and School Improvement, 22*(2), 175–191.

Stenberdt, V. A., & Makransky, G. (2023). Mastery experiences in immersive virtual reality promote pro-environmental waste-sorting behavior. *Computers and Education, 198,* Article 104760.

Strahan, C., Gibbs, S., & Reid, A. (2019). The psychological environment and teachers' collective-efficacy beliefs. *Educational Psychology in Practice, 35*(2), 147–164.

Stroud, H. S. (2022). *Collective Efficacy, Teacher Expectations, and Reading Achievement in High-Poverty Elementary Schools.* Trevecca Nazarene University.

Taheri, M., Motealleh, S., & Younesi, J. (2022). Workplace fun and informal learning: The mediating role of motivation to learn, learning opportunities and management support. *Journal of Workplace Learning, 34*(3), 229–241.

Tarzian, M., Ndrio, M., & Fakoya, A. O. (2023). An introduction and brief overview of psychoanalysis. *Cureus, 15*(9), Article e45171.

Tasa, K., Sears, G. J., & Schat, A. C. H. (2011). Personality and teamwork behavior in context: The cross-level moderating role of collective efficacy. *Journal of Organizational Behavior, 32*(1), 65–85.

Theeboom, T., Beersma, B., & van Vianen, A. E. M. (2014). Does coaching work? A meta-analysis on the effects of coaching on individual level outcomes in an organizational context. *The Journal of Positive Psychology, 9*(1), 1–18.

Torres, K., Rooney, K., Holmgren, M., Young, S. Y., Taylor, S., & Hanson, H. (2020). *PLC at Work in Arkansas: Driving achievement results through school transformation and innovation.* Portland, OR: Education Northwest.

Tschannen-Moran, M., & Barr, M. (2004). Fostering student learning: The relationship of collective teacher efficacy and student achievement. *Leadership and Policy in Schools, 3*(3), 189–209.

Tschannen-Moran, M., & Hoy, A. W. (2007). The differential antecedents of self-efficacy beliefs of novice and experienced teachers. *Teaching and Teacher Education, 23*(6), 944–956.

VanSlander, J., Sharpe, S. W., & Cardullo, V. (2022). Increasing the effectiveness of novice teachers: Constructing vicarious and mastery experiences through a collaborative support model. In B. S. Zugelder & M. L'Esperance (Eds.), *Handbook of research on the educator continuum and development of teachers* (pp. 313–337). Hershey, PA: IGI Global.

Varela, D. G., & Fedynich, L. C. (2021). Teaching from a social distance: Teacher experiences in the age of COVID-19. *Research in Higher Education Journal, 39.* Accessed at https://files.eric .ed.gov/fulltext/EJ1293887.pdf on July 14, 2024.

Ventura, S., & Ventura, M. (2022). *Achievement teams: How a better approach to PLCs can improve student outcomes and teacher efficacy.* Alexandria, VA: ASCD.

Versland, T. M., & Erickson, J. L. (2017). Leading by example: A case study of the influence of principal self-efficacy on collective efficacy. *Cogent Education, 4*(1), Article 1286765.

Voelkel, R. H., Jr., & Chrispeels, J. H. (2017). Understanding the link between professional learning communities and teacher collective efficacy. *School Effectiveness and School Improvement, 28*(4), 505–526.

Wang, C., Kim, D.-H., Bai, R., & Hu, J. (2014). Psychometric properties of a self-efficacy scale for English language learners in China. *System, 44,* 24–33.

Wang, L. (2022). Exploring the relationship among teacher emotional intelligence, work engagement, teacher self-efficacy, and student academic achievement: A moderated mediation model. *Frontiers in Psychology, 12,* Article 810559.

Ware, H., & Kitsantas, A. (2007). Teacher and collective efficacy beliefs as predictors of professional commitment. *The Journal of Educational Research, 100*(5), 303–310.

Warner, L. M., Stadler, G., Lüscher, J., Knoll, N., Ochsner, S., Hornung, R., et al. (2018). Day-to-day mastery and self-efficacy changes during a smoking quit attempt: Two studies. *British Journal of Health Psychology, 23*(2), 371–386.

Watson, J. B. (1913). Psychology as the behaviorist views it. *Psychological Review, 20*(2), 158–177. https://doi.org/10.1037/h0074428

Wells, M. S., Widmer, M. A., & McCoy, J. K. (2004). Grubs and grasshoppers: Challenge-based recreation and the collective efficacy of families with at-risk youth. *Family Relations, 53*(3), 326–333.

Wertheimer, M., & Puente, A. E. (2020). *A brief history of psychology* (6th ed.). New York: Routledge.

Wilde, N., & Hsu, A. (2019). The influence of general self-efficacy on the interpretation of vicarious experience information within online learning. *International Journal of Educational Technology in Higher Education, 16*(1), 1–20.

Will, M. (2022a, March 22). Fewer people are getting teacher degrees. Prep programs sound the alarm. *Education Week.* Accessed at www.edweek.org/teaching-learning/fewer-people-are -getting-teacher-degrees-prep-programs-sound-the-alarm/2022/03 on November 27, 2023.

Will, M. (2022b, April 14). Teacher job satisfaction hits an all-time low. *Education Week.* Accessed at www.edweek.org/teaching-learning/teacher-job-satisfaction-hits-an-all-time-low/2022/04 on November 27, 2023.

Williamson, R., & Blackburn, B. R. (2023). *Improving teacher morale and motivation: Leadership strategies that build student success.* New York: Routledge.

Wilson, C., Marks Woolfson, L., & Durkin, K. (2020). School environment and mastery experience as predictors of teachers' self-efficacy beliefs towards inclusive teaching. *International Journal of Inclusive Education, 24*(2), 218–234.

Withy, H. (2019, September 23). Strategies for developing and maintaining self-efficacy in teachers. *The Education Hub.* Accessed at https://theeducationhub.org.nz/strategies-for-developing-and-maintaining-self-efficacy-in-teachers on November 28, 2023.

Wood, E. (2022). *The degree of influence leadership style has on collective efficacy* [Unpublished doctoral dissertation]. Caldwell University.

Wray, E., Sharma, U., & Subban, P. (2022). Factors influencing teacher self-efficacy for inclusive education: A systematic literature review. *Teaching and Teacher Education, 117,* Article 103800.

Wu, H., Li, S., Zheng, J., & Guo, J. (2020). Medical students' motivation and academic performance: The mediating roles of self-efficacy and learning engagement. *Medical Education Online, 25*(1), Article 1742964.

Yin, H., Tam, W. W. Y., & Lau, E. (2022). Examining the relationships between teachers' affective states, self-efficacy, and teacher-child relationships in kindergartens: An integration of social cognitive theory and positive psychology. *Studies in Educational Evaluation, 74*(3), Article 101188.

Yurt, E. (2022). Collective teacher self-efficacy and burnout: The mediator role of job satisfaction. *International Journal of Modern Education Studies, 6*(1), 51–69.

Zakeri, A., Rahmany, R., & Labone, E. (2016). Teachers' self- and collective efficacy: The case of novice English language teachers. *Journal of Language Teaching and Research, 7*(1), 158–167.

Zee, M., & Koomen, H. M. Y. (2016). Teacher self-efficacy and its effects on classroom processes, student academic adjustment, and teacher well-being: A synthesis of 40 years of research. *Review of Educational Research, 86*(4), 981–1015.

Zelenak, M. S. (2015). Measuring the sources of self-efficacy among secondary school music students. *Journal of Research in Music Education, 62*(4), 389–404.

Zhu, X., Law, K. S., Sun, C. (T.), & Yang, D. (2019). Thriving of employees with disabilities: The roles of job self-efficacy, inclusion, and team-learning climate. *Human Resource Management, 58*(1), 21–34.

INDEX

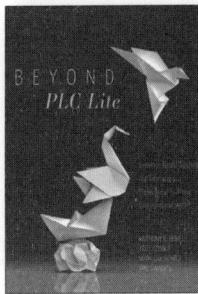

Beyond PLC Lite
Anthony R. Reibel, Troy Gobble, Mark Onuscheck, and Eric Twadell
Move your school teams beyond "PLC Lite" with ten evidence-based actions that will center student agency and efficacy in curriculum, assessment, instruction, and intervention practices. Gain access to rubrics, protocols, and templates designed to build a culture of continuous improvement.
BKF913

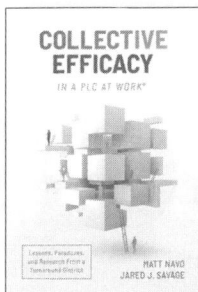

Collective Efficacy in a PLC
Matt Navo and Jared J. Savage
How did one of California's lowest-performing districts become a top turnaround district? It all came down to building collective team efficacy. Dive into this resource to find parallels to your own story and apply the lessons learned at Sanger Unified to the school community you serve.
BKF973

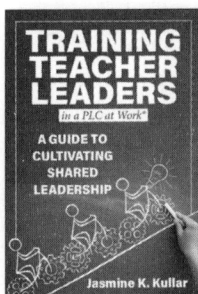

Training Teacher Leaders in a PLC
Jasmine K. Kullar
In this book, author Jasmine K. Kullar empowers teacher leadership teams with the knowledge to implement the PLC process successfully while developing ten essential leadership skills that will help influence their colleagues to advance student achievement.
BKG201

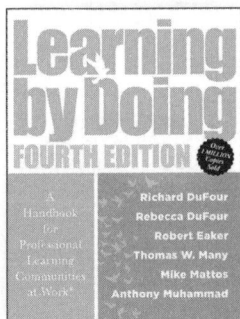

Learning by Doing, Fourth Edition
Richard DuFour, Rebecca DuFour, Robert Eaker, Thomas W. Many, and Mike Mattos
In this fourth edition of the bestseller *Learning by Doing*, the authors use updated research and time-tested knowledge to address current education challenges, from learning gaps exacerbated by the COVID-19 pandemic to the need to drive a highly effective multitiered system of supports.
BKG169

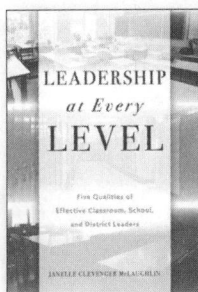

Leadership at Every Level
Janelle Clevenger McLaughlin
Nurture your leadership skills and grow as a lifelong learner with the support of *Leadership at Every Level*. Ideal for book studies, this resource shares practical, research-based strategies for strengthening leadership capacity at the classroom, school, and district levels.
BKG014

Solution Tree | Press   *a division of* Solution Tree

Visit SolutionTree.com or call 800.733.6786 to order.

Wait! Your professional development journey doesn't have to end with the last pages of this book.

We realize improving student learning doesn't happen overnight. And your school or district shouldn't be left to puzzle out all the details of this process alone.

No matter where you are on the journey, we're committed to helping you get to the next stage.

Take advantage of everything from **custom workshops** to **keynote presentations** and **interactive web and video conferencing**. We can even help you develop an action plan tailored to fit your specific needs.

Let's get the conversation started.

Call 888.763.9045 today.

SolutionTree.com